More Praise for The Triple Bottom Line

"An engaging mix of powerful ideas and practical advice. Values matter and Savitz shows how profitability and responsibility can and must go hand in hand."
—Michael Morris, chairman, president, and chief executive officer, American Electric Power

"Andy Savitz gets it. He also happens to be witty, sensible, and a good writer as well as a good business strategist—sort of a modern Ben Franklin. That makes this book a joy to read as well as indispensable for businesspeople who wish to succeed in this new age."
—Walter Isaacson, president and chief executive officer and former chairman, Aspen Institute; author, *Benjamin Franklin: An American Life*

"'Some circumstantial evidence is very strong,' Savitz and Weber recall Thoreau saying, 'as when you find a trout in the milk.' The flood tide of corporations they profile provides powerful evidence that the triple bottom line is going mainstream."
—John Elkington, founder and chief entrepreneur, SustainAbility

"A timely contribution to why big corporations engage in sustainable development and how managers can implement it in their companies."
—Bjorn Stigson, president, World Business Council for Sustainable Development

"Must-reading for any corporate manager or investor seeking the 'sweet spot' where financial and stakeholder interests meet. It provides powerful arguments, cogent analysis, great stories, and dozens of real-world insights into how companies are enhancing profits through sustainability strategies."
—Mindy Lubber, executive director, CERES; former regional administrator, United States Environmental Protection Agency

"Savitz and Weber's *The Triple Bottom Line* offers a perspective that is already influencing the wisest and most socially responsive corporations in the world. This well-written, insightful, and practical book will guide executives for decades to come. "
—Max Bazerman, Jesse Isador Straus Professor of Business Administration, Harvard Business School

"Amidst the proliferating number of books on corporate sustainability topics, Savitz's *The Triple Bottom Line* is a refreshing relief. Its accessible style, jargon-free language, and thematic organization avoids the tendency toward cheerleading and case study overdose characteristic of the field. Savitz speaks with clarity, authority, and good humor."
—Allen White, senior fellow, Tellus Institute; cofounder, Global Reporting Initiative

"*The Triple Bottom Line* is full of practical advice based on Savitz's hands-on experience working with corporate managers. This book is a very readable guide for those who want to build a successful and sustainable business for the twenty-first century."
—Arnold S. Hiatt, former chairman and CEO, the Stride Rite Corporation

"Most executives have a superficial or misguided understanding of sustainability. *The Triple Bottom Line* should be required reading for business leaders who seek to enrich their shareholders, society, and themselves."
—Scott Cohen, editor and publisher, *Compliance Week*

"Responsible leadership ensures that what we have today will be around for future generations. This book shows us both what it takes to lead responsibly and what happens when people fail to do so. An insightful book for those who seek how they can personally make a difference."
—Samuel DiPiazza, global chief executive officer, PricewaterhouseCoopers LLP

"Andy Savitz puts *sustainability* in a clear, practical framework supported with real business examples."
—Travis Engen, former president and chief executive officer, Alcan, Inc.; chair, Prince of Wales' International Business Leaders Forum; chairman, World Business Council for Sustainable Development

The Triple Bottom Line

How Today's Best-Run Companies Are Achieving Economic, Social, and Environmental Success— and How You Can Too

Andrew W. Savitz
with Karl Weber

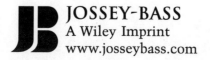
JOSSEY-BASS
A Wiley Imprint
www.josseybass.com

Published by Jossey-Bass
A Wiley Imprint
989 Market Street, San Francisco, CA 94103-1741   www.josseybass.com

Readers should be aware that Internet Web sites offered as citations and/or sources for further information may have changed or disappeared between the time this was written and when it is read.

Jossey-Bass books and products are available through most bookstores. To contact Jossey-Bass directly call our Customer Care Department within the U.S. at 800-956-7739, outside the U.S. at 317-572-3986, or fax 317-572-4002.

Jossey-Bass also publishes its books in a variety of electronic formats. Some content that appears in print may not be available in electronic books.

Library of Congress Cataloging-in-Publication Data

Savitz, Andrew W.
   The triple bottom line : how today's best-run companies are achieving economic, social, and environmental success—and how you can too / Andrew W. Savitz and Karl Weber.
       p. cm.
   Includes bibliographical references and index.
   ISBN-13: 978-0-7879-7907-2 (cloth)
   ISBN-10: 0-7879-7907-4 (cloth)
   1. Success in business. 2. Social responsibility of business. 3. Industrial management—Environmental aspects. I. Weber, Karl, 1953- II. Title.
   HF5386.S346 2006
   658.4'08—dc22

                                                                          2006012329

Printed in the United States of America
FIRST EDITION
HB Printing   10 9 8 7 6 5 4 3

Contents

To Penelope
And to our children, Noah and Zuzzie; their cousins, Louis,
Sarah, Daniel, Olivia, Julianna, Elliot, Sophia, Jacob, and Jonah;
and their offspring, who will hold us accountable

INTRODUCTION

The whaling industry personified American prosperity for over one hundred years. It employed seventy thousand sturdy New Englanders and fueled hundreds of thousands of homes and businesses here and abroad, earning fortunes for boat owners and more than a few enterprising crewmates. The intrepid whaler was celebrated in song, story, and even high art, including what is arguably the greatest American novel, Melville's *Moby-Dick*. Whaling was a tale of courage and initiative—a tale of America.

Today nearly all the whales are gone, and so is the industry built around them. The decline began in the mid-1840s, when hunters ignored decreasing stocks and continued harpooning grays, rights, humpbacks, and other species of this enormous, elegant mammal. Within a few years, the industry that had thrived for a full century collapsed entirely. The era of American whaling still stands as a symbol—but now it represents the shortsightedness of businessmen whose thirst for profit made their enterprise unsustainable.[1]

Sadly, contemporary fishing fleets don't seem to have absorbed the lessons of their past. Fishing grounds the world over are being closed as the industry exploits valuable species to the point of extinction. Commercial populations of cod, hake, haddock, and flounder have fallen in the North Atlantic by up to 95 percent during the last decade, prompting calls for zero catches as the only way for stocks to regenerate.[2] Another once-great industry, it seems, may be on the verge of becoming unsustainable.

This is a book not about the whaling or fishing industries, but about how to avoid their fate. It is a look at how businesses can prosper financially while protecting and renewing the social, environmental, and economic resources they need—and how they can fail if they do not tend to those resources.

The centerpiece of this book is the concept of *sustainability*. The term originated around a growing awareness, in the 1980s, that nations had to find ways to grow their economies without destroying the environment or sacrificing the well-being of future generations. Sustainability has since become a buzzword for an array of social and environmental causes, and in the business world it denotes a powerful and defining idea: *a sustainable corporation is one that creates profit for its shareholders while protecting the environment and improving the lives of those with whom it interacts*. It operates so that its business interests and the interests of the environment and society intersect. And as we will show, a sustainable business stands an excellent chance of being more successful tomorrow than it is today, and remaining successful, not just for months or even years, but for decades or generations.

Sustainable organizations and societies generate and live off interest rather than depleting their capital. Capital, in this context, includes natural resources, such as water, air, sources of energy, and foodstuffs. It also includes human and social assets—from worker commitment to community support—as well as economic resources, such as a license to operate, a receptive marketplace, and legal and economic infrastructure. A company can spend down its capital for a while, but generally not for long. A firm that honors the principles of sustainability, by contrast, is built to last.

Sustainability in practice can be seen as *the art of doing business in an interdependent world*. Sustainability in the broadest sense is all about interdependence, which takes several forms.

Sustainability respects the interdependence of living beings on one another and on their natural environment. Sustainability means operating a business in a way that causes minimal harm to living creatures and that does not deplete but rather restores and enriches the environment. The whalers of the nineteenth century failed to respect this form of interdependence and decimated their industry as a result.

Sustainability also respects the interdependence of various elements in society on one another and on the social fabric. Sustainability means operating a business in a way that acknowledges the needs and interests of other parties (community groups, educational and religious institutions, the workforce, the public) and that does not fray but rather reinforces the network of relationships that ties them all together.

Sustainability also respects the interdependence of differing aspects of human existence. Economic growth and financial success are important and provide significant benefits to individuals and society as a whole. But other human values are also important, including family life, intellectual growth, artistic expression, and moral and spiritual development. Sustainability means operating a business so as to grow and earn profit while recognizing and supporting the economic and noneconomic aspirations of people both inside and outside the organization on whom the corporation depends.

The only way to succeed in today's interdependent world is to embrace sustainability. Doing so requires companies to identify a wide range of stakeholders to whom they may be accountable, develop open relationships with them, and find ways to work with them for mutual benefit. In the long run, this will create more profit for the company and more social, economic, and environmental prosperity for society.

The concept of sustainability is sometimes confused with other terms that are widely used in business today. Many businesspeople, authors, and experts use the expression *corporate social responsibility* (CSR), for example, to refer to a company's obligations to society at large. It's a useful term, and we will occasionally use the expressions "responsible business" or "corporate responsibility" as shorthand for the kinds of managerial practices we recommend. We prefer the term *sustainability*, however, because responsibility emphasizes the benefits to social groups *outside* the business, whereas sustainability gives equal importance to the benefits enjoyed by the corporation itself.

Similarly, the term *business ethics*, which is commonly used to describe the social and moral responsibilities of businesspeople, is too narrow in its focus for our purposes. Business ethics emphasizes specific choices made by individual managers: What should I do when I'm asked or tempted to pay a bribe, cut corners on safety, or fudge the corporate accounts? It doesn't address broader operational questions, such as the following: Who should be consulted when decisions are being made that affect large numbers of people outside the company? To whom are business managers responsible? How should companies systematically measure the impact of their activities on society?

Sustainability has developed as a unified way of addressing a wide array of business concerns about the natural environment, workers' rights, consumer protection, and corporate governance, as well as the impact of business behavior on broader social issues, such as hunger, poverty, education, health care, and human rights—and the relationship of all these to profit.

Most books about sustainability focus on how society can benefit if companies take a more responsible approach. This book turns that lens around, examining how companies can become more profitable by doing the right thing. One powerful way to grasp this connection is the concept of the Triple Bottom Line, originally proposed by sustainability guru John Elkington. Elkington suggests that businesses need to measure their success not only by the traditional bottom line of financial performance (most often expressed in terms of profits, return on investment (ROI), or shareholder value) but also by their impact on the broader economy, the environment, and on the society in which they operate.[3]

In conducting their businesses, companies use not only financial resources (such as investment dollars and sales revenues) but also environmental resources (such as water, energy, and raw materials) and social resources (such as community employees' time and talents, and infrastructure provided by governmental agencies). A sustainable business ought to be able to measure, document, and report a positive ROI on all three bottom lines—economic, environmental, and social—as well as the benefits that stakeholders receive along the same three dimensions.

The Triple Bottom Line (TBL) captures the essence of sustainability by measuring the impact of an organization's activities on the world. A positive Triple Bottom Line reflects an increase in the company's value, including both its profitability and shareholder value and its social, human, and environmental capital (see Figure I.1).

The table shown in Figure I.1 is an oversimplification, of course. Just as meaningful financial reporting cannot be reduced to one number, so sustainability does not sum precisely. There is yet no way to accurately or completely describe consumer benefits or community benefits using a number, and some of the numbers themselves require a great deal of explanation, which is precisely why most financial reports include pages of management discussion and analysis.

The Triple Bottom Line exists currently as a kind of balanced scorecard that captures in numbers and words the degree to which any company is or is not creating value for its shareholders and for society.

Figure I.1 The Triple Bottom Line

	Economic	*Environmental*	*Social*
Typical Measures	Sales, profits, ROI	Air quality	Labor practices
	Taxes paid	Water quality	Community impacts
	Monetary flows	Energy usage	Human rights
	Jobs created	Waste produced	Product responsibility
	TOTAL	TOTAL	TOTAL

Elkington's formulation is central to understanding sustainability. Whereas the practice of sustainability is still an art, the measurement of sustainability is becoming a science, including specific goals and parameters by which businesses can measure and judge their own progress. As we'll explain in detail later, thousands of companies around the world have been measuring and reporting their performance in the environmental, economic, and social spheres. And growing numbers of institutional and individual investors, consumers, and workers are beginning to evaluate companies according to the Triple Bottom Line.

Sustainability, then, is *not* simply a matter of good corporate citizenship—earning brownie points for reducing noxious emissions from your factory or providing health care benefits to your employees. Nor is it merely a matter of business ethics—of doing the right thing when confronted with a particular moral dilemma that arises in the course of doing business. Sustainability is now a fundamental principle of smart management, one that's all too easy to overlook or take for granted in a world where the financial bottom line is often treated as the *only* measure of success. And as we will show, even well-run companies with good intentions and with years of success behind them can now fall hard if they ignore the principles of sustainability.

If sustainability is more important today than ever before, it's probably because corporations have, over the past few decades, entered what we call the Age of Accountability. They are increasingly being held responsible not only for their own activities, but for those of their suppliers, the communities where they are located, and the people who use their products. They are being called to account not only by investors and shareholders but by politicians, whistleblowers, the media, employees, community groups, prosecutors, class-action lawyers, environmentalists, human rights advocates, public health organizations, and customers. These stakeholders come from every corner of the world, armed with both the traditional media and that global megaphone called the Internet.

As a result, businesses are being forced to respond to social, economic, and environmental changes in the world around them. Just as global warming is fundamentally altering the commercial and regulatory landscape for energy and auto companies, so the advent of HIV/AIDS, SARS, and persistent malaria is changing the basic business model for pharmaceutical companies. Just as Nike was transformed by the discovery of children working in its overseas factories, so Wal-Mart is now coming face-to-face with "the high cost of low wages," and McDonald's with obesity. No sooner had Dell, Apple, and IBM created the personal computer than they had to bridge the digital divide.

The best-run companies, large and small, are responding to these challenges. Toyota develops the gas-electric hybrid engine, and the Prius becomes the world's fastest-selling car. BP moves "Beyond Petroleum." DuPont moves away from chemicals to become the world's largest producer of soy protein. Procter & Gamble (P&G) goes head-to-head with Unilever to figure out how to develop and sell products to the desperately poor, in ways that will help lift them out of poverty. And some of these moves are generating enormous financial benefits. PepsiCo claims annual revenue increases of $250 million from new purchasing programs that seek out companies owned by women and minority-group members, and 3M saves over a billion dollars through its Pollution Prevention Pays program.

Perhaps most significant, corporations are reaching out to their harshest critics, demanding to know how they can improve and seeking new forms of collaboration, innovation, and partnership to improve their results—many with startling success. And they are publishing TBL reports, asking to be judged on the basis of detailed information.

This book will show you how and why they are doing it and provide you with the tools you need to start or speed your own journey.

We come at these issues not as though they were abstractions, but through a decade of working on them with some of America's biggest, most robust corporations. Andy Savitz led the environmental practice at PricewaterhouseCoopers, one of the world's foremost financial advisory services companies, and has helped senior executives and mid-level managers apply the Triple Bottom Line at their firms and in their departments, in the process making them more sustainable. Karl Weber gained similar insights through his research and writing on a series of books exploring business strategy, corporate decision making, and the innovative practices of many of the world's most successful companies.

In these pages, we'll provide you with a set of tools—must-dos, don't-dos, and simple charts and lists—and stories to carry you down the road to sustainability for your business. In the end, you should emerge with an understanding of why and how this transformation is occurring and what you can do to become part of it.

Correctly understood and applied, sustainability is about strategy, management, and profits. But in today's interconnected world, thinking about profits as if they were unrelated to the economic and social impacts of what you do to get them is shortsighted and counterproductive. Social and environmental issues are creating risks and opportunities that fundamentally change the playing field for individual firms, industries, and business itself. The best-run companies see this and are turning these trends to their advantage. *The Triple Bottom Line* will help you apply the same advanced thinking to your own business.

May 2006
Boston, Massachusetts   ANDREW W. SAVITZ
Chappaqua, New York   KARL WEBER

The Triple Bottom Line

Part One

THE SUSTAINABILITY IMPERATIVE

1

SELLING HERSHEY

A Business Fable for Our Times

I think what makes a good CEO today is what will always make a good CEO and what has in the past: strong values, great personal integrity, and a willingness to make the tough calls. But it certainly requires an openness and transparency with the multiple constituents, whether it be shareholders, the board, employees, customers, or suppliers. And those characteristics don't have a shelf life in terms of when it's good or not good to apply them.

—*Rick Lenny, CEO, Hershey Foods Corporation*[1]

Trouble in Utopia

July 25, 2002, was a day like any other in the picture-perfect town of Hershey, Pennsylvania, home of the world-famous Hershey bar.[2] Tourists strolled Chocolate Avenue, gawking at streetlights shaped like Hershey Kisses and shopping for candy-themed souvenirs at the dozens of gift shops. Bedazzled children and obliging parents lined up for tours of Hershey's Chocolate World and squealed with delight on the ten roller coasters at nearby Hersheypark. Those with more sedentary tastes relished a whipped cocoa bath or chocolate hydrotherapy at the Hotel Hershey's pricey spa, or simply savored the sweet aromas from the factory whose assembly lines generated a nonstop supply of Mr. Goodbars, Reese's Peanut Butter Cups, and Kit Kat Bars. All these pleasures had one thing that united them even more than their chocolate flavor: the steady stream of income they produced for Hershey's twelve thousand residents, nearly all of whom had a connection to the company after which their town was named.

It was a day like any other—until the news that turned July 25, 2002, into what the townspeople of Hershey still call Black Thursday. It came in a story in the *Wall Street Journal*, which revealed that the board of the Hershey Trust, the charitable organization that owned a controlling stake in the Hershey Foods Company and thereby in the future of everyone in town, was planning to sell the company to the highest bidder.[3]

The news flashed through town. The questions followed in an instant. Who might the new owners be? What would they do with the Hershey plant, the theme park, the spa and hotel and gardens, and all the other attractions that had made their town a center of tourism? What would happen to the chocolate-related jobs that drove the local economy? Would Hershey, Pennsylvania, become a ghost town?

No one could say.

It is a story that has been told in one company town after another all across America: corporate interests, under pressure to pursue short-term gains, decide to sacrifice the local economy, culture, and tradition in pursuit of profit. And in some towns, after a period of dismay and anger, the citizens quietly accept their fate.

Not in Hershey.

A coalition of angry citizens formed within hours. It included former CEOs of Hershey who hated the idea of selling the company they'd nurtured; leaders and members of Chocolate Workers Local 464 of the Bakery, Confectionery, Tobacco Workers and Grain Millers International, the union that represented twenty-eight hundred employees at the Hershey plant; alumni of the Milton Hershey School, the remarkable educational center for orphans created by company founder Milton S. Hershey himself; and thousands of business owners and residents of central Pennsylvania who feared the death of a town they cherished.

A week later, five hundred townspeople converged on Chocolatetown Square for the first protest rally in the history of bucolic, conservative Hershey. The protestors clustered under the trees in the little plaza, handed out leaflets, carried signs reading "Derail the Sale" and "Milton's Dream Has Become a Nightmare," and cheered a series of fiery speeches as startled tourists looked on. Former Hershey chairman and CEO Dick Zimmerman angrily denounced the sale idea as unnecessary and unwise. The president of the Hershey School Alumni Association, New York attorney Ric Fouad, appealed to Milton Hershey's founding vision. And union leader Bruce Hummel mocked the board as sacrificing the community for profit. "You don't sell the children to save the house," he roared. The crowd roared back.

The rally was only the start of a series of headaches for the top brass of Hershey Foods and the leaders of the trust. And it came as quite a shock. The emergence of a broad coalition of activists vowing to fight the sale was the last thing they had expected. How had it happened? And how on earth had Hershey's leaders so badly misgauged the reaction to their plan?

Patriarch of Chocolate

The connection between the town of Hershey and its largest employer is more than geographic or even economic. The fate of the company and that of the community are closely entwined, and that's the way Milton S. Hershey wanted it. The deeply religious Hershey, a member of the socially conservative Mennonite sect, wanted his wealth to be used "for a purpose of enduring good," and he viewed his little Pennsylvania town as a Utopian community, designed and managed for the good of all its inhabitants.[4]

Hershey built the town in the early years of the twentieth century. Through his Hershey Improvement Company, he founded most of its leading institutions, including the local bank, department store, zoo, and public gardens modeled on those at the French royal court in Versailles. He laid out the bucolic street design, built a trolley company, and designed houses for factory workers and bigger houses for corporate executives. He even founded a community college that local residents and company employees could attend free of charge. During the Great Depression, despite a 50 percent drop in chocolate sales, he kept the workers from his factory busy building a hotel, a community center, a sports arena, and public schools—all, of course, bearing the Hershey name.

Milton also founded the Hershey Industrial School—now known as the Milton Hershey School—which provides free room and board, clothing, medical care, and schooling for some thirteen hundred disadvantaged children. The charitable trust that Hershey created in 1909, which owns and operates the school, also owns or controls over three-quarters of the voting shares of Hershey Foods.

The result: the town of Hershey and the students and teachers at Milton Hershey School are completely dependent on and closely linked with the company Hershey founded. For decades, Hershey Foods executives managed the business accordingly. "I was always told that we had a fiduciary responsibility to the trust," says John Dunn, who rose over the course of thirty years from a Hershey sales-man in Chicago to the company's director of marketing. "And I was always reminded that we must never do anything that would com-promise our business or our financial success—because the Trust was relying on us."[5]

Logic would dictate that, in such circumstances, the management of the company would never lose sight of the profound connections among the business, the school, and the community that houses and sustains them both. That, after all, is what Milton Hershey had made clear he wanted. But company managers were governed by neither Milton's dreams nor simple logic.

The remarkable battle for control of Hershey Foods that erupted in the summer of 2002 illustrates many of the central themes of this book and raises a host of questions that business lead-ers everywhere need to consider—questions like these:

- Do the responsibilities of a business manager go beyond earn-ing the highest possible profits? If so, what are those responsi-bilities, and how should they be balanced with the pursuit of profits?

- What responsibilities does a company have to its workers, their families, the community where they live, and society at large? Is it enough to pay fair wages, provide competitive benefits, and supply needed goods and services—or should a company do more?

- What information should be disclosed about corporate decisions and activities to those who have a stake in them? How should the leaders of a company take into account the viewpoints and concerns of those stakeholders? And who should have a say about the fate of the company?

Hershey Foods and the Hershey Trust are, by almost any measure, well-run and well-meaning organizations. Their leaders, who had jointly reached the decision to sell the company, were upstanding citizens of the corporate world and the local community. Yet when challenged to chart a course for future decades in a rapidly changing world, they stumbled, hurting the company financially and leaving Wall Street and the American public with an abiding image of a big chocolate-covered mess.

The Responsible Thing to Do

To understand that meltdown, we must go back seven months to December 2001, when a deputy attorney general for the state of Pennsylvania met with the board of the Hershey Trust to probe allegations of mismanagement and conflicts of interest by its seventeen members. The state's investigation would soon fizzle, but this meeting would be remembered for a very different reason. Mark Pacella, the deputy attorney general, warned the board members that it was high time they found ways to diversify their gigantic, $5.4 billion holdings, a full 52 percent of which were in Hershey Foods. To do anything else would be foolhardy and irresponsible. It might even be illegal.

The board had sound financial reasons to make such a move. As any investment manager can confirm, having one's holdings heavily concentrated in the shares of a single company is not sound practice. It left the trust vulnerable to any downturn in the prospects of Hershey Foods. The emergence of a new and powerful competitor in the chocolate market, or a large increase in the price of cocoa, could decrease the value of the trust fund and seriously impair its charitable works. The deputy attorney general's suggestion was based on good business logic, and the board promised to take it under advisement.

The board of trustees acted three months later, voting 15 to 2 to sell its entire interest in Hershey Foods.

It was a cataclysmic decision. The board could have pursued diversification by selling only a portion of its Hershey holdings, which is what Mike Fisher, Pennsylvania's attorney general and Mark Pacella's boss, would later say his office had had in mind when Pacella urged the trust to diversify.[6] But the board realized that selling the entire block would bring a significant price advantage—the so-called control premium that investors usually are willing to pay for a controlling share of a company.

Focused exclusively on their fiduciary responsibility to maximize the trust's profits to benefit the Milton Hershey School, the board members decided to sell Hershey Foods in its entirety, all at once, in hopes of realizing the largest possible profit. They also refrained from saying they would require any buyer to maintain the company's local operations. Again, their goal was to maximize the sale price.

Convinced they were doing the responsible thing, board members quietly began making arrangements to sell the company, until that sunny day in late July when the news hit the streets of Hershey and the rest of the world.

The Chocolate Hits the Fan

The news that Hershey Foods was in play was big news on Wall Street. Hershey's stock rose from $63 a share into the seventies, and a list of potential buyers quickly emerged, including such international business powerhouses as Kraft Foods, Nestlé, and Cadbury Schweppes. Sale prices of up to $12 billion were mentioned in the press, and lawyers, bankers, and fund managers began licking their chops at the prospect of enormous fees and profits.

But in Hershey, Pennsylvania, the news produced shock and dismay. Bruce Hummel, business agent for the union, recalls being stunned when he heard the news. "We'd just gotten though negotiating a new contract," Hummel says, "and NLRB rules stipulate that the company is supposed to inform the union when a major change like a sale is in the works. They never said a word to us."[7]

Local folks also wondered: Why had Hershey kept them completely in the dark? That isn't how people in small-town America treat their friends and neighbors . . . unless they are ashamed or embarrassed about what they are doing.

In retrospect, some Hershey residents felt that the decision to sell the company must have been in the works for months. Rick Lenny had been the first outsider named CEO of Hershey Foods. Shortly after his arrival in March 2001, a number of long-term company executives had been quietly pushed toward early retirement in what some employees called "the purge." Now that the sale plan had been announced, many concluded that Lenny had been hired specifically to clean house and make the company more attractive to a would-be buyer. Hershey confirmed no such thing. But under the circumstances, the locals were now unwilling to accept the company's word.

Stunned and angry townspeople felt they had no choice but to launch a grassroots campaign to oppose the sale, including the formation of a watchdog group they called Friends of Hershey.

As an ambitious state politician, Pennsylvania attorney general Mike Fisher was soon caught up in the controversy. On August 12, Fisher filed a petition with the seemingly named-for-TV Orphans' Court Division of the Court of Common Pleas of Dauphin County, Pennsylvania, calling for prior court approval of any deal to sell Hershey. This was an ironic turn of events, considering that the impetus for selling Hershey seemed to have originated with a suggestion by a member of Fisher's own staff. Fisher's recent decision to seek the governorship undoubtedly played a role: riding to the rescue of the state's beloved Chocolatetown was clearly an image-enhancing move. Fisher downplayed the politics, however, insisting that he was simply trying to protect the interests of the community, something the Hershey board had failed to do.

The World Is Watching

The international fame of Milton Hershey's charming town had always drawn positive attention to Hershey Foods. Now it fueled controversy. People from around the world took an interest in the fate of the much-loved company and the town that millions had visited as tourists. Columnists and commentators who had recently gorged on the greed and duplicity of companies like Enron, WorldCom, and Adelphia found the Hershey story a tempting treat, writing feature stories on the saga with zinger headlines like "A Bittersweet Deal," "Putting the Bite on Hershey," and the seemingly irresistible "Kiss of Death."

Everyone had something to say about the proposed sale, most of it negative. *Business Week*'s feature story "How Hershey Made a Big Chocolate Mess" excoriated the trust's handling of the sale, citing its failure to anticipate public protests, failure to win advance support from key constituencies, and failure to study the impact of any sale on the Milton Hershey School and its students.[8]

Outside groups connected the Hershey controversy to their own causes. A closely linked trio of not-for-profit organizations— the Campaign for Tobacco-Free Kids, Essential Action, and Global Partnerships for Tobacco Control—weighed in with a strong protest against the sale. One of the potential buyers was Kraft Foods, whose parent company was the tobacco firm Philip Morris. "It would be terribly ironic if the School Trust were to effectively force the sale of Hershey Foods to a company associated with the orphaning of thousands upon thousands of children worldwide," wrote Matthew Myers, the president of the Campaign for Tobacco-Free Kids, in a September 12, 2002, letter to Robert C. Vowler,

CEO of the trust. "Hershey and Philip Morris go together like chocolate and poison."

Soon Essential Action's website featured an "Action Alert" urging readers to support its efforts with a series of specific actions:

1. SEND AN EMAIL to Robert Vowler, CEO of the Hershey Trust Company. . . .
2. SEND LETTERS AND POSTCARDS to Hershey Trust Board Members. . . .
3. SIGN PETITION TO REMOVE HERSHEY TRUSTEES! . . .
4. ADD YOUR VIEWS TO THE LOCAL DEBATE. Submit letters-to-the-editor to local newspapers. . . .[9]

Executives at the company and the trust hunkered down. Apparently stunned by the reaction of the town and bewildered by the avalanche of bad press, they refused comment when besieged by newspaper and TV reporters, and failed to provide spokespeople to air their side of the controversy at public forums. The investment world, initially delighted, began to voice displeasure and doubts. In early August, two Wall Street analysts downgraded Hershey shares as a result of the mishandling of the company sale. Others, certain that the sale would go through despite the controversy, began bidding up the stock price—typical behavior, of course, when a company is in play. Hershey stock reached a high of $79.49 on July 29, then stayed in the upper seventies as the company management began weighing potential offers, while all around them protests and legal maneuverings swirled.

About-Face

Community outrage grew steadily. A petition demanding the ouster of the trust's board grew to 3,000 signatures, then to 6,500, then to 8,000—in a town whose total population was only 12,000. The protests attracted all sorts of unlikely allies, from staunchly

Republican small-business owners who contributed truckloads of pizzas and bottled water to sustain picketing union workers, to prosperous local realtors who showed up wearing fur coats to take lessons in carrying protest signs from union leader Bruce Hummel.

Attorney General Fisher continued to throw up legal roadblocks to a sale. On September 4, after a full day of hearings, Senior Judge Warren G. Morgan of the Orphans' Court surprised most observers by issuing a temporary injunction blocking any deal to sell the company. Morgan chastised board members for showing "a capriciousness that is an abuse of their discretion." As townspeople rejoiced, the trustees appealed, and the case began to travel rapidly through the Pennsylvania court system. Legal advisers to the trust and the company predicted that the injunction would ultimately be overturned, allowing the sale to go ahead.

The trust set a deadline of September 14 for prospective buyers to submit bids. Nestlé, Kraft, Cadbury Schweppes, and even Coca-Cola and PepsiCo were reported to be the leading contenders to win Hershey. But in mid-September, an unexpected suitor appeared—the William Wrigley Jr. Company. Wrigley was smaller than Hershey, with revenues of $2.4 billion and 10,800 employees compared with Hershey's $4.6 billion and 14,400 employees, and was known as "a debt-free, keep-your-head down chewing gum company." For Wrigley to make such a huge acquisition, said one analyst, would be "like a guy who's never had alcohol before drinking a keg of beer."[10]

Nonetheless, on September 17, 2002, a deal was all but finalized to sell Hershey to Wrigley for $12.5 billion. The sale price represented a 42 percent premium over the price of the stock prior to the sale announcement. It was also a full billion dollars richer than the only other offer on the table, a joint bid from Nestlé and Cadbury Schweppes. All in all, it was an excellent financial package, reflecting confidence that the Pennsylvania courts would ultimately have to approve the deal.

But as in any good small-town drama, there was a surprise ending. Just before midnight, Hershey Foods issued a terse statement:

> Hershey Foods Corporation announced today . . . that the Trust's Board of Directors has voted to instruct the company to terminate the sale process that the company initiated at the direction of the trust.[11]

The board had decided to kill its own deal—despite the $12.5 billion on the table and the $17 million in banking and other fees it had already invested in the scheme.

Board members refused to explain their reasons for quashing the sale, just as they had for putting it on the auction block. But media leaks from sources close to the board indicated that the overwhelming and continuing protests from the community had eventually split the board in two. Feeling like pariahs among the angry employees and people of Hershey, first one, then several board members had backed away from the plan. Finally, support for the sale utterly collapsed.

Hershey Foods CEO Rick Lenny, who had negotiated the deal with Wrigley, was deeply embarrassed and furious at the sudden turnaround, reportedly screaming at board members, "We had a deal! You told me if I brought you a deal that was acceptable we would all go ahead."[12] The investment bankers involved in arranging the deal were equally angry. One banker barked, "This has nothing to do with anything other than the politics."[13]

Media around the world reported the startling outcome of the business battle in David-slays-Goliath tones. Thousands of Hershey employees, residents of Hershey, and Hershey School alumni celebrated, feeling they had saved *their* company and *their* community through the power of protest.

The mood at Hershey Foods headquarters was somber. Hershey stock fell nearly 12 percent to $65 the day after the sale was cancelled. By contrast, Wrigley stock fell just eight cents; conservative investors who favored Wrigley may have been relieved to be taken off the hook by the bride's last-minute cold feet. The *Wall Street Journal* observed, "Hershey now is left to chart a course as a stand-alone player that effectively can't be sold—but whose controlling shareholder [the Trust] has shown it is ambivalent about its long-term commitment to the company."[14]

Two months later, under pressure from the community, the employees, and the Pennsylvania attorney general's office, ten members of the board of the Hershey Trust were ousted. A new eleven-member board was created that included four members not on the earlier board, all inhabitants of Hershey or nearby communities. Two months after that, as the dust was finally settling, *Business Week* magazine enshrined the Hershey Trust Company among its "Ten Worst Managers of 2002."[15]

Lessons from the Chocolate Mess

Business managers of all kinds, in all industries, can learn some basic lessons of sustainability from the Hershey fiasco.

Focusing on profit alone can backfire. The managers who made the decision to sell Hershey Foods were doing the right thing by purely financial yardsticks. They were trying to maximize returns to the trust. But in today's business world, the financial bottom line is not the only or even the most important measure of success. Executives also must consider the social, economic, and environmental impacts on anyone with a stake in the outcome.

The protests that derailed the Hershey sale were based on non-financial concerns: the economic impacts of the sale on company employees and their families; the social disruption it would cause to the community; and long-term effects on students, teachers, and alumni of the Milton Hershey School. Those nonfinancial concerns ultimately trumped the financial ones, causing what looked like a good deal to crater.

Businesses are accountable to more people than they may realize. Hershey management acted as if their fiduciary duty was the only interest that mattered. They forgot about other crucial individuals and organizations—stakeholders—with a vested interest in their actions. Some stakeholders had obvious connections to the company—the employees of Hershey Foods, residents of Hershey, alumni of the Milton Hershey School. Others proved to be equally important: the citizens of Pennsylvania; the media; and millions of Americans who knew, loved, and patronized the company and town. Board members even managed to overlook the legacy of Milton S. Hershey himself, whose vision for his company and town was repeatedly invoked against the sale.

The Hershey deal had aspects that appear unique, especially the roles of the Hershey Trust and the attorney general. But almost every company these days faces special circumstances that can disrupt its plans. Some are subject to activist investors who push hard in the opposite direction from where they want to go. Others rely on government contracts or public permits that can be held hostage by politicians or threatened by environmentalists or the media. Some executives wake up to a demonstration by animal rights activists, a camera held by Michael Moore, their headquarters being occupied by Greenpeace, or a call saying, "Eliot Spitzer's office holding for you on line two." Many rely on sensitive natural resources or suppliers in distant places who can upset the apple cart in dozens of ways.

So don't lull yourself by thinking, "Nothing like this can happen to me, because my stock isn't owned by a trust." Chances are good that the world is still watching what you do and will react— strongly—if you make a Hershey-style blunder.

Bad things can happen to good companies that fail to take a broad view of accountability. Well-intentioned, well-managed organizations like the Hershey Trust and Hershey Foods that focus exclusively on shareholders as if they were the only stakeholders that matter are headed for trouble just as certainly as those that knowingly violate societal norms in pursuit of profit.

It could have been different. John Dunn, the former marketing executive at Hershey, emphasizes that the board could have succeeded if they had understood and managed their accountability: "In the end, it's really not that important for Hershey Foods to stay in the hands of the trust. They could have sold the company if they'd handled it properly. But by blundering ahead without communicating with the community, they sent the message that they were willing to endanger the sense of continuity and tradition that the people and businesses of central Pennsylvania had been counting on. That was just plain dumb."[16]

Stakeholder engagement is an increasingly critical component of successful management. In this case, openness and inclusion on the part of the deal-makers were necessary conditions for success. But the Hershey Foods Company was completely incapable of sharing information or bringing stakeholders to the table, even after they announced the deal! To do so would have cut against one hundred years of paternalism and a track record of operating in secrecy and solitude.

Hershey keeps to itself. Hershey's website, for example, contains a lot of fun facts about candy bars but is otherwise less informative by far than any of its competitor's sites. In writing this book, we spoke to numerous sources in and around the town of Hershey, including former employees and officers of the company—yet no company spokesperson or current executive would speak about the firm or its botched sale. Even such basic information as the identity of the products made in Hershey's various chocolate plants is treated as a closely guarded company secret. And when we asked a Hershey spokesman to describe the company's corporate responsibility programs, he replied airily, "Oh, there's so much I could explain if I had the time . . . ," and shortly thereafter hung up the phone.

Companies have legitimate reasons for keeping secrets and for confining decisions to a small circle of insiders and Wall Street bankers, as did Hershey and the trust. But bringing your stakeholders inside the tent on matters that might affect them is increasingly a matter of responsible corporate citizenship *and* sophisticated risk management.

When Hershey sprang its proposed sale on the general public, it was taking an unnecessary business risk, especially in light of recent warning signs (including a rare strike settled just weeks before the announcement). The furious reaction that derailed the sale was driven, in large part, by the fact that everyone except the bankers had been kept in the dark. According to John Dunn, "The way the company handled the controversy compounded the prob- lem. Instead of reaching out, they went into a bunker. They refused to make any public statements, failed to show up at community meetings, ignored calls for an open forum or debate."

It's hard not to agree with Dunn's conclusion that this "was a textbook example of what *not* to do in a corporate controversy."

A year after the showdown, Hershey Foods CEO Rick Lenny was asked to name the most important qualities of a good chief executive. He emphasized "openness and transparency with the multiple constituents" (the full quotation appears at the head of this chapter). It's excellent advice, even if Lenny and his leadership team ignored it during their crisis and there is reason to believe they still don't practice it today.

Politics is an inescapable part of business. The anonymous invest- ment banker who complained bitterly that the cancellation of the sale "has nothing to do with anything other than the politics" was not wrong. The board's decision to pull back *was* a political one, in the sense that it was motivated by the belated recognition that most concerned stakeholders opposed the deal and would, in various ways, have withdrawn their support from the company if the sale had gone through. To a doctrinaire advocate of the free market, the fact that business leaders must consider the political impact of their decisions may be abhorrent. But it's a reality. Hershey's lack of political judg- ment and skills was a direct cause of the company's misfortune.

Hershey and Sustainability

How does the concept of sustainability apply to the Hershey story? From its beginnings, Hershey had made enormous investments in its employees and its town. Yet over a period of several months in 2002, the Hershey Trust squandered much of that valuable social capital. The company inevitably paid a substantial price, as did shareholders. Management even now is working to rebuild the trust and support wasted during that period of confusion. It is unclear whether the community will ever acquiesce even to a partial sale of the company, and the lingering distrust is an anchor that restricts the firm's freedom of action and depresses its business prospects.

A sustainable company manages its risks and maximizes its opportunities by identifying key nonfinancial stakeholders and engaging them in matters of mutual interest. The board's failure to do so harmed the company, the trust, and the employees and local citizens, who quickly realized that their win was illusory. They are stuck with a board and company that have priorities that appear to be directly at odds with their interests.

It is instructive to compare Hershey's corporate culture with the more savvy and responsible approach of one of Hershey's biggest competitors and former suitors, Cadbury Schweppes. The British-based firm is considered one of the world's most socially responsible companies. Among other enlightened practices highlighted in the company's two-hundred-page sustainability report for the year 2004 (titled "Working Better Together") is this description of how Cadbury Schweppes managed the closing of a plant that manufactured cough drops and chewing gum in Avenida, Brazil:

> To increase production, logistics and distribution efficiencies and support our plans for growth and innovation, we decided to consolidate the Avenida production site into the modern facility at Bauru [also in Brazil]. We began the transition in October 2003 and aim to complete it by July 2004. While the closure of Avenida do Estado involves the loss of 300 jobs, 212 new jobs will be created in Bauru.
>
> We have managed the impact of the changes by being open and transparent about what has to be done and by working with employees to do it in the right way. We informed all employees in advance of the closure and hired a firm that specializes in supporting large scale

restructuring. The firm devised a programme, New Professional Project, to coordinate the redeployment of employees in the most supportive way. The programme included researching job vacancies with local companies and matching employees' capabilities, wishes and ambitions within the current job market and business environment.[17]

Comparable openness and responsiveness by Hershey Foods in regard to the possible loss of jobs in Hershey, Pennsylvania—a community that is far more tied to the history and reputation of Hershey Foods than Avenida, Brazil, is to those of Cadbury Schweppes—might have defused resentments stirred up by the proposed sale and paved the way for its completion.

The Hershey story shows that even a well-run company with good intentions and with a proud history of business and philanthropic achievement can stumble or fall when the principles of sustainability are ignored. Why has sustainability become such a crucial issue for today's businesses? And what must they do to address it successfully and avoid the kinds of mistakes that Hershey made? The rest of this book will answer those questions.

2

THE SUSTAINABILITY
SWEET SPOT

How to Achieve Long-Term Business Success

> It's up to us to use our platform to be a good citizen.
> Because not only is it a nice thing to do, it's a
> business imperative. . . . If this wasn't good for
> business, we probably wouldn't do it.
> —*Jeffrey Immelt, CEO, General Electric*[1]

Where Profit Meets the Common Good

Business leaders with a superficial understanding of sustainability think of it as a distraction from their main purpose, a chore they hope can be discharged quickly and easily. "We're responsible corporate citizens, so let's write a check to the United Way or allow employees to volunteer for the local cleanup drive or food kitchen and get back to work."

This approach reveals a fundamental misunderstanding. Sustainability is *not* about philanthropy. There's nothing wrong with corporate charity, but the sustainable company conducts its business so that benefits flow naturally to all stakeholders, including employees, customers, business partners, the communities in which it operates, and, of course, shareholders.

It could be said that the truly sustainable company would have no need to write checks to charity or "give back" to the local community, because the company's daily operations wouldn't deprive the community, but would enrich it. Sustainable companies find areas of mutual interest and ways to make "doing good" and "doing well" synonymous, thus avoiding the implied conflict between society and shareholders.

The vision of a company that renews society as it enriches its shareholders may seem remote, and for most companies it is. But we propose a way to think about your company's current operations that might suggest an avenue for moving in that direction.

Think about sustainability as the common ground shared by your business interests (those of your financial stakeholders) and the interests of the public (your nonfinancial stakeholders). This common ground is what we call the sustainability sweet spot: the place where the pursuit of profit blends seamlessly with the pursuit of the common good (see Figure 2.1). The best-run companies around the world are trying to identify and move into their sweet spots. And they are developing new ways of doing business in order to get there and stay there.

General Electric (GE) has long been considered an environmental scofflaw. It fought the U.S. Environmental Protection Agency (EPA) for years, trying in vain to avoid responsibility for polluting the Hudson and Housatonic Rivers with over one million pounds of toxic waste.[2] Jack Welch, GE's CEO and chairman, personally led the attack, which included arguing over settled science and challenging the entire federal hazardous waste cleanup program as unconstitutional, tactics widely considered irresponsible.

When Welch retired, many of the flattering reviews referred to GE's environmental record as Welch's one black eye. Now Jeffrey Immelt, his successor, appears to be plotting a new course—not because he and the company are born-again environmentalists, but because being pro-environment is smart business for GE.

In 2005 GE announced an initiative called Ecomagination. It is a powerful example of finding and working toward the sweet spot. It's "action that goes beyond compliance to benefit both society and the long term health of the enterprise," according to Ben Heineman, GE's senior vice president of law and public affairs.[3]

Ecomagination's main thrust is to create clean technology to help GE's customers reduce their environmental impacts, primarily carbon emissions. GE has announced it will double its annual investment in clean energy technologies to $1.5 billion by 2010

Figure 2.1. The Sustainability Sweet Spot

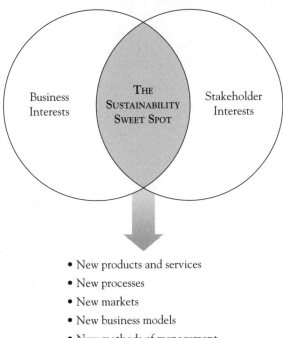

- New products and services
- New processes
- New markets
- New business models
- New methods of management
  and reporting

and will also double its revenues from eco-friendly products during the same time period.[4]

Addressing climate change presents GE with a huge business opportunity. GE's wind energy business has already quadrupled in revenues since it was acquired in 2002 from Enron, and its fuel-efficient jet and locomotive engines and natural gas turbines are proving to be essential to customers needing additional ways to reduce their emissions.[5] GE has sold over $1 billion worth of wind and natural gas turbines to China since 2003.[6]

GE has found a significant overlap between its business interests and protecting the environment. And to expand the area of overlap, the company appears to be saying that the time has come for climate change regulations that will ultimately impose carbon restrictions on businesses in the United States.[7] GE is thus working to nudge the circle representing stakeholder concerns closer to the circle representing its business interests. The bigger the overlap, the better for GE (see Figure 2.2).

GE's Ecomagination embodies the observation by Ian Davis, managing director of the management consulting firm of McKinsey & Company, that "large companies need to build social issues into strategy in a way that reflects their actual business importance."[8] GE has also spent large sums of money advertising Ecomagination, creating some suspicion that the campaign will be more hype than strategy—but that remains to be seen.

The overlap between winning increased market share and supporting healthier lifestyle habits is a sweet spot for PepsiCo (see Figure 2.3). If the idea of healthy products sounds like a stretch for

Figure 2.2. GE's Sustainability Sweet Spot

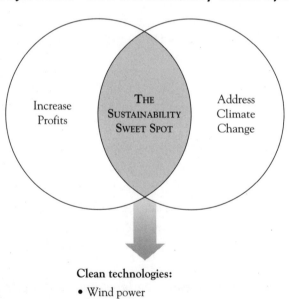

Clean technologies:
- Wind power
- Gas turbines
- Hybrid locomotive engines
- Efficient jet engines

Figure 2.3. PepsiCo's Sweet Spot (Products)

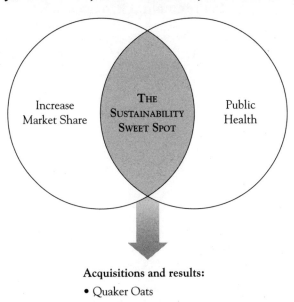

Increase Market Share

THE SUSTAINABILITY SWEET SPOT

Public Health

Acquisitions and results:

- Quaker Oats
- Tropicana
- Rapid sales growth in healthy-product segment

a company famous for its sugary sodas and salty snacks, think again. Having purchased Tropicana and Quaker Oats, PepsiCo has made the healthy-product sweet spot the fastest-growing segment of PepsiCo's North American product portfolio by far, with 2005 revenue growth about 2.5 times that of its traditional products. Social responsibility has thus helped PepsiCo earnings per share grow at a prodigious 13 percent in 2004 and to surpass Coca-Cola in market cap for the first time in history.[9]

PepsiCo is working toward other sweet spots. Its business goal of cost reduction overlaps with a series of environmental improvements to reduce energy, waste, and packaging (Figure 2.4). Its goal of risk reduction overlaps with steps to address long-term water supply and quality concerns for communities in which its plants are located and for its crucial suppliers (such as farmers who supply corn

Figure 2.4. PepsiCo's Sweet Spot (Environmental Processes)

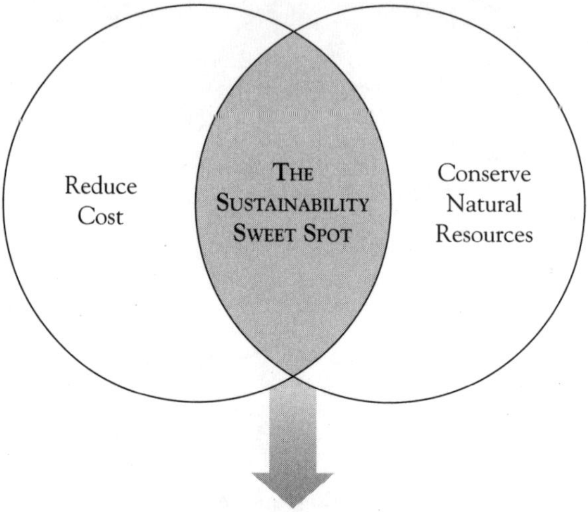

Reduce Cost

THE SUSTAINABILITY SWEET SPOT

Conserve Natural Resources

Process improvements:

- Reduced water use
- Greater energy efficiency
- Reduced packaging
- Enterprise-wide environmental metrics
- Centralized technical assistance

for Frito-Lay brand chips) (Figure 2.5). These responsible actions will benefit the environment and PepsiCo's neighbors and business partners even as they increase shareholder value and put the company's operations on a more sound, sustainable footing for decades to come.

The sweet spot embodies the literal meaning of "sustainability," making your company *viable for the long term* by managing according to principles that will strengthen rather than undermine the company's roots in the environment, the social fabric, and the economy. A business that occupies the sustainability sweet spot (or that strives to fit as much of its activities into that favored zone as possible) should have real long-term advantages over its rivals.

Figure 2.5. PepsiCo's Sweet Spot (Risk Management)

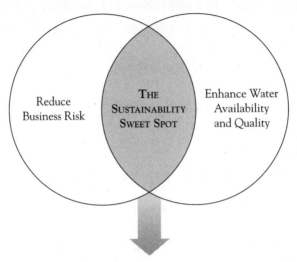

Risk management steps:
- Assessments of community water supply and quality
- Assessments of supplier water
- Programs to reduce water requirements on all affected parties

Imagine a company that historically earns its profits from a finite resource whose extraction and use degrades the environment—providing oil or coal, for example, which exist in limited supplies and generate harmful pollution. Such a business isn't sustainable in the long run; either the resources or the social tolerance for pollution on which it relies will eventually run out. Costs will rise as supplies dwindle and as social concerns translate into higher taxes, additional cleanup costs, and increased liability.

If it were possible for such a company to shift its business so as to eventually supply clean and renewable energy (such as wind or solar power) or conservation services while maintaining or even increasing revenues, that would be a responsible and profitable choice.

This is not a hypothetical case. British Petroleum (BP) adopted this long-term strategy when it rebranded itself "Beyond Petroleum" in 1998. BP has since reduced greenhouse gas emissions from its own production processes (saving an estimated $650 million thanks to improved efficiencies along the way) and has invested heavily in alternative energy sources, including solar power. BP is not yet sustainable by any means, but it is acting responsibly as it marches toward an ever larger sweet spot.

A Map to the Sweet Spot

Every action you take in business has two components: an impact on profits and an impact on the world. This can be represented by a four-celled matrix with two axes, which represent profitability and social benefit (see Figure 2.6).

The northeast corner of the map is conceptually similar to the sweet spot, where stakeholders' interests and corporate interests overlap. Your goal is to get as much of your business activity into that quadrant as possible. You want every business decision to push you north and east. The value of the map emerges when you use it to plot the location of various businesses or activities in order to determine ways to move them in a northeasterly direction, or to generate ideas for quantum strategic change.

Suppose you own a business or manage part of one that is currently located in the northwest quadrant (profitable but not

Figure 2.6. The Sustainability Map

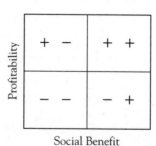

sustainable). Is it possible to devise ways of moving the business eastward (more sustainable) without moving south (less profitable)? DuPont has done so by moving from the chemical business toward the soy protein business without sacrificing revenues or profits. If you have a business in the southwest corner (neither profitable nor sustainable), can you find ways to base a turnaround on moving both north and east?

Your goal should be to develop strategies and change operations to move toward the northeast corner of the map. For example, an energy company that profits from burning dirty coal could devote its short-term research dollars toward clean-coal technology and its long-term effort toward a future in which most energy is derived from such renewable sources as solar, wind, hydroelectric, and geothermal power. Both initiatives embody migration toward the northeast corner of the map, where both profitability and social benefit are high.

Both small and large companies have changed their businesses to move further toward the northeast corner of the sustainability map.

Country Lanes is a tiny UK tour company that offers day trips and holiday travel, by bicycle or on foot.[10] Patrons must somehow find their way to the rendezvous point at which the tour begins. Country Lanes recently redesigned all its tours to begin at railway stations, with the result that 85 percent of their customers now use rail travel to get there. This has eliminated a million miles of automobile travel and 328 tonnes of carbon dioxide emissions per year. Business is up because customers now find it easier to get to the tours. Country Lanes also supports local business by encouraging its customers to spend money on snacks, drinks, and lunches from neighborhood pubs and shops.

When Toyota revealed its intention to create a new form of gasoline-electric car, one that would capture and use braking energy, the company was derided as an environmental do-gooder that would surely lose money. "We wondered if anyone would want one," admitted Takehisa Yaegashi, the senior Toyota engineer now known as the father of the hybrid.[11] Today Toyota can't manufacture the Prius fast enough to meet demand. The car is peppy, durable, and easy to drive, and gets up to 52 miles per gallon of gas in city driving. Waiting lists are sixteen months long in some parts of the United States and Japan. Over one hundred twenty thousand of the hybrids were shipped to the United States in 2005, more than doubling the previous year's figure, and hybrid versions of Toyota's Highlander and Lexus SUVs have entered the market.

Toyota now views hybrids as a central part of its strategy to become the number one car manufacturer in the world and break into the Big Three in the United States. The company recently announced that it will focus on selling one million hybrid vehicles a year worldwide (including six hundred thousand in the United States) by early in the next decade.[12]

Toyota made two bets at once: that both the price of gas and concern about air pollution would rise. Winning either bet might have made the car a success, but Toyota appears to have won both, making the Prius a worldwide phenomenon. The car is both good for Toyota's shareholders and good for the environment—a remarkable example of finding the sweet spot.

"Prove It!"

Many businesspeople find the simple logic behind the sweet spot compelling, but others require proof that sustainability creates financial benefits. They seek an assurance that's as good as gold—incontrovertible evidence that they can and will make more money practicing sustainable management than they will with good old-fashioned, short-term, profit-only thinking.

Let's start then with the testimony of those that help companies create gold. Goldman Sachs, Deutsche Bank, Credit Suisse, Banco do Brasil, and fifteen other multinational investment banks recently reported the following:

> [We] are convinced that in a more globalized, interconnected and competitive world the way that environmental, social and corporate governance issues are managed is part of companies' overall

management quality needed to compete successfully. Companies that perform better with regard to these issues can increase shareholder value by, for example, properly managing risks, anticipating regulatory action, or accessing new markets, while at the same time contributing to the sustainable development of societies in which they operate. Moreover, these issues can have a strong impact on reputation and brands, an increasingly important part of company value.[13]

Empirical evidence includes the share prices of companies listed in the Dow Jones Sustainability Index and the FTSE4 Good Indexes, two listings of sustainability companies that have outperformed various market indexes. Companies that belong to the World Business Council for Sustainable Development outperformed their respective national stock exchanges by 15 to 25 percent over the past three years. From 1999 through 2003, the Winslow Green Index of one hundred "green-screened" companies increased in value by over 73 percent, whereas the members of the comparable benchmark Russell 2000 Index increased by less than 17 percent.[14]

"Companies pursuing growth in the triple bottom line tend to display superior stock market performance with favorable risk-return profiles," according to John Prestbo, president of Dow Jones Indexes. "Thus sustainability becomes a proxy for enlightened and disciplined management—which just happens to be the most important factor that investors do and should consider in deciding where to buy a stock."[15]

Exemplary environmental performance, long considered a proxy for good management, is now being touted by investment advisers as a measure of value—perhaps of hidden value, the savvy investor's favorite kind. UBS, the Swiss-based investment bank, recently opined, "Environmental performance indicators appear to be a possible indicator of strong operational performance. Strong environmental indicators in the presence of below-average profitability may signal an investment opportunity, in our view."[16]

It cannot be proved that sustainability is *the* reason behind the strong market performance of the companies that have embraced it, but when similar results continue year after year, the correlation implies causation. (As Henry D. Thoreau, the American essayist and philosopher, famously remarked, "Some circumstantial evidence is very strong, as when you find a trout in the milk.")

Those seeking the gold standard should recall that the cases for such strategic initiatives as Total Quality Management, Six Sigma, and reengineering were not proved before thousands of businesses invested billions of dollars in them. These concepts won widespread support because of case studies that illustrated their effectiveness, endorsements from well-known business leaders, their resonance with the *zeitgeist* of their times, and eventually (in some cases) because of financial results. The initial evidence supporting those programs was largely anecdotal, but, as Travis Engen, recently retired CEO of Alcan, once observed, the plural of *anecdote* is *data*.

Like most business strategies, sustainability is not a guarantee of financial success. It requires commitment, resources, and a change of direction, which entail costs and risks. The real question, as with all important business decisions, is this: Is sustainability a good bet for me and my company?

Sustainability is quickly becoming mainstream. Socially responsible initiatives, from the Prius to natural foods, from green buildings to eco-friendly clothes and cosmetics, from windpower to the beneficial reuse of industrial waste, have migrated from being considered heretical, to impractical, to visionary, and finally to common sense—usually as soon as they begin to turn a profit. Eventually they become part of business as usual, their controversial origins all but forgotten.

When Ralph Nader first began to argue that cars could be made much safer, he was dismissed by Detroit and most of the public as an agitator and a nutcase. Now all car companies strive for increased safety, and some, such as Volvo, have made it the centerpiece of their marketing.

Can a sustainable business strategy enhance profitability? Of course, but when it does, it usually travels on our mental maps from the space now labeled "sustainability" into the one more simply known as "good business."

Three Ways Sustainability Enhances Your Business

Whether you find or even look for the sweet spot, the principles of sustainability can improve the management of your business in three fundamental ways—by helping you *protect* it, *run* it, and *grow* it.[17]

Protecting the Business

Protecting the business includes reducing risk of harm to customers, employees, and communities; identifying emerging risks and management failures early; limiting regulatory interventions; and retaining the explicit or implicit license to operate granted by government or by the community at large.

Biotechnology giant Monsanto made a concerted push into the field of bioengineering crops in the mid- to late 1990s. Monsanto's genetically modified (GM) seeds were supposed to offer farmers enormous competitive benefits—corn containing natural insecticides, and soybeans able to withstand potent weed killers. Monsanto had a powerful sweet spot proposition: that its pioneering efforts would give the company a leading position in a major new marketplace and provide a powerful new weapon in the battle against world hunger. "Monsanto is in a unique position to contribute to the global future," declared biodiversity advocate Peter Raven.[18]

But Monsanto executives, like those at Hershey, failed to work with stakeholders in their development of the new initiative—a core principle of sustainable business. Monsanto dismissed early critics of GM products as antitechnology fanatics and failed to mount a concerted effort to educate consumers about the science behind genetic engineering.

Monsanto consequently found itself beset by a variety of attacks. A British scientist claimed that rats eating GM potatoes failed to grow properly, and a Cornell university study published in 1999 appeared to show that monarch butterfly caterpillars died after ingesting pollen from bioengineered corn. The accuracy of both claims was quickly challenged, but public fears about "Frankenfoods" now seemed to be bolstered by science.

Several European supermarket chains as well as American natural-food retailers announced that they would remove GM foods from their shelves, and major food companies, such as baby-food maker Gerber, vowed to keep their products free of GM ingredients. Embarrassingly, even the staff canteen at Monsanto's own UK headquarters announced it would ban GM food from its menu "in response to concern raised by our customers."[19]

Nonengineered soybeans began to sell at a premium over their modified counterparts—a sign that the market was rejecting GM foods. By the end of 2000, the stock market valued Monsanto's $5 billion-a-year agricultural business unit at less than zero, despite billions the company had invested in highly advanced science over the previous decade.[20]

Today the entire biotech industry is still struggling to win acceptance for bioengineered products in Europe and around the world—largely because of Monsanto's early failure to consider the demands of sustainability before launching this major business initiative.

Running the Business

Running the business includes reducing costs, improving productivity, eliminating needless waste, and obtaining access to capital at lower cost.

Eco-efficiency is a basic component of sustainability that applies to running your business. It means reducing the amount of resources used to produce goods and services, which increases a company's profitability while decreasing its environmental impact. The underlying theme is simple: pollution is waste, and waste is anathema because it means that your company is paying for something it didn't use. Given the clarity of this logic, it's amazing how few companies have diligently pursued eco-efficiency.

Consider the financial benefits from eco-efficiency enjoyed by STMicroelectronics (ST), the Swiss-based firm that is one of the world's largest manufacturers of semiconductors, with 2003 revenues of $7.2 billion and close to forty-six thousand employees worldwide. ST earmarks 2 percent of its annual capital investments for environmental improvements. The resulting efficiencies have trimmed the company's electricity use by 28 percent and its water use by 45 percent, with cost savings of $56 million in 2001, $100 million in 2002, and $133 million in 2003. Energy conservation projects pay for themselves within 2.5 years on average—an extraordinary return on investment. Former CEO and honorary chairman Pasquale Pistorio notes, "this proves the validity of the stance we have taken for years: ecology is free."[21]

Growing the Business

Growing the business includes opening new markets, launching new products and services, increasing the pace of innovation, improving customer satisfaction and loyalty, growing market share by attracting customers for whom sustainability is a personal or business value, forming new alliances with business partners and other stakeholders, and improving reputation and brand value.

Sustainability is a powerful engine of economic and business growth, driving innovation and new technologies. In 2004, $5.8 billion was spent on "green building" initiatives, the design and construction of eco-friendly, healthy, and efficient buildings.[22] Entire new businesses have been developed in support, including energy-saving home appliances, low-flow toilets, ultraefficient heating, solar heating and electricity, and superefficient cooling and insulation systems.

The sustainability mind-set is also helping companies think creatively about how to gain access to vast new markets that were once dismissed as unprofitable or even impossible. Significant businesses are being built at the "bottom of the pyramid," among the four billion people living on less than $2 per day, who collectively represent enormous untapped buying power. Companies that figure out how to sell goods and services to the poor will reap huge rewards in the decades to come and create new opportunity for those in need.

C. K. Prahalad, the business consultant who, along with Professor Stuart Hart, has studied opportunities at the bottom of the pyramid, explains how companies that respect the rights, needs, and interests of the poor can create new business models that in turn create economic opportunity for business and society.[23]

Prahalad cites Casa Bahia, a Brazilian retailer with sales of over $1.2 billion and over twenty thousand employees, which operates exclusively in the *favelas*, or shantytowns, where the poorest people of Brazil are found; Annapurna Salt, a Unilever brand that has captured a significant share of the market in India, Ghana, Kenya, Nigeria, and other African nations with small, low-priced packages of iodized salt specifically designed to help combat rampant iodine deficiency disorder among the poor; and Hindustan Lever Ltd., the largest soap producer in India, which has achieved sales of over $2.5 billion through innovative production, packaging, and marketing techniques that reach into many of the smallest and poorest villages in the subcontinent. This is pure sweet spot, creating profit while providing access to needed and affordable consumer goods, thereby stimulating economic growth and improving the quality of life.

It takes ingenuity and creativity to find ways to reach customers at the bottom of the pyramid. But the effort is worthwhile, not just because of the sizeable profits to be earned in the short run but because of even greater long-term benefits to companies that win the patronage and loyalty of this huge group of consumers at the start of their march toward middle-class status—a transition that bottom-of-the-pyramid programs will help accelerate.

Additional Business Benefits of Sustainability

So far we've focused on the hard side of the case for sustainability— the direct and measurable costs, primarily financial, of ignoring your stakeholders and their concerns, and the economic benefits that companies are enjoying by managing themselves or producing goods and services to assist others in the pursuit of the principles of sustainability.

There's also a soft side, one that turns on opportunities and risks that may be harder to quantify: company reputation, employee satisfaction, customer good will, and the value of being considered a leader in your industry.

Wegman's, a privately held grocery chain with sales of $3.4 billion in 2004, was named the best company to work for in America by *Fortune* magazine.[24] The company offers higher-than-average wages, high-end training programs, college tuition assistance, and, perhaps most important, jobs designed to empower workers to make decisions to help customers. Wegman's commitment to these practices is expensive: the company spends 15 to 17 percent of sales on labor costs as opposed to the industry average of 12 per cent. Wegman's has also spent over $54 million in tuition assistance over the past twenty years.

But employee satisfaction creates sizeable financial benefits for Wegman's. The company's costs related to turnover (for example, unemployment insurance, severance, training, lost productivity) are 6 percent of revenues compared to the industry average of 19 percent, which translates to a savings of approximately $300 million per year, far more than needed to cover the costs of the programs.

Moreover, the family-owned company is thriving in the face of competitive pressure from companies like Wal-Mart and Costco, and sees its employee retention programs as fundamental to its success. Wegman's margins are double those of America's four biggest grocery firms, and its sales per square foot are twice the industry average.

Hard Cases

Unfortunately, sustainability isn't always an easy win-win. Many situations arise, especially in the short term, where being sustainable imposes additional costs or redirects money away from shareholders and toward other stakeholders. Some of these situations are resolved as being in the long-term interest of shareholders, but others represent genuine, perhaps permanent conflicts of interest between shareholders and other stakeholders. These are the hard cases.

Many companies try to avoid those situations by seeking new sweet spot opportunities or concentrating on activities that will move them closer to the northeast corner of the Sustainability Map. But avoidance isn't always possible. The realities of the U.S. automobile industry, for example, include both consumer demand for gas-guzzlers and a cost structure that currently makes big cars more profitable than hybrids. It's impossible, not to mention highly unsustainable, for a company to act against its own financial interest. Demanding that the car companies or their executives do so is, to put it kindly, counterproductive.

There's a useful distinction between being *sustainable* and being *responsible*. The responsible action is for the automakers to meet the current demand for SUVs while working to alter consumer preferences and preparing to make hybrids profitable. Thus, when Bill Ford Jr. publicly describes the environmental downsides of SUVs and works to make the hybrid Ford Escape a winner in the marketplace, his behavior can be considered highly responsible even though his industry, his company, and his main products are not yet sustainable.

Similarly, we can't expect, nor do we want, the energy companies to give up on oil and gas production today because extracting and burning fossil fuels is unsustainable in the long term. But we can and should expect them to work hard to help society make the transition to renewable energy sources—as BP is doing, even while it maintains a high percentage of its current operations in oil and gas extraction.

Hardest of all is when there is *no* sustainable or responsible action to be taken. If, for example, genetically modified food is conclusively proved to be dangerous for consumers and bad for the planet (like leaded gasoline or asbestos-based insulation), the only responsible approach for companies in that business will be to close down their operations as fast as possible while trying to mitigate the adverse impacts of doing so. Any other choice would be socially irresponsible, making them the legitimate target of activists, responsible businesses, and society, while at the same time exposing their shareholders to ever-growing liability risks.

Why Now?

We believe that sustainability enhances profitability for the vast majority of companies. It serves as a road map for doing business in an interdependent world. It offers new ways to protect your company from environmental, financial, and social risks, to run your company with greater efficiency and productivity, and to grow your company through the development of new products and services and the opening of new markets. It provides intangible benefits that include an improved corporate reputation, higher employee morale, and increased customer goodwill. Sustainability will set you and your organization on the path to long-term success.

So far, so good. But if these assertions are correct, why has sustainability only recently made its way onto the agenda? What is different about *today*'s business environment that is making sustainability a crucial factor in twenty-first-century business success? To answer this question, we need to make a brief detour into business history and examine the emergence of some of the most potent trends now at work on the global stage.

3

THE AGE OF ACCOUNTABILITY

Sorry, I can't talk right now—I'm uploading a live
satellite feed onto the Web. We're watching
Greenland break apart.
—*Kert Davies, research director, Greenpeace,*
during a telephone conversation with Andrew W. Savitz

Sustainable Business—An Old Idea
Made New Again

Practices that promote certain aspects of sustainability have been
around for a long time. Some great companies have always tried to
behave responsibly in terms of their resources and impacts. But the
areas that make up today's sustainability movement—the environment, community relations, labor practices, social responsibility,
and others—were historically seen in isolation from one another,
with companies addressing specific issues based on their special circumstances or business requirements, or because of the personalities of their leaders. So when we try to trace the history of
sustainable business, we find scattered, disconnected anecdotes that
describe the pioneering efforts of a few organizations in a few areas.
In retrospect, these efforts foreshadow the much more powerful,
widespread, and integrated sustainability movement that is transforming business today.

None of the companies that deserve a place in the early history
of sustainability have scored consistently high marks over the years

in all three areas of social, environmental, and economic responsibility. DuPont, for example, is only now transforming itself from a company notorious for polluting the environment in the 1960s into a more environmentally responsible business and ultimately sustainable enterprise. But in terms of safety and community involvement, the leaders of the new DuPont can draw historical connections to the earliest days of the company.

DuPont's sustainability philosophy dates back over two hundred years to when the firm was an explosives manufacturer.[1] The first DuPont plant was housed in a three-sided building designed to funnel unplanned explosions toward the neighboring Brandywine River. The underlying social principle was simple and suited to the times: "Don't blow up the workers—and mind the town as well." Thus company founder E. I. DuPont and the other early leaders of the firm embraced two basic aspects of sustainability—worker and community safety—from the company's earliest days. (Undoubtedly they also recognized the financial price they'd pay if a disastrous accident occurred, as it did in 1818, when an explosion attributed to a foreman's drinking killed forty workers, which forever ended any drinking on DuPont sites.) To this day, safety is DuPont's number one priority, and the company draws on its legacy to reinforce a safety culture.

It took another two hundred years for DuPont (and society at large) to develop a comparable concern for the environment. By then, DuPont had helped create more than 250 hazardous waste sites, which it has so far spent $1.2 billion to clean up. Today the company faces fresh environmental concerns related to the possible impacts of the chemicals used to manufacture Teflon.

Ford Motor Company pioneered the element of today's sustainability movement that centers on economic benefits to workers and the community.[2] In 1913, when hourly wages for skilled workers ran as low as $.15, the company's founder, Henry Ford, startled the world by announcing that he would pay a guaranteed daily wage of $5 to every worker, because "everyone who works at Ford should be able to afford the product he produces." It was a shrewd business move as well as a humane one. Labor turnover at Ford virtually disappeared, with the result that the company's total labor costs *fell*, enabling Ford to lower the price of a Model T while increasing profits.

Ford can't claim an unblemished record on labor relations, however. During the Great Depression, Ford engaged union-busting thugs to beat up striking workers, and it has used enormous, disruptive layoffs to control payroll costs during business downturns. Yet Ford now works to find the sustainability sweet spot, generally facing its challenges straightforwardly and often in collaboration with other affected parties.

Every company would like to claim that the products and services it provides offer some positive benefit to the broader community, and, in that sense, the idea that businesses have a responsibility to serve society is far from new. But prior to the 1990s only a handful of companies made social benefits an explicit part of their overall management approach.

Johnson & Johnson (J&J), the venerable maker of medical equipment, drugs, and other health care supplies, is the preeminent pioneer in this area.[3] In 1943, Robert Wood Johnson Jr., the CEO of J&J and son of the company's founder, wrote a credo that codified the firm's socially responsible approach to conducting business. The credo has since been updated and revised, but its hierarchy of values remains the same. The company's first responsibility is to the people who use its products and services; the second, to its employees; the third, to the community and environment; and the fourth, to the stockholders. In the view of J&J's leadership, "if the Credo's first three responsibilities are met, the stockholders will be well served."

Many companies plaster their values on the walls. Within J&J, the credo defines the culture. Employees at every level of the company frequently debate its meaning and turn to the credo for guidance in solving daily problems.

The credo's value was vividly illustrated during the 1982 Tylenol crisis, when a handful of capsules of the popular painkiller were laced with cyanide by a still-unidentified criminal and placed on drugstore shelves in the Chicago area, causing seven deaths. The company's response to this crisis might have been defensive or self-serving, designed to minimize financial damage to the company. But at J&J the well-being of customers came first. The corporation immediately removed all Tylenol products from sale across the United States (at an estimated cost of $100 million) and mobilized a 2,500-person communications effort to get out all the facts as openly, honestly, and rapidly as possible. As a result, nationwide panic was contained, the endangered Tylenol brand was saved, and public confidence in J&J was completely restored, even bolstered. CEO Jim Burke and his associates were quick to credit the forty-year-old credo for their surefooted response to the crisis.

The companies we've cited here—DuPont, Ford, and J&J—were sustainability pioneers, each developing a specific aspect of corporate responsibility based on their specific circumstances. All three are now actively engaged in the full range of economic, social, and environmental activities defined by sustainability and measured by the Triple Bottom Line. As companies of enormous stature and long-term financial success, they show that a commitment to sustainability—to managing in a socially responsible fashion—is fully consistent with profitable growth over the long haul.

New Pressures on Business

In philosophical terms, the notion of corporate responsibility probably originated in the form of business philanthropy in the 1920s, as exemplified by the charitable foundations created by the great capitalists John D. Rockefeller, Henry Ford, and Andrew Carnegie. Having created huge business empires—often using competitive methods that many considered ethically questionable—these moguls moved, in their later years, toward returning some of their wealth to the communities that created it, building universities, hospitals, museums, libraries, schools, and churches that enhance the quality of life to this day.

At the same time, many businesses were building entire communities around their factories, creating housing, stores, recreational facilities, and churches for their workers. In some cases, the business owners were motivated by an idealistic desire to create a better world. That was the case with Milton S. Hershey and his beloved Chocolatetown. In other cases, greed and the desire to control the lives of workers were more powerful motivations. In some mining, steel, and factory towns, living conditions were squalid or dangerous. The legacy of company towns whose environment was despoiled by irresponsible businesses lives on today in such communities as Anniston, Alabama, and Bethlehem, Pennsylvania, which are still working to restore the damage done by decades of toxic dumping.

In the 1930s and 1940s, corporate responsibility expanded to include workers' rights. Labor unions battled to organize workers, achieve recognition by management, and win concessions, such as increased wages, shorter hours, and improved working conditions. Roosevelt's New Deal pushed through a series of laws protecting the rights of labor, including the National Labor Relations Act (1935), which guaranteed the right to collective bargaining, and the Fair Labor Standards Act (1938), which established the minimum wage and the forty-hour work week. However, unions and the federal government were the primary forces behind these efforts; many businesses fought against the expansion of workers' rights.

During this period, business thinkers were not focused on the social implications of *how* businesses operated. Business's social responsibility was considered a matter of making charitable donations to organizations like the local Community Chest. As Peter Drucker put it in his classic *Management,* "Where an earlier generation had looked to the 'rich businessman' to endow a hospital, post–World War II big business was expected to support worthy causes. Emphasis was still on [supporting] outside 'causes' rather than on the behavior and actions of business itself."[4]

The focus on the impact of business on society intensified in the 1960s, as part of a general social awakening. Rachel Carson's book *Silent Spring* (1962) galvanized a generation of political activists, spearheaded the campaign to ban the pesticide DDT, and is widely credited with launching the modern environmental movement.

The two decades that followed saw a series of landmark events that exemplified the growing power of environmentalism, including (in the United States) the creation of the Environmental Protection Agency (EPA) and passage of a host of laws—the Clean Air Act, the Clean Water Act, the Superfund, the Resource Conservation and Recovery Act, the Safe Drinking Water Act, and others—that focused on *how* businesses operated.

Consumer rights and product safety also emerged as major corporate issues, driven by the groundbreaking work of Ralph Nader. His dramatic congressional testimony about auto safety and the revelations in his book *Unsafe at Any Speed: The Designed-In Dangers of the American Automobile* (1965) led to a series of auto safety laws and launched the consumer movement. In 1972, Congress established the U.S. Consumer Product Safety Commission, and subsequent years saw a series of trends that continued to put the spotlight on business, including the rise of product safety litigation focused on consumer goods from the Dalkon Shield contraceptive device to asbestos to tobacco. Attention had shifted to the responsibility of companies for the impacts of their products and how they were made.

As the 1970s, 1980s, and 1990s unfolded, more social movements emerged, each creating new pressures on businesses to fulfill newfound social responsibilities: the civil rights movement (focused initially on equal rights for blacks, and later broadened to include Latinos or Hispanics, Native Americans, and other ethnic groups); the women's rights movement; the anti-apartheid movement focused on South Africa; the gay rights movement; and other similar efforts.

Today the business environment continues to evolve in ways that make the increasing demand for corporate responsibility dangerous to ignore and profitable to embrace. In the rest of this chapter, we'll look at some of the most important trends contributing to this evolution.

A Freer World

When World War II ended in 1945, only about twenty-two nations had democratic forms of government. The rest were either totalitarian or authoritarian. And even these few democratic governments operated in a style of benign paternalism, exemplified by the Eisenhower administration, in which major decisions were made by a handful of political leaders who took advice almost exclusively from the heads of large, established institutions—major corporations, leading universities, the military. Western governments weren't under pressure to be responsive to the people, who were just glad to have survived a brutal world war and mainly wanted government to jump-start their economies and protect them from the new threat of Communist domination.

Today, an estimated 117 nations are democratic. And with the spreading worldwide acceptance of free enterprise and democracy as the way of the future, people everywhere are taking it for granted that they deserve more say about their own futures.

The government paternalism of the 1950s has long since been replaced by activism and citizen involvement. Groups that were once effectively disenfranchised—women, racial and religious minorities, gays, students, consumers, and the elderly—have forced their way into the political dialogue, claiming rights and influence once enjoyed only by powerful elites. This spreading democratic spirit underlies the explosion of rights movements touched on earlier in this chapter, and the trend feeds on itself: the more freedom and power people have, the more they expect and are in a position to demand.

For businesses, this change offers fabulous opportunity. The demise of communism has opened up new markets all around the world. The widespread acceptance of free enterprise has liberated vast industries from nationalization and created broad new horizons for business in the former Soviet Union and its erstwhile satellites. Vast new markets have opened in once-destitute nations, such as India and China. And in the United States, working women, blacks, Latinos, Asians, and gays have become far more significant in the consumer marketplace.

But these new opportunities carry a price. Main Street now has a vested interest in corporations' financial and social performance. The newly empowered people who are your customers, your workers, your investors, and your neighbors are demanding a voice in how your business is run and its impact on their lives.

A More Interdependent World

The world in which we live and do business is also becoming more closely interdependent, a profound change created by several related trends.

Products and services, distribution, and marketing are all becoming more complex, demanding that companies and individuals work more closely together both within and between enterprises and also across regional and national borders. Many of the world's most successful companies today operate not as centrally controlled monoliths but as networks of loosely connected units, each with a high degree of autonomy. P&G, for example, has thousands of business relationships, gets lots of business ideas from outside the company, and uses joint ventures at a global, regional, and local level to bring them to fruition. As A. G. Laffey, the company's chairman and CEO, says, "It's pretty clear we will work with anybody."[5] A generation ago it's unlikely that any Fortune 500 CEO would have made such a statement.

Even as these relationships multiply, they are becoming more complicated. The relationship between vendors and purchasers, once a simple zero-sum game in which each fought for a larger piece of the pie, has become far more complex. P&G and Wal-Mart, for example, recognizing their financial and operating interdependence, now work closely together to develop information and logistics technologies that will benefit both.

What does all this have to do with sustainability? As companies become increasingly dependent on one another, their interests become more closely entwined. The traditional doctrines of "buyer beware" and "arm's-length transactions" work less well in a world where your company's long-term health requires stable business relationships and economically healthy and ethically responsible partners, joint venturers, suppliers, distributors, and marketers with whom to do business. And when those parties may be located anywhere in the world, you and your company suddenly have good reason to care about the practices of companies and nations far from corporate headquarters.

Mutual dependence isn't merely financial. It is also reputational and legal. Two thousand vendors contribute parts or services to Ford automobiles, and another nine thousand assist Ford to run as a company.[6] Any one of those suppliers or vendors that uses prison labor, employs a ten-year-old worker in one of its factories, or dumps toxic waste into a river can create embarrassment as well as political and legal problems for Ford. And advocacy groups are prepared to exploit the new interdependence to put pressure on companies. "We attack the weakest link in the company's value chain," says Kert Davies, director of research at Greenpeace.[7]

Most managers don't yet realize that they may be held responsible for the illegal or irresponsible actions of their suppliers and vendors, or that their customers may be held responsible for those actions. Management of social issues all the way up and down the supply chain is one of the new challenges posed by the sustainability imperative in an interconnected world.

A Wired World

The spread of freedom, the growth of a worldwide economy, and the business interdependence we have just described are all being driven by an astounding explosion of global communications advances.

Social critics were surprised by the impact of television on American culture and politics in the early 1960s. The Kennedy-Nixon presidential debates demonstrated that in the television age, image is all-important. Voters who listened on radio felt that Nixon won on the strength of his rhetoric, whereas those who saw the debate on TV gave Kennedy the edge because of his more youthful, confident, and attractive appearance. Many voters turned against U.S. involvement in Vietnam, the "living room war," because it was the first war whose horrible reality could be viewed every evening on the TV news. Electronic media had begun to turn the planet into a global fishbowl.

Today, as the quotation from Kert Davies at the head of this chapter suggests, anyone concerned about the impact of global warming on the polar ice cap can literally watch it happening via live satellite feed on the Internet. Anyone concerned about, or aggrieved by, the activities of any corporation can easily find and join with like-minded people on the World Wide Web. Bad news can circle the globe in an instant, with potentially devastating effects—as the makers of Kryptonite locks recently discovered.

Kryptonite makes a popular brand of U-shaped bicycle lock with a tubular cylinder locking mechanism.[8] At least, it *was* a popular brand until an obscure design flaw suddenly leaped into prominence. It seems that a high percentage of the locks could be easily opened without a key by using the plastic barrel of a Bic-style ball-point pen. The flaw had been noticed and written about as early as 1992, but few people knew about it until a bike-loving security specialist named Chris Brennan posted an item about it on a cyclists' Internet bulletin board in September 2004.

Suddenly it seemed that everyone in the world had heard about the problem. Within a week, hundred of messages raising the alarm about the "Bic-pick" maneuver were flying through cyberspace. Bike shop owners saw sales of Kryptonite products plummet. One retailer commented, "At first I didn't believe it. Then I tried it—wow—there it is—easier than a lock pick. The Bic thing has shaken my faith in any of the tubular cylinder locks, and we are pulling all of them from the shelves."

Thankfully for Kryptonite, the company had already designed a new disc-style cylinder with improved pick-proof attributes. When the public relations disaster struck, Kryptonite rushed huge quantities of the new lock into production. Within weeks, they'd replaced the old locks on store shelves—and probably saved the company. It was a near-death experience made possible mainly by the global reach of the Internet and the power it places in the hands of consumers.

Of course, companies can also use the new media technologies to their advantage. (Today, Kryptonite studiously monitors the blogosphere and has considered launching a blog of its own to stay in touch with avid users, retailers, and critics of bicycle security systems.) But the communications media are so decentralized that it's impossible for any company, no matter how large, rich, and powerful, to control the messages being disseminated about it. And fragmented media outlets with niche audiences (such as bicycle enthusiasts) are easily leveraged by advocacy groups—at a cost close to zero.

You are now doing business in a world where what you say can easily be drowned out by a multiplicity of voices over which you have no control. It's not just the Internet. The proliferation of twenty-four-hour news services, from the cable networks down to the lowliest blogger, means that companies are becoming increasingly transparent, whether they want to or not. How much longer will it be before CNN, Fox, and MSNBC demand the right to "embed" reporters on permanent assignment within huge, influential companies like General Motors, Microsoft, and Wal-Mart?

Transparency is increasing just as corporate reputation, brands, and other intangible assets are becoming dominant value drivers. A sport-shoe company like Adidas, which outsources 83 percent of its global manufacturing to Asian companies, owns almost no tangible assets. What the company does own is intangible: ideas and patents, financial and management resources, business relationships, brands, knowledge, and goodwill—most of which, in turn, depend on its reputation. And if 75 percent of your assets are intangible, as is now the case on average for the Fortune 500, it's obvious that an attack on your reputation can be financially devastating.

This vulnerability is increased because many more people than ever before now follow the markets, glued to business channels around the clock. Bad news, true or false, is apt to prompt investors to flee first and ask questions later. Companies like Arthur Andersen, Martha Stewart Omnimedia, and Wal-Mart illustrate the power of bad publicity to depress a firm's values and business prospects—fairly or not.

An Imperiled World

The sense of living in a world of physical limits was profoundly underscored for billions of people by the first pictures of Earth taken from Apollo 8 as it circled the moon in December 1968. The image of our home planet rising above the empty lunar landscape against the infinitely deep background of space proved beyond any doubt that we were stewards of a small and precious vessel.

A number of events and trends have since reinforced that sense of a shared and fragile world:

- The discovery of acid rain, which was creating "dead lakes" over hundreds of miles across state or national borders
- The growing damage to the global ecosystem caused by carbon dioxide and other greenhouse gases, with impacts thousands of miles from their source
- The felling of rain forests in the Amazon Basin and around the world, driven by economic forces that originate in North America and Europe and producing climatic effects around the world
- Repeated oil shocks in which political, military, or financial troubles in a handful of Middle Eastern countries create economic dislocations in Japan, the United States, Europe, and dozens of other nations
- Ecological disasters, such as the Exxon *Valdez* oil spill, the Bhopal chemical disaster, and the Chernobyl nuclear accident in Ukraine, which produced radioactive fallout and health damage across thousands of square miles in Europe
- The hole in Earth's ozone layer that has increased solar radiation for sunbathers in the Caribbean, ranchers in Patagonia, and monks in Tibet
- The HIV/AIDS catastrophe, with the prospect of other global pandemics, such as SARS and Avian flu, spread via expanded international travel, trade, and migration

- The 2004 tsunami disaster, which destroyed thousands of lives in countries across a wide swath of the southern hemisphere
- The persistence of poverty, disease, hunger, and lack of drinking water and sanitation in large regions of the world, affecting more than two billion people—one-third of the world's population
- Underlying and exacerbating these trends, the continuing growth of world population, which mushroomed from around four billion in 1975 to more than six billion in 2000 and is projected to reach nine billion by 2050[9]

In what seems a much smaller and highly imperiled world, it is difficult for any business, much less the business community, to say that social, economic, or environmental problems across the state, nation, or globe are irrelevant or "not our concern." People assume that anything that happens anywhere on Earth may affect them, directly or indirectly, sooner or later—and that therefore they must take it all seriously, looking closely at how their actions may affect others (and even, potentially, the fate of the world). And many are extending the same assumptions to the businesses they patronize or for which they work.

A Socially Conscious World

It's natural that today's young people, who were born and raised in a world whose sustainability has been questioned for as long as they can recall, should be especially conscious of these issues. It seems obvious that younger people are more in touch with the smallness of our planet, having grown up with the Internet and the globalization of communications and culture, as well as with constant reminders of its fragility; today's twenty-five-year-olds grew up watching the televised stories of Bhopal (1984), Chernobyl (1986), and the Exxon *Valdez* (1989).

Popular culture reinforces these concerns. Movies from *Silkwood* (1983) to *A Civil Action* (1998) to *Erin Brockovich* (2000) have lionized environmental heroes or heroines and vilified polluters. Every young adult knows that Academy Award–winning actor Leonardo DiCaprio drives a hybrid Toyota Prius, that rock star Bono is on a crusade to alleviate poverty and debt in the developing world, and that Richard Gere is deeply involved in the fight against HIV/AIDS. The mind-blowing outpouring of funds in response to the 2004 tsunami in South Asia was unprecedented in scope, but it followed naturally on the heels of similar outreach efforts—Live Aid, Band Aid, Farm Aid. Tens of millions of today's young people know what's happening around the world, and they care.

In response to this burgeoning of interest, courses on environmentalism, CSR, and sustainability have taken root in colleges. The Triple Bottom Line is now being taught at business schools all over the world, and over half of U.S. business schools mandate courses in corporate responsibility. As a result of this expanded consciousness, we're seeing the birth of organizations like Net Impact, an eleven-thousand-member network of business students and young professionals, whose mantra is that "it is possible to use business to effect positive social, environmental and ethical change."[10]

Social activism is also on the rise among the young. According to a recent survey from the Higher Education Research Center at UCLA, the percentage of entering U.S. college freshman who reported taking part in an organized demonstration in high school rose from 35 percent in 1988 to over 45 percent in 2001. This is a higher percentage than during the 1960s, when only about one-quarter of students participated in protests. Volunteerism on campuses has also reached new heights.[11]

Younger generations to come will be even more sensitive to these issues. While we were writing this chapter, Andy's six-year-old son, Noah, asked him, "Dad, where's Brazil? Does it have rain forests? Are they okay?" These are questions that come naturally to today's youngsters—who are, of course, tomorrow's consumers, activists, and corporate leaders.

A Corporate World

Even as our world increases in complexity and interconnectedness, governments in many regions are in retreat—practically, philosophically, and politically—from some of their traditional social responsibilities. This is a natural outgrowth of the triumph of laissez-faire capitalism and the collapse of socialism that occurred throughout Europe, Asia, and much of the developing world during the past fifteen years.

In much of the developed world, government regulation of business is declining. Eager to provide an attractive climate for business, many countries are deregulating industries, privatizing businesses that were once government controlled, reducing trade restrictions, opening their borders, adopting regional or global rather than local or national standards, and shifting from the traditional command-and-control model of regulation to free-market mechanisms or jointly negotiated settlements between the private and public sectors.

As these trends unfold, businesses—especially large corporations—are becoming richer and more powerful than ever. When the world's one hundred largest economic entities are ranked in terms of gross domestic product (that is, the value of goods and services produced) just sixty-three are countries—the other thirty-seven are multinational corporations. The combined sales of the world's top two hundred corporations are bigger than the combined outputs of all but the world's ten richest countries.[12] This is an enormous concentration of wealth and power—not in the hands of presidents or parliaments, but in the hands of CEOs and corporate boards.

A graphic example of the shift in power and efficacy from the public to the private sector came in the immediate aftermath of the Hurricane Katrina catastrophe on the U.S. Gulf Coast in 2005. While the entire U.S. government, notably the Federal Emergency Management Agency, fumbled the disaster relief effort, giant companies with powerful logistical capabilities, such as Wal-Mart, Home Depot, PepsiCo and Federal Express, not only got their own operations up and running but also provided more effective relief than the Feds, getting emergency supplies of water, food, and building materials to law enforcement officials and the stranded masses days before the U.S. government could respond.

Many advocacy organizations devoted to social and political causes have thus shifted their efforts away from lobbying government to lobbying the free market and the businesses that operate in it. Pressure on companies to develop and adhere to high standards of behavior when it comes to the environment, labor practices, human rights, and other social issues is consequently at an all-time high.

As if to mark this role reversal, businesses are even being pressured to change or resist the behavior of governments, as when advocacy groups demand that companies use their influence to promote change in countries whose policies they deem unacceptable. Human rights groups attacked Yahoo's Beijing division for assisting the Chinese government in identifying an email user—a journalist who was ultimately sentenced to ten years in jail for emailing documents related to the Tiananmen Square protest.[13] And Microsoft and Google have come under attack for cooperating with the Chinese government in making it harder for activists to use their search engines to research political issues.

The shift in power from the public to the private sector means that societies at large will be looking to business to help solve social, environmental, and economic problems that were once considered solely the province of government. These new pressures will be felt in every sector of the business world. And if you run or work for a small or medium-size company, don't assume you will escape. As we'll explain later, many large companies have transferred these new requirements to suppliers, distributors, marketers, and others throughout their value chains. Although your small company may be less visible to the public eye than McDonald's, Ford, or IBM, the chances are good that you will ultimately be subject to exactly the same demands for corporate accountability now faced by the global giants, especially if you do business with them.

A World of Investor Activists

Corporate shareholders are becoming more engaged with social issues. From mainstream investors to endowment managers for religious and educational organizations, investors have begun to push corporations to pay more attention to nonfinancial risks. The Interfaith Center on Corporate Responsibility, which represents religious pension funds, maintains a database of shareholder resolutions related to sustainability issues. Recent resolutions cover a mind-boggling range of topics that includes "sexual orientation discrimination," "weaponization of space," "parabens in beauty products," "glass ceiling," "smokefree facilities," "HIV reporting," "report global warming impact on operations," "China business principles," "drilling in the Arctic Wildlife Refuge," "amusement park safety," "foreign military sales," "limit CEO pay," "diversity on the board of directors," and many more.

Both the number of resolutions and their success at drawing votes from shareholders have been steadily increasing. Between 2001 and 2004, shareholder resolutions related to social responsibility increased by 51 percent, from 739 to 1,116. At one time, a 2 percent approval vote for a proxy resolution was considered significant; today, votes of 10, 20, and even up to 40 percent are not uncommon.[14] And each year, dozens of resolutions are withdrawn by corporate dissidents after negotiated settlements are reached in which the companies yield to most or all of the demands.[15]

In addition, more and more investors are choosing investment opportunities on the basis of companies' environmental and social records, a practice commonly referred to as *socially responsible investing* (SRI). SRI started to take off in the United States during the Vietnam War, when investors who opposed U.S. participation moved their money out of companies that profited from war-related contracts. During the 1970s, the list of issues gradually expanded to include labor rights and the environment.

But it was the struggle against apartheid in South Africa that first demonstrated the growing social and political clout of SRI.

Centered on the Sullivan Principles (a set of guidelines for business practices that emphasized human rights and rejected racial discrimination, first proposed in 1977 by Leon H. Sullivan, an American minister and social activist), the anti-apartheid movement called on U.S.-based businesses, higher education institutions, and other major investors either to divest their South African holdings or to insist that they be operated in accordance with nondiscriminatory policies. Those behind the Sullivan Principles exerted significant economic pressure on the apartheid regime, helping accelerate its collapse in 1993 and its replacement by the current majority-rule government.

The dramatic impact of the South Africa divestment campaign drew increased interest in SRI. So did the gradual accumulation of research demonstrating that corporations with good social records tended to outperform corporations with bad social records, as did investment portfolios created using SRI selection systems (often called screens). Managers of the portfolios of many churches, universities and colleges, and state and city pension funds began to follow SRI principles; and the number of bond, equity, mutual, and money market funds that used some type of social screening increased from just a handful in the early 1980s to well over one hundred by 1997. SRI mutual funds, such as the Dreyfus Third Century Fund, the Neuberger & Berman Socially Responsible Fund, the Parnassus Fund, and the Pax World Fund, began to attract large numbers of investors, and their positive investment results drew increasing respect from investment analysts and the press.

By the late 1980s, interest in SRI had spread from North America to Australia, Japan, Austria, France, Germany, Switzerland, and many other countries. Today approximately two hundred SRI mutual funds screen using the Triple Bottom Line, and SRI portfolios account for an estimated $2 trillion in investment capital. According to one estimate, one dollar in eight in the United States is invested, in part, according to SRI principles.[16]

SRI has become an important presence in the world of investing. Any public company that wants access to the widest possible pool of investment capital must look for opportunities to participate in this burgeoning market. That involves, of course, making one's company an attractive investment according to all the traditional financial benchmarks. But it also entails solid performance according to the social, environmental, and economic indicators that complete the Triple Bottom Line.

A World of Stakeholders

The term *stakeholder* was introduced in 1984 by Professor R. Edward Freeman, who defined a stakeholder as anyone who is affected by, or can affect, an organization.[17] It includes internal stakeholders (such as your employees), stakeholders in your value chain (from your suppliers to your customers), and external stakeholders (communities, investors, nongovernmental organizations [NGOs], government agencies, regulators, the media—even future generations who may be affected by your company's actions today).

Today the network of stakeholders that affect every business has become more vocal, skillful, influential, tenacious, and effective than ever before. Hence stakeholder concerns—the environment, labor and human rights, community relations, consumer protection, and social responsibility—are becoming more important to corporations.

Many nonfinancial stakeholders are gaining credibility, influence, and power thanks to their access to the mass media and their roots among the general population. In a recent survey that sought to measure public perceptions of the trustworthiness of major world organizations, Amnesty International, the World Wildlife Fund, and Greenpeace outranked the leading multinationals in Europe and were ranked among the top fifteen most trusted organizations in the United States.[18] Thus when one of these groups denounces a particular company, it's likely that most of the public will immediately assume that the charges are correct and that the company's attempts to defend itself are self-serving and probably dishonest.

That's only the beginning of the public relations challenges for many corporations. Certain stakeholder organizations believe they have a vested interest in fomenting crises for businesses. A dramatic confrontation with a major corporation—a multibillion-dollar lawsuit, a demonstration or strike that threatens to shut down a factory, a journalistic exposé of alleged corruption or abuse of power—draws enormous publicity to the stakeholders' cause, supports fundraising and membership drives, and puts business on the defensive. A world of empowered stakeholders is thus inevitably a world of ticking time bombs for business.

In this new environment, even one stakeholder can sometimes have incredible power. In December 1996, in Humboldt County, California, Julia "Butterfly" Hill climbed a redwood tree (which she dubbed Luna) to prevent Pacific Lumber from cutting down sequoias. The company played into her hands, threatening to cut down Luna with Hill in it and even sending helicopters to threaten her perch. By playing Goliath, the company transformed Hill into a heroic, media-beloved David. She lived in Luna on a platform 150 feet above the ground for two years until Pacific Lumber agreed to preserve the tree and the surrounding forest.

The whistleblower phenomenon is another example of growing stakeholder power. Insiders who expose corporate malfeasance of many kinds are now protected against firing or other punishment by numerous laws, with additional protections and incentives recently conferred by the Sarbanes-Oxley Act. When their accusations lead to fines or money recovered, whistleblowers can even collect a piece of the settlement—up to 30 percent of sums recovered—under the Federal False Claims Act. Since that law was passed in 1986, over $1.3 billion has been paid to corporate insiders who turned in their companies.[19] Popular culture has glorified the role of the whistleblower. *The Informer, Silkwood,* and other films have idealized whistleblowers, transforming the image from snitch to hero. *Time* magazine put a collection of notable whistleblowers on its cover as its "People of the Year" in December 2002.

Stakeholders embody the new expectations on corporations to be more responsible, and the near universal use of the term indicates that companies are more accountable, not just to shareholders, but to others who have a stake in their activities.

Perhaps the simplest and most visceral way to sum up these new challenges is this: for every issue your company has to deal with, imagine someone—perhaps *many* someones—in your face, pulling at you, demanding action and refusing to go away or let go until they are satisfied.

Welcome to the new world of stakeholders.

When Global Trends Arrive on Your Doorstep

The trends we've just enumerated describe in broad terms the challenging business environment in which companies must operate today, as well as changes that will only intensify the challenges in the years to come. Many industries and businesses are grappling with these issues already, but even the most forward looking can't possibly see what the future holds for them. What is clear is that these trends will eventually affect your industry and your company in a powerfully focused fashion at a time and in a way that no one can accurately predict. The resulting risks and opportunities are enormous, and you need to be prepared.

It's clear, for example, how the growing power of stakeholders, the increased power of modern communications media, and the emergence of new tactics and strategies in the legal community have led to massive suits involving thousands, even millions of plaintiffs, arrayed against collections of large corporations in a particular industry. One by one, major business sectors have been targeted by such enormous lawsuits: chemicals (Agent Orange, the gasoline additive MTBE), pharmaceuticals and health care (the Dalkon Shield, DES, and Vioxx), construction (asbestos, mold, "sick building syndrome"), tobacco, and, it appears, the fast-food and snack industry (in connection with obesity).

Plaintiffs are successfully reaching further and further back in time. Holocaust victims are demanding and receiving compensation

from German companies for their illicit profiteering and expropria-
tion of property 70 years ago; descendants of American slaves are
suing companies for the enslavement of their ancestors 160 years
ago; and Indian tribes have received redress for claims going back
even further.

The dramatic expansion of legal liability, the explosion of lawsuits, the remuneration of whistleblowers, and the piling on by public prosecutors are important wake-up calls for corporations
everywhere, not just in the United States. Shareholder lawsuits
against Parmalat in Italy and Ahold in Holland and the criminal
prosecution of a German CEO for an excessive compensation package are early warning signals of a similar transformation in Europe.

Moreover, these changes in law reflect a far broader transformation of societal expectations related to corporate behavior. Thus
when Judge Warren G. Morgan of the Orphans' Court issued his
injunction against Hershey, halting the sale of the company, he did
so because aspects of the sale ran contrary to what he viewed as the
legitimate expectations of the employees and the community—a
factor that might not have carried much weight if the case had
arisen a generation earlier.

What does the future hold? How will corporate responsibilities
expand in the years to come? Will hospitals and insurance companies be sued over shortages of affordable health care or care for the
elderly (as pharmaceutical companies have already been forced to
make HIV/AIDS medication accessible to the poor)? Will coal-
burning utility companies be held liable for the deaths of coal min-
ers or for harm to entire neighborhoods if their emergency response
plans fail to protect surrounding communities in the event of fore-
seeable emergencies or natural disasters? How will the changing
expectations of society translate into new risks and liabilities for
your industry or company?

The expansion of corporate responsibility is like the buildup of
carbon dioxide in the atmosphere—gradual, almost imperceptible.
But just as global warming is expected to ultimately produce sudden,

local effects that are shockingly destructive—droughts, tornadoes, tsunamis, and hurricanes—so these growing expectations are already causing major disruptions in specific industries and specific companies. That is why you can't afford to ignore them, even if your own business has (so far) remained unaffected.

Doing business in this emerging world—freer, more interdependent, wired, and filled with powerful, vocal stakeholders—demands a high degree of accountability. You can't pretend you are operating in a vacuum. Instead you're in a crowded neighborhood where everyone knows your business, has an opinion about it, and feels that he or she has the right to express that opinion and try hard to change your behavior. Call this period the Age of Accountability, a new era for business in which responding to the demands of sustainability is a necessity, not an option.

4

BUSINESS RESPONDS

We thought we could sit in Bentonville, take care
of customers, take care of associates—and the
world would leave us alone. It doesn't work that
way any more.

—*Lee Scott, CEO, Wal-Mart[1]*

Sustainability Reaches the C-Suite

The rising generation of leaders is uniquely positioned to respond to today's sustainability crisis. They are highly educated, globally conscious, technology savvy, and the most diverse generation of corporate chieftains in history. As they enter their forties and fifties and assume leadership in business, politics, social causes, academia, religion, the arts, and every other sphere, they bring along their generational sensibility, forged in the political, social, and economic crises of the 1960s and 1970s as well as, more recently, in the epoch-making traumas of September 11, 2001, the tsunami of 2004, and Hurricane Katrina in 2005.

The result: a new cohort of business leaders and managers who are looking for social, philosophical, even spiritual meaning and satisfaction in their lives and their work.

The 1980s was the decade of Gordon Gekko ("Greed is good"). The 1990s was a decade of evolving global markets, empowering technology, and a giddy stock market that created unprecedented wealth. Today the joyride is over. In its wake is a new sobriety, as business leaders recognize the need to create organizations that will survive and thrive not just for a quarter or two (the philosophy of the quick killing) but for years, decades, and generations.

Furthermore, as the boomers age, they are becoming more sensitive to legacy issues, such as environmentalism, poverty, business ethics, and social progress—the very currents that are pushing sustainability into the mainstream. The wave of religious and personal searching reflected in a spate of philosophically centered best sellers, from Rick Warren's *The Purpose-Driven Life* to Po Bronson's *What Should I Do with My Life?* mirrors the same trend.

A generation of people in search of deeper meaning in their lives is now taking over the corporate suites. Their personal quests are intersecting with the drive toward sustainability, making it part of the daily mission of companies around the world.

Many CEOs and CFOs understand the demands of today's Age of Accountability. The accounting and reporting scandals, Sarbanes-Oxley and its European analogues, and the clamor for better governance underscore that sustainability and stakeholder engagement are now crucial elements of business leadership.

Motivations vary among CEOs who have endorsed sustainability. Some, like Chad Holliday of DuPont, Travis Engen of Alcan, and Bertrand Collomb of Lafarge, have made sustainability a personal mantra. They have strong personal concerns about the environment and society, driven in some cases by direct involvement or something they heard from their spouse or their children. The youthful Bill Ford (just forty-nine years old in 2006) represents a new generation of CEOs who grew up in an era of recycling, organic food, and Earth Days, for whom environmentalism is a core personal value.

Other CEOs recognize the image benefits, for their companies and themselves, of being in the forefront of the sustainability movement. Some have been persuaded by colleagues or highly motivated employee groups. Many see the business risks involved in ignoring sustainability; others are excited by the economic opportunities sustainability offers. And in many cases, the personal satisfaction of trying to put their enterprise on the side of the angels plays a role.

In the end, the reasons are unimportant. What is crucial is that more and more CEOs are driving sustainability harder and harder, making it a key focus of their management style and corporate strategies.

We've noted the generational shift at GE from the feisty Jack Welch who battled the EPA to Jeffrey Immelt— twenty-one years younger—whose signature initiative is Ecomagination. Some call Ecomagination mainly an image-buffing exercise, but the benefits to the company and the environment will be no less real.

Exxon is at a different stage in the generational cycle. The giant oil company is an arch-villain to environmentalists, and former CEO Lee Raymond seemed to enjoy playing the skeptic on climate change, although he insisted that politics is not involved: "We're not playing the issue. I'm not sure I can say that about the others." In fact, Exxon's use of paid media to distort public policy on the issue recalls the obscurantist efforts of the tobacco companies in the 1950s. No wonder environmental organizations all over the world have united in a campaign against the oil giant, calling Raymond and his company the "number one climate criminal."[2]

The sixty-six-year-old Raymond recently retired. We're betting that, as at GE, a younger CEO will eventually work to set Exxon on a different course, for practical business reasons if for no others.

More and more CEOs today are following this path. As of this writing, twenty-two hundred CEOs have signed the UN Global Compact. Launched by UN Secretary General Kofi Annan in January 1999, this initiative aims, "to unite the power of markets with the authority of universal ideals . . . to reconcile the creative forces of private entrepreneurship with the needs of the disadvantaged and the requirements of future generations"[3] (in other words, to encourage businesses to seek the sweet spot). The compact captures these universal ideals under four headings: human rights, labor standards, environment, and anticorruption. Together they describe a sustainability agenda that a growing number of CEOs have adopted as their own.

At the same time, more and more leaders within specific indus-tries are working together to develop sustainability definitions, guide-lines, and practices for their industries. This group includes some of the world's most controversial industries, often viewed as inherently unsustainable, such as forestry, cement, oil, and mining. Even the nuclear energy industry, once uniformly reviled by environmentalists, is trying to define itself as offering a sustainable, carbon-free alterna-tive to today's environmentally dangerous reliance on fossil fuels.

Sustainability is now a regular focus at the annual World Economic Forum at Davos, where many of the world's most power-ful business and political leaders gather annually to reflect on the key challenges of the year ahead. And surveys of corporate leaders by PricewaterhouseCoopers and others consistently show that a high percentage of CEOs are ready to sacrifice short-term profits in the interests of long-term sustainability.

The growth of executive leadership associations and programs focused on sustainability is both a sign and a driver of change. The World Business Council for Sustainable Development is the lead-ing CEO organization dedicated to sustainable development. Founded after the 1992 Earth Summit in Rio de Janeiro, it includes some 180 international corporations based in thirty-five nations, among them many of the world's best-known and most-respected companies. The U.S. Conference Board now hosts four conferences a year on corporate citizenship. Business for Social Responsibility, created in the 1980s, was a relatively small organization until about five years ago. Now its membership is growing rapidly, and its annual conference draws standing-room-only crowds.

One sure indication that the message is penetrating throughout the corporate world will be when CEO compensation is routinely tied to social and environmental as well as financial performance—that is, the Triple Bottom Line. Little by little, this is beginning to happen. Xerox and low-price retailer Dollar General are already amending their executive compensation policies to reflect social per-formance. Even Halliburton, the controversial, politically connected firm that has been accused of everything from bilking taxpayers through overpriced no-bid contracts in Iraq to employing illegal immigrants for rebuilding after Hurricane Katrina, may be moving toward a similar policy. After a recent meeting between Halliburton and Christus Health, a Catholic health care organization based in Texas that invests in Halliburton, the company expressed its willingness "to continue talking to Christus Health about developing mutually agreeable social responsibility criteria and a reasonable approach to applying such criteria when determining executive compensation."[4]

If executive pay for social responsibility catches on, it will indicate a significant shift by business toward the rebalancing of financial and nonfinancial objectives, and catalyze further interest in sustainability at the executive level. In that case, middle managers will want to pay close attention. As an ambitious manager once remarked, "What interests my boss fascinates me."

A Job for Every Manager

As companies and their CEOs make commitments to adopt sustainable practices, an understanding of how sustainability applies to your job is increasingly important for any aspiring business leader. If your company hasn't yet incorporated sustainability into your job description, just wait. In the years to come, leaders aware of and committed to sustainable management will have a distinct advantage over their less enlightened colleagues in the race to the top of the corporate pyramid.

It would therefore be a mistake for managers below the executive level—business unit or division heads, plant or departmental managers, and vice presidents or directors in charge of particular functions—to assume that sustainability is irrelevant to them. As sustainability grows in importance, the skills, knowledge, experience, and mind-set associated with it will be an increasingly necessary part of every manager's portfolio.

Structural shifts in business are also increasing the burdens carried by middle managers. The sustainability challenges of the next two decades will be addressed by corporations that have already downsized, reengineered, and reorganized themselves to be flatter, more open, more flexible, and more responsive than traditional businesses. Most middle managers now have more accountability, responsibility, and power than their counterparts a generation or two ago. They will use these tools to help drive the sustainability movement from the middle of the organization—in many cases abetted by enlightened CEOs working supportively from the top down.

Virtually every business function is being linked into the sustainability movement:

- *Production and manufacturing.* Environmental protection, worker safety, and product liability have long been at the forefront for operations managers. Today, eco-efficient manufacturing processes, the beneficial reuse of waste, pollution prevention, and cradle-to cradle manufacturing (whereby products and materials are designed with ultimate recycling in mind) are driving new waves of design, engineering, and management change.

- *Marketing.* Marketing managers will have to deal with social and political questions around the promotion of their products, as have the tobacco, alcohol, guns, and adult entertainment industries. They'll be challenged regarding marketing appeals to children and such dilemmas as marketing goods to customers in the developing world for whom costly developed-world products may be inappropriate or even harmful.

- *Sales.* Sales professionals at all levels and in both business-to-business and business-to-consumer markets will be confronted with a wide range of customer concerns regarding the sustainability of their offerings.

- *Research and development.* Companies are analyzing environmental issues from the conception and design phase of a new product, using sophisticated tools such as life cycle analysis, which evaluates the environmental impact of a product throughout its history. Some companies are expanding the use of these tools to forecast social and economic impacts as well.

- *Customer relations.* No department is more intimately connected to the customers, with both the potential risk of damaging the company's relationship to the wider community and the opportunity to improve it. Now companies and managers are figuring out how to partner with their customers in the pursuit of sustainability.

- *Human resources.* A host of companies have incurred huge political, social, and financial costs by violating shifting legal and cultural norms that affect hiring, firing, promotion, and training in such areas as diversity, human and labor rights, privacy, and, most recently, child labor.

- *Risk management.* Companies with specialists in insurance risk (to guard against disasters) and financial risk (to guard against interest and currency fluctuations) will also need expertise in evaluating today's complex, changing array of sustainability risks.

- *Information technology (IT).* As stakeholders' demands for information related to management and sustainability grow, IT specialists will be called on to integrate and customize information systems that meet these needs.

- *Purchasing.* Large companies now realize they face both legal and reputational liability for the labor and human rights practices of their suppliers. Thus purchasing agents are being challenged to develop new business criteria for selecting and managing partners, and new monitoring mechanisms to ensure compliance.

- *Supply-chain management.* Contractual issues related to sustainability are hitting the desks of supply-chain managers, creating new complexity and challenging them to meet the changing requirements of those to whom they supply goods and services or from whom they obtain them.

- *Investor relations (IR)*. Although socially responsible investing (SRI) has been around for thirty years, many IR specialists have previously been able to avoid this niche marketplace. Now, as SRI grows in popularity and importance, entirely new areas of knowledge and skill are required.

- *Finance and accounting*. Over one-third of the social and environmental indicators typically included in sustainability reports involve information that is either created by or rolls up to the CFO. Financial professionals face enormous challenges related to sustainability, including finding ways to track, verify, and present TBL information that is meaningful and credible to stakeholders.

- *Public relations (PR)*. PR professionals are in a pickle. They need to play a key role in stakeholder engagement regarding sustainability and make sure the company gets appropriate credit for its efforts—but they must do so without making those efforts appear to be "just a bunch of PR." It's a difficult balance to strike.

- *Environment health and safety (EHS)*. EHS plays a key role in managing sustainability, and many EHS professionals have built careers trying to integrate environmental concerns into general management practices. Yet many EHS departments and managers, stuck in a command-and-control mind-set, have trouble making the transition to today's broader, market-based sustainability platform.

- *Legal and governmental affairs*. Given our increasingly litigious world, it's inevitable that lawyers, lobbyists, and governmental experts will play a critical role in companies' journey toward sustainability. Lawyers will have to learn not only about whole new areas of risk but also how to enable outreach, reporting, accountability, and transparency without increasing legal liability.

It's hard to imagine any corporate office, department, or business unit that won't somehow be involved in your company's sustainability efforts. No manager can afford to ignore sustainability issues. In fact, these issues are already landing on your lap every day, whether you realize it or not.

Further, in today's extended enterprise, where businesses rely on multiple partnerships and networks with outsiders, managers at every level are expected to partner with others up and down their own value chains and outside the business world altogether, from government, social and community organizations, and academia. Sustainability thus poses challenges for you not just as a manager manipulating the usual levers of corporate control (pay, budgets, performance objectives, management systems, and so on) but also as an ambassador, politician, and negotiator seeking ways to reach out to and communicate with stakeholders of all kinds, some of whom will be friendly and supportive, others anything but.

For every manager, then, sustainability presents both opportunities and risks. From the risk perspective, a manager might well ask, *Given the environmental, social, and economic impacts of my operation, who is in a position to ruin my day—or maybe my career?* For most managers, the answer is "many people." For a director of EHS or a plant manager, it might be the maintenance shift worker who mistakenly empties a waste tank into the sewage system; for a purchasing agent or a head of IR, it might be the overseas supplier who has twelve-year-old children working in the factory; for a store manager or a manager in human resources, it might be the cashier who uses racial slurs while addressing customers.

The opportunities may be less obvious, but they are more important. They include, for example, the opportunity to reduce costs by trimming waste or to create revenue by turning your waste into someone else's source material; the opportunity to expand into new markets by redesigning, repackaging, or repurposing products; or the opportunity to hire talented and committed employees who are attracted to an organization devoted to sustainability.

Many managers are already helping their companies achieve these benefits. Some are doing so as part of formal companywide programs; others have taken the initiative within their own domains. Either way, you ought to get on board.

Business Support for the Sustainability Movement

Just as individual businesses are responding to sustainability, so are many institutions that support business—a sign of the staying power and growing long-term impact of the movement. In turn, this burgeoning institutional base offers powerful support to companies and managers who want to pursue sustainability but aren't sure how to get started. If you or your company is in this category, this section will highlight some vital resources for you.

Colleges and business schools have dramatically expanded coverage of sustainability issues in their curricula. Some universities have academic centers focused on corporate responsibility that work with and develop case studies about affiliated companies. A 2005 survey of MBA programs by the Aspen Institute and World Resources Institute found that more than half required students to take courses on corporate responsibility, an increase from approximately one-third in 2001.[5]

Corporate reporting is another way sustainability is being incorporated by the business sector. Approximately three thousand companies around the world voluntarily issue reports covering environmental, social, or other sustainability issues, and the number grows every day. Endorsing this trend, stock exchanges in France, the United Kingdom, South Africa, and many of the Scandinavian countries now require or strongly recommend broad nonfinancial disclosure as a condition of listing.

The Dow Jones Sustainability Index (DJSI), created in 1999, tracks the financial performance of the leading sustainability-driven companies worldwide, helping investors examine sustainability as a defining measure of corporate performance. Currently the DJSI World Index (the dominant brand in the DJSI portfolio) includes 250 firms drawn from fifty-nine business sectors in twenty-three countries, including such industry giants as GE, Toyota, Hewlett-Packard, Citigroup, Pfizer, Unilever, 3M, and P&G. Other indexes that are part of the same family are the DJSI World Index Ex Alcohol,

Gambling, Armaments and Firearms (which excludes companies that derive revenues from the cited business areas) and the Dow Jones STOXX Sustainability Index, which focuses on European companies.

The two newest DJSI indexes, launched in September 2005, focus on North America: DJSI North America and DJSI United States. DJSI North America is drawn from the six hundred largest North American companies and includes firms rated in the top fifth of each industry sector in terms of DJSI's economic, environmental, and social criteria—currently a total of 111 companies. DJSI United States is simply made up of the U.S. firms that qualify for DJSI North America, a total of 93 companies.

Companies listed on the DJSI World Index enjoy benefits including improved access to investment capital (because shares of DJSI members are recommended for sustainability investing), prestige, and brand enhancement (because recognition as a global sustainability leader can enhance a company's reputation in the eyes of stakeholders, financial analysts, and the public at large). Most important, DJSI-listed companies are a good investment. As noted in Chapter Two, DJSI stocks have outperformed the market since the launch of the index in 1999.

It isn't easy to make it onto the DJSI World select list. You must fill out a long questionnaire analyzing your company's behavior on economic, environmental, and social dimensions, and provide relevant documentation to the Sustainable Asset Management Group (SAM), the Zurich-based investment-advisory firm that serves as the sustainability rating bureau for DJSI. SAM also analyzes media coverage, stakeholder reports, press releases, and other sources of independent information about the company that have appeared during the past year, and may also conduct interviews with company employees. The media and stakeholder analysis may amount to as much as 50 percent of your company's score in a given business area.

Your company's chances of making the DJSI World list are based not only on its absolute score but also on how it ranks within your industry, as well as on how your industry ranks in the world of global business. To be eligible, an industry group must have at least one company that attains a specified minimum performance score; and from each eligible industry group, only companies with a performance score at least one-third that of the highest-ranked company in the group are eligible for DJSI World. Thus, even if your company is the best of a bad lot—let's say, a relatively "clean" business in an exceptionally "dirty" industry—you may find it difficult to earn a high enough ranking to win a spot in DJSI World.

Governmental and quasi-governmental agencies have also come to recognize the importance of the sustainability movement. The U.S. Environmental Protection Agency now has an office of sustainability and is starting to look at possible regulatory drivers. The UK government also has a minister for sustainability.

Perhaps most telling, the International Organization for Standardization (ISO), a network of national standards institutes of 148 countries with a central secretariat in Geneva, Switzerland, plans to issue guidelines for social responsibility in 2008 similar to those it has issued on quality (ISO 9000) and environmental management (ISO 14001). ISO standards are so influential in the business world—for example, playing a major role in determining the kinds of goods that can be sold on international markets—that the mere announcement of forthcoming ISO guidelines for sustainability indicates a long-term change is under way.

Clearly the sustainability movement is reaching critical mass. As a manager, you need to understand this transformation and be prepared to turn it to your advantage. If you don't, you may lose out—and so will your company.

5

EMBRACING ACCOUNTABILITY

To understand what's going on, you have to get in a
conversation with the people trying to put you out
of business.

—Edward Shultz, former CEO,
Smith & Wesson Holding Company[1]

From Confrontation to Cooperation

In 1997, Michael G. Morris was the newly appointed president and
CEO of Northeast Utilities (NU), a Fortune 500 electric company.
NU was going through tough times. The company's financial performance had been mediocre, and employee morale was at an all-
time low. Worst of all, the energy giant was under federal criminal
investigation for violating rules set by the Nuclear Regulatory
Agency and the EPA in the operation of its Millstone nuclear power
plant. Having appeared on the cover of *Time* magazine not once but
twice as an environmental scofflaw, the company had a reputation
for being feisty and combative with regulators, a tone that had been
set by Morris's longtime predecessor at the helm of NU.

Morris's first internal meeting, four days after he arrived at the
company, took place in the main auditorium. A group of four hundred employees came expecting to get a routine update on the legal
proceedings. The new CEO was the surprise opening speaker.

"I've just come from a meeting with the Connecticut attorney
general," said Morris. "He told me that some of his lawyers were trying to obtain documents from us related to the environmental

investigation. When asked for those documents, one of our in-house lawyers told the deputy attorney general that he had no intention of doing her work for her, and that she could obtain a copy of those documents from the EPA's public records office, which, if she didn't know it, was located in Washington, D.C."[2]

There were a few sarcastic chuckles in the room, but Morris didn't smile. Instead he paused and looked directly out at his audience. They went stone silent. Finally, Morris continued. "The next time one of our people is disrespectful or makes it more difficult for an employee of any public agency to do his or her job," said Morris slowly, "that person is no longer with our company. The public agencies have their job to do, and we have our job to do. But the mantra at this company, from now on, is cooperation, not confrontation. Not only is confrontation the wrong attitude, but it's a losing strategy. We're going to stop playing that game today."

One year later, the company pleaded guilty to twenty-five felonies and paid $10 million in penalties, fines, and "mitigation" fees, a record at the time. Morris entered the guilty plea personally, appearing in federal court to face the judge along with twenty mostly longtime senior NU officers, who he insisted accompany him that chilly November morning. From a PR standpoint, this was a low-water mark for the company and its nine thousand employees.

But the business reality was far different. Several days after the settlement, an article appeared in the *New London Day* describing the company as having taken the "high road by admitting guilt, paying a fine, and emphasizing the improvements that have been made" in its environmental programs. Rather than bash the company for its admittedly criminal operation of the local nuclear reactor, the *Day* called the guilty plea "a good business decision."[3] Soon thereafter, the company sold the Millstone power station, now staffed with an outstanding environmental compliance department, for $1.3 billion, nearly twice what analysts had predicted it would sell for a year earlier when its name was automatically preceded by the word "troubled."

NU continues to have an exemplary environmental compliance record to this day. It has also performed well financially: 2005
represents the fifth consecutive year in which NU increased its dividends paid to shareholders. These financial returns, related to the
highly lucrative sale of the Millstone nuclear power plant, are, in
part, the payoff for Mike Morris's counterintuitive new policy of
embracing the company's toughest perceived adversaries—in this
case, environmental regulators.

Stakeholder Engagement—You Have a Choice

As we've seen, the world in which we live today is more complexly
interconnected than ever before. It's a world in which a growing array
of individuals, interest groups, and organizations view themselves as
stakeholders in your business with a legitimate interest in how you
operate and a right to influence your decisions. Challenging? Yes—
even scary. But stakeholders are here to stay and growing more powerful all the time.

The expanding importance of stakeholders is perhaps the single
most important element in what we have called the Age of
Accountability. In fact, it's possible to examine most or all of the crucial sustainability issues you and your company will face in terms of
stakeholder relationships. In most cases, the problems and opportunities you'll encounter in connection with your firm's economic,
social, and environmental performance will land in your inbox
because they reflect the interests and concerns of stakeholders. And
as we'll see, both solving the problems and maximizing the opportunities will require communicating with and working with your stakeholders. Hence the description of sustainability that we proposed in
the introduction—a description that's not complete but, we think,
quite useful: *the art of doing business in an interdependent world.*

Sustainability requires a detailed understanding of your interdependence in relation to those with whom you interact—whether
as a company, a department, a plant, or an individual manager. It
means embracing and partnering with your stakeholders rather than

assuming that they are adversaries to be defeated, skeptics to be lectured to, or, at best, temporary allies to be held at arm's length. Only by making stakeholder engagement a systematic and permanent element of your management style can you hope to shepherd *all* the resources you and your company depend on—environmental, social, and economic—to achieve lasting success in today's interdependent world.

Stakeholders Have a Vote on Your Future

The notion that you must partner with your stakeholders may seem counterintuitive at first. Most companies maintain a distant, if not outright antagonistic, relationship with nonbusiness stakeholder groups, such as environmentalists, community organizers, social justice advocates, and shareholder activists seeking changes in corporate governance. In most cases, these external stakeholders have been kept outside the tent. Why should business leaders and managers want to invite them in now?

The reasons may be obvious in some cases. Many stakeholders have ways to influence your decisions. In some cases, they have a direct vote: shareholders aligned with activist groups have been increasingly successful at forcing proxy votes on social and environmental issues. Outside the corporate structure, citizens in the city, state, or nation where you operate can vote for or against your company indirectly by electing or defeating government officials who are friendly to your company's interests, or otherwise seeking to influence the kinds of regulations, tax policies, and labor and environmental rules with which you must deal.

Other stakeholders wield different forms of influence over your future. Customers can vote with their wallets by choosing to shop elsewhere when they are offended or by flocking to patronize you when they consider you supportive of their values. Activist groups can orchestrate rallies or organize boycotts against you; employees can stage walk-outs or sick outs. Nowadays, more and more people and groups have a vote in how your business is run— and they are increasingly eager to use that vote to hinder or help you.

Stakeholders can make a real difference in your company's freedom to operate. Therefore, recognizing their power and managing with their interests in mind is obviously smart business. The giant retailer Wal-Mart, for example, is now beginning to reach out to labor groups, environmentalists, community organizations, and others whom it previously scorned. Realizing that the attitudes of these stakeholders will influence the company's growth prospects in the future, Wal-Mart launched an expensive advertising campaign and created a communications "war room" to present its side of the controversies in which it has become embroiled. "We're getting past the idea that anyone who criticizes you has an ulterior motive and wants you to fail," says CEO Lee Scott.[4]

But partnering with stakeholders involves more than press releases, advertisements, charitable donations, and aggressive media tactics. The true spirit of partnership means involving stakeholders in the decisions and activities that define your business. And doing so can help you by reducing the risks from stakeholder opposition and by creating new value that all the partners can share. Examples are cropping up all over the business world. Here is one.

In the rain forests of Borneo in Indonesia, logging has long been controversial. Teak and other exotic hardwoods flourish there, and the profits from harvesting them are important to the local population. But logging, like other so-called extractive industries, can be environmentally and economically destructive. Timber companies concerned more about immediate profits than about long-term growth sometimes wipe out vast stands of trees so ruthlessly that regrowth is almost impossible. Once the companies move out, they leave behind thousands of suddenly unemployed local workers and an environment denuded of the plant and animal species that once were the life blood of the region.[5] (As geographer and biologist Jared Diamond has documented in his best-selling book *Collapse*, deforestation has been a major factor in the economic and social downfall of a number of advanced human civilizations.)[6] As a result, such environmental groups as the Rainforest Action Network and Greenpeace International have called for a boycott of Indonesian timber.

In response, a consortium of Asian logging companies set to work in 2003 with a wide-ranging coalition of partners to establish a sustainable Indonesian logging initiative. The largest of the logging firms is Sumalindo Lestari Jaya, owned by the Hasko Group, a big Indonesian corporation. Sumalindo had earlier been driven out of Borneo by locals over payment disputes and accusations of improper cutting of valuable trees. In an effort to save its business, Sumalindo joined forces with stakeholder groups that included local village leaders; the Nature Conservancy, a Virginia-based environmental organization; and a group of major retailers of wood and wood-based products, such as Ikea and Home Depot, whose customers had been urging them to buy lumber only from sustainable sources.

Under the new program, logs and boards are tagged with a bar code to confirm that they were logged properly. Sumalindo is also investing heavily in efforts to lessen the environmental impact of its logging activities. For example, the company is building an aerial tram (cost: half a million dollars) to lift logs out of valleys rather than drag them through the forest, destroying undergrowth and causing erosion. It is also sending its workers to classes run by the Nature Conservancy on eco-friendly logging techniques, including lessons that show how to fell trees so that they fall close to the road, further minimizing the need for dragging.

Sumalindo's goal is certification of its products and processes by the German-based Forest Stewardship Council, an influential player on the world environmental scene. Such certification will open the way for more teak and other woods produced in Indonesia (and by Sumalindo specifically) to flow freely onto world markets, benefiting both the loggers and the people of Borneo who share in the profits.

This story beautifully illustrates the concept of sustainability in its original, environmental meaning: sustainable logging will help prolong the life of the forest and enhance the natural inheritance of future generations. But the partnership between Sumalindo and an array of stakeholders also illustrates how sustainable management improves a company's prospects for long-term success. Both the people of Borneo and worldwide consumers of wood products had rebelled against the notion of ravaging the rain forest for the sake of harvesting timber. Sumalindo had even been forced by public pressure to abandon the business. Partnering with stakeholders to develop a viable, environmentally sound system of logging has enabled Sumalindo to reestablish its business on a secure footing, with the potential of being profitable (as well as politically and socially acceptable) for decades to come.

As the Sumalindo example demonstrates, the sustainable business seeks to partner with a wide range of stakeholders, including those who may seem to have little direct power over its operations.

Many managers shy away from significant engagement with stakeholders because the idea of opening up to outsiders or working with them seems dangerous. Partnering with stakeholders certainly has potential pitfalls. But sustainable companies are discovering that outside stakeholders can be among their most loyal, creative, and helpful business partners. Companies like Shell, DuPont, and P&G have figured out that they have a much better chance of getting where they want to go in the long term by learning to be open and even to share certain decisions with outsiders. Forty years ago, these multinational corporations and others like them could make unilateral decisions to shape their futures. Now they are creating multilateral partnerships to accomplish the same.

Balancing Act

Of course, it's easy to say, "Just run your business in the interests of all its stakeholders and you will do fine." But those interests don't always coincide—at least not on the surface. What if there is no overlap between your business interests and the demands of your stakeholders? What do you do when different stakeholders make different, even strongly conflicting, demands on you and your business?

The first rule is to look for hidden areas of potential connection between benefits to society and the profit imperative. Investors in

Wegman's may not have been thrilled, initially, to hear that the company was providing tuition assistance in the millions to its employees, money that could just as well have been returned to them. But it's hard to complain when that investment produces employee loyalty with financial benefits far greater than the cost.

There are times, however, when maximizing profits and creating social benefits do conflict. When a utility company chooses to generate electricity by burning cheap, high-sulfur coal, the shareholders may be pleased because profits are high, but environmentalists and people living downwind are highly displeased because of the resulting air pollution.

And sometimes the interests of outside stakeholders may collide. When Wal-Mart argues that its low prices create social value by making good products affordable, it pits its employees against its customers. Wal-Mart claims that its average prices are 8 percent lower than at other retailers, saving U.S. consumers some $16 billion each year.[7] Yet Wal-Mart creates that value largely by squeezing money from its employees by keeping wages and benefits low.

In other situations, environmentalists may be at odds with antipoverty or public health activists. Recently, J. P. Morgan, the third-largest investment bank in the United States, adopted voluntary guidelines that restrict its lending for development projects with possible adverse environmental impacts. "This is increasingly becoming the way all banks operate," said Steve Lippman, vice president of Trillium Asset Management, a socially oriented investment firm that helped lobby for the change. J. P. Morgan is on the side of the angels, right? Not so fast. Niger Innis, a spokesman for the Congress of Racial Equality, a civil rights group that advocates investment in the developing world, responded angrily, accusing J. P. Morgan of "political correctness and cowardice. A lot of these projects that banks finance have real health benefits." Again, the stakeholder conflict is real, not merely a matter of perception, creating a genuine dilemma for managers.[8]

Conflicts exist even within narrowly defined stakeholder categories, such as the environmental community. The current controversy over the Cape Wind proposal to generate power using

130 large windmills in the waters off the coast of Nantucket, Massachusetts, pits local nature-lovers (including prominent liberal residents of the island, such as retired newscaster Walter Cronkite and Senator Edward Kennedy) concerned about birds and the visual impact of the rotating blades on their favorite seascapes against many environmental groups that favor the project as an important step toward more renewable energy sources.

Although balancing the needs and desires of your various stakeholders is rarely easy, it can be done. When environmentalists demand that Detroit build fuel-efficient cars while car buyers demand SUVs and shareholders demand profits, is it possible to satisfy all three groups? Quite possibly, by developing and marketing a fuel-efficient hybrid SUV, as Lexus, Honda, and Ford have done. Companies often must develop new technologies, new ways to market and distribute their products, even new business models to reach the sweet spot—a challenge that the philosophy and practice of sustainability work to address.

Every business executive or manager *must* take on the challenge of balancing various stakeholder interests—and in fact is probably *already doing so*. The only real question is this: Will you take on this challenge consciously and willingly, using the full array of tools, techniques, and strategies available to you? Or will you do it grudgingly, semi-intentionally, and probably ineffectively? The choice is yours.

Playing Politics: A Reality of Business

The investment banker who resented the fact that the Hershey sale fell through because of "politics" reflects the view that businesspeople shouldn't have to worry about something as sordid or trivial as politics. That attitude is narrow-minded and ultimately self-defeating. Politics is the process by which power is shared and decisions are made in a society—a process that every successful business needs to master.

We aren't talking about government relations, which is handled for most large companies by a separate department that hires lobbyists and other professionals to implement legislative strategy. We are talking about human relations, the art of finding common ground with your stakeholders, which is handled at most large companies by thousands of managers and employees on a day-to-day basis.

Some managers are natural politicians. They seem to have a personal relationship with everyone they need to know, inside and outside the company, to get the job done and make things go smoothly. They get better results by virtue of basic political skills, which are often simply a matter of being open to those outside their immediate circle and treating people honestly, fairly, and with courtesy and respect. They cultivate good habits like returning phone calls and remembering people's names. This kind of "small P" politics can be an important lever of power in an interdependent world. So rather than fight it, make the choice to become *good* at it.

At a corporate level, some companies are seemingly tone-deaf when it comes to the politics of corporate responsibility. Exxon, for example, has made itself a lightning rod for resentment by the world environmental community, not only because it rejects the overwhelming scientific consensus on the role of carbon-based fuels in climate change but also because of the way it has gone about saying so. The company contributed $100 million to Stanford University, apparently to sponsor scholarship designed to overturn or confuse this consensus, wasting its money and getting nothing but more negative attention on the issue.

Exxon made a more subtle but similarly counterproductive move when it published a 2004 corporate responsibility report defiantly titled "Staying the Course." The company seems to enjoy sticking its thumb in the eyes of the people who care most about the environment and corporate social responsibility.

Exxon has sought to portray its position on climate change as a principled stand against "political correctness." Yet it's hard to see how this position has helped the company. (Exxon has been enjoying record profits along with the rest of the energy industry, thanks mainly to the 2005 spike in oil prices, so its environmental skepticism isn't a calculated effort to shore up its conservative investment base.) The company has now been targeted by what many activists are calling the first unified anticompany campaign in the history of the environmental movement. "Everyone is banding together on this one," says Kert Davies of Greenpeace, who is leading the charge.[9]

It's inevitable that the anti-Exxon campaign will be a painful and potentially costly distraction from the company's business. Exxon could have chosen a path of engagement with its environmental adversaries or simply taken a less confrontational tone. It would still have benefited from the current run-up in oil prices, while *also* enjoying the potential benefits from positive PR and saving itself $100 million in the process.

Businesspeople need to become more capable and sensitive politicians, in the best sense of that word. This includes recognizing that sometimes being right—from a scientific or technical perspective—may be valueless if public opinion is solidly against you. Look at what happened when Greenpeace took on Royal Dutch Shell, the global network of oil, gas, and chemical companies active in 140 nations around the world, over the Brent Spar offshore oil drilling facility.

Brent Spar came to public prominence in 1995, when Shell applied for permission to dispose of the giant rig in deep Atlantic waters approximately 250 kilometers from the west coast of Scotland. Claiming that the oil rig contained thousands of tons of dangerous toxins, Greenpeace ran a high-profile media campaign against the plan, including calls for boycotts of Shell service stations, and its activists occupied Brent Spar for more than three weeks.[10]

In the face of public and political opposition in northern Europe (including some physical attacks on service stations in Germany), Shell continued to insist that deep-sea disposal was the safest and most environmentally appropriate means of disposal for the used rig. Shell stuck to its position, door closed, long after it was obvious to everyone else that the company simply needed to back off.

Seduced by the steady flow of dramatic images from the protesters, the media lapped up Greenpeace's claims, and Shell got a huge black eye in the international press, from which it took years to recover. Belatedly, the company switched its position and announced it would abandon its plans to dispose of Brent Spar at sea.

But afterward, when independent Norwegian consultants Det Norske Veritas assessed the rig's inventory, their findings vindicated Shell. The rig was actually empty and devoid of toxins. Greenpeace issued a hasty apology, acknowledging that sampling errors had led to a substantial overestimate of the oil remaining in Brent Spar's storage tanks.

In the words of German environmentalist Dirk Maxeiner, "As we know today, the sinking of Brent Spar would have had practically no ecological impact on the marine system in the North Atlantic. In 1995, however, Greenpeace had the credibility and Shell only had the truth, so the oil company didn't have the slightest chance against Greenpeace." Shell made matters worse by being rigid and closed during the controversy, much as Hershey did.

It may be unfair that businesses should suffer political or financial damage when it's undeserved. But life, as they say, is tough. Community members may be completely wrong, in your view, about how they want you to build your plant or whether they want you there at all, but it's their community, and you can expect them to have their say—and maybe their way. Smart management is about effectively navigating the world as it is, not the world as we might wish it to be. Well-run companies and successful managers use all the clubs in their bag, including political skills, to achieve their objectives.

Sometimes, compromise with adversarial stakeholders may *not* be possible. Some advocates will not even talk to you, much less compromise. The Southern Baptist Convention (SBC), for instance, refused to compromise with Disney when the company began to provide equal benefits to gay partners of their employees, a concession to gay rights that conservative Baptists considered anathema. The SBC launched a boycott of Disney.[11]

How should you respond if your company is targeted by an extreme organization unwilling to engage in good faith? Disney's strategy was to stay the course, despite suffering what the Baptists claimed were "hundred of millions in losses." The company eventually outlasted their opponents, who called off the boycott after eight years.

Win or lose, this kind of cold war can be a painful option, but it may be the only one available to you. In the vast majority of cases, however, engaging your adversarial stakeholders is possible and will be far more effective than simply ignoring or combating them. Your goal should be to head off conflicts before they arise, but in the event they do arise, become engaged as soon as possible.

Getting Ahead of the Curve

Sustainable businesses seek to understand these transformational realities and to anticipate problems before they arise, heading them off when they can and gaining strength from them when they cannot. This takes practiced judgment and political skills.

Let's look at how Shell has learned to manage political risks in the aftermath of its Brent Spar debacle.

Today, every Shell business unit is required to create and implement a stakeholder engagement plan. This plan spells out the specific stakeholder groups that the company will seek to work with, from environmental, labor, and energy NGOs to local community organizations and suppliers, and describes the precise role each stakeholder organization will hopefully play to help develop, monitor, evaluate, comment on, and improve Shell programs for expanding and maintaining its businesses in a sustainable fashion.

The stakeholder groups Shell works with are not "front" organizations, captive to Shell's interests—far from it. In support of their independence, Shell offers these groups space in the company's annual sustainability report to comment on Shell's efforts, free of censorship or spin. Shell's 2004 report, for example, describes the work of an independent scientific review panel, organized under the auspices of the World Conservation Union, that assessed the impact on endangered western gray whales of oil and gas production by Sakhalin Energy (SEIC), in which Shell owns a 55 percent share. Alongside Shell's own statement about its efforts to comply with recommendations made by the scientific panel, the report includes a statement by Dr. Randall Reeves, the chair of the panel: "Whilst acknowledging the substantial resources invested by SEIC in gray whale research, the Panel concluded that in several important respects SEIC's assessment of risks and proposed mitigation and monitoring measures fall short of a precautionary standard." The statement goes on to enumerate the ways in which Shell's efforts fell short.[12]

The panel continues to meet and monitor Shell's operations and presumably will continue to put heat on the company to comply with its own highest environmental standards—while also enjoying a forum to criticize Shell in the pages of a report that is produced and published by Shell itself. It's an impressive gesture of corporate transparency that enhances Shell's credibility.

Shell now benefits from its open relationships with stakeholders, gaining access to valuable expertise and insight on the environmental, social, political, and economic challenges that the company faces or might face in the future while enhancing its ability to head them off. Stakeholder engagement also helps Shell in more subtle, but equally important, ways.

Shell faced a major corporate embarrassment during 2004. It was forced to reissue and correct its financial statements after an independent audit revealed that the company's oil reserves had been overstated by the equivalent of nearly 4.5 billion barrels. The U.S. Securities and Exchange Commission (SEC) hit Shell with a $120 million civil penalty, and the United Kingdom's regulatory body weighed in with a £17 million penalty. Phillip Watts, a past president of the World Business Council for Sustainable Development and leading corporate proponent of sustainability, was asked by Shell's board to step down.

This is the kind of misstep that under most circumstances would be a public relations disaster, and for a time Shell experienced a bumpy ride in the global media spotlight. Yet among environmental activists at least, the public criticism of Shell was muted and short lived. One reason for this, we believe, is that Shell had built up a reservoir of goodwill over the years through its environmental efforts and nurturing of positive stakeholder relationships. Having established a significant degree of trust with the NGO community, Shell received the benefit of the doubt when the bad news hit. In an ironic reversal from the norm, the financial community was up in arms about the behavior of a big oil company, but there was hardly a bad word from environmental or social activists.

It's easy to imagine that another oil company with a less benign reputation—say, Exxon—would have been sliced and diced for the same mistake. The relatively mild reaction to Shell's error by the advocates suggests a subtle but invaluable benefit that companies with strong stakeholder relationships enjoy.

An obvious opportunity, one that companies continually pursue, is to work with stakeholders to influence public opinion and persuade lawmakers to act in ways that will increase the demand for their products, or decrease the demand for their competitor's. GE is trying to increase its chances of success on its clean technology investments by working with newfound allies in the environmental movement to push for climate change regulations, and to reinforce the growing public perception that action is needed to protect the environment.

The ability to work with, rather than against, your stakeholders, represents a significant competitive advantage for responsible companies that are open to stakeholder engagement. Companies that find the sweet spot are certain to garner goodwill and political support, increasingly valuable forms of capital in our interdependent world.

To quote management guru Peter Drucker, "In the next society, the biggest challenge for the large company—especially for the multinational—may be its social legitimacy: its values, its missions, its vision."[13] The sustainability movement aims to address this biggest challenge to the corporation in the years ahead, and for this reason alone is something no manager can afford to ignore.

6

THE BACKLASH AGAINST SUSTAINABILITY

Sustainability is a pernicious fad.
—*One manager's reply to PricewaterhouseCooper's*
2002 sustainability survey

Critics on the Left and the Right: The Cynics and the Skeptics

In Newtonian physics, the Third Law of Motion states, "For every action, there is an equal and opposite reaction." Any major cultural, social, and economic shift in today's interdependent, wired, and political world also seems to invite a response. The enormous movement toward sustainability by businesses around the world has produced an inevitable backlash, most of it from one of two camps.

First, there are cynics, often associated with the politics of the left, who deride the sustainability movement as mere hype. They call for significant corporate reform in dealing with environmental and social issues, but regard current efforts by business to achieve such reform as inadequate at best, dishonest ploys to obscure continued corporate malfeasance at worst. The cynics usually want government to mandate more responsible behavior rather than relying on corporations to change themselves.

In the other camp are the skeptics, often associated with the politics of the right, who attack the concept of sustainable business on the grounds that business leaders have no business getting involved with the environment or social responsibility. The sole job of business managers is to maximize profits, and if they focus single-mindedly on that, the world will be better off in the long run.

In this chapter, we'll focus on the arguments being made against sustainability from both sides. Some of these may reflect your concerns; others may be arguments you've heard from colleagues inside or outside your organization. We believe that the principles of sustainability are supported by facts, experience, and logic, and in this short chapter we hope to convince you that sustainability stands up well to the best arguments against it.

The Cynics: "Sustainability Is Corporate Hype"

First, let's consider the criticisms raised by the cynics, who consider it unlikely or impossible that businesses in a capitalist society will ever voluntarily manage themselves in a socially and environmentally responsible fashion.

The cynics say that as long as investors reign supreme and Wall Street is the chief arbiter of a company's value, corporate leaders and managers will direct their every waking moment to increasing shareholder value, often at the expense of all other stakeholders. Until companies are valued in a different way, on the basis of their social as well as financial performance, nothing will change unless mandated by law.

In factual terms, this is simply not true, as 3M or any company that has saved money through conservation will attest. Countless corporations have voluntarily improved their environmental performance for financial reasons. And, like Wegman's and J&J, many companies have also found ways to invest in workers, consumers, or the community that provide excellent financial returns. So even in a world of short-term profit maximizers, companies may behave responsibly, and they often do.

The cynics say that these changes have come at the margins, that they have not gone nearly far enough to save the world. This is true, but we see reason to be hopeful in the fact that business leaders are now realizing that many more forms of corporate responsibility can help maximize profits and minimize risk in the long run. And as that idea takes hold, more dramatic, positive changes are in store.

It will be a long time before Wall Street switches over to the Triple Bottom Line. But as TBL risks are seen as increasingly material to a company's financial bottom line, Wall Street must and will take notice. And as investment banking powerhouses like Goldman Sachs and UBS start advising clients that they are undervaluing risks associated with social responsibility, corporate behavior will shift.

The cynics also argue that most of today's supposed investments in sustainability efforts are really spent on advertising and public relations. They point to GE's Ecomagination initiative, launched with millions of dollars spent on slick television commercials even while the company's actual environmental plans remain somewhat vague.

It's true that many companies have specific PR objectives underlying their responsibility programs. And we would also agree that GE has a very long road to go before its actions speak as loudly as the singing and tap dancing elephants in its ads.

But we think that fewer and fewer responsibility programs are just about PR. As the scrutiny, research, ratings, and comparisons intensify, companies whose sustainability programs are phony will either get real or get exposed. Corporations are already coming under legal pressure to demonstrate that their sustainability claims are valid—for example, Nike was sued because of allegedly false claims about its human rights record and was forced to settle the case, after a long period of negative publicity.

The cynics also claim that widely publicized sustainability programs are designed to fend off calls for additional government regulation. By putting a happy face on self-regulatory efforts, industries can convince government leaders and the general public that tougher mandates are unnecessary. Accordingly, the cynics see many responsibility initiatives as minimal, jerry-rigged efforts to avoid aggressive new regulations.

Again, there's some truth in this charge. Most business executives would prefer to retain control over their own sustainability practices rather than be dictated to by a government agency. (For many businesspeople, maintaining control in every area is *the* key criterion of success. Jack Welch's view was summarized in the title of a well-known book on his management style, *Control Your Destiny or Someone Else Will*.) But many of today's sustainability initiatives go far beyond the minimal efforts that would be needed to satisfy government regulators.

In any case, the motivations of business leaders are probably less important than the fruit of their efforts. After the Bhopal disaster, the entire chemical industry was understandably fearful of the likelihood of draconian government regulations being imposed on their factories and other facilities. So they created Responsible Care, a self-regulatory program that has assisted the industry in achieving a 70 percent reduction in emissions and an employee safety record that is four times better than the average for the U.S. manufacturing sector. Responsible Care may have originated as a way of fending off government regulation, but it has proved to be a meaningful step toward sustainability by an industry that was once among the world's most dirty and dangerous.[1]

The most fundamental line of criticism, represented by such proponents of sustainability as Paul Hawken, author of *The Ecology of Commerce*, faults today's businesses—even those that are energetic and committed—on the ground that their sustainability efforts are woefully inadequate to address the scope of tomorrow's environmental and social crises. Ray Anderson, founder and CEO of Interface, Inc., and author of the book *Mid-Course Correction*, eloquently expressed this point of view in a fire-breathing 1998 speech: "The first industrial revolution, of which we are still beneficiaries, is flawed, it is not working, it is unsustainable . . . it is *the* mistake. And we must move on to another, better industrial revolution, and get it right this time."[2]

From today's perspective, no one can say whether this criticism is valid or not. But even if today's efforts toward sustainability prove to be inadequate, that does not invalidate them or suggest they should be abandoned until far more dramatic, radical steps are possible. Neither businesses nor the public are likely to support extreme shifts in business practices until they've tested and become accustomed to the changes produced by more modest initiatives.

Someday we may look back on today's sustainability programs and regard them as mere baby steps. But baby steps are necessary when you're learning to walk.

The Skeptics: "The Business of Business Is Business"

The skeptics argue against the very idea of sustainable business on grounds of principle, most often in the name of laissez-faire capitalism, the economic theory described originally by Adam Smith and elaborated and defended by such modern economists as F. A. Hayek and Milton Friedman. It would take an entire book to address their arguments in detail. But the challenges they raise are critical. In the next few pages, we'll address those that are most commonly heard.

Isn't profitability, not social responsibility, the primary objective of business? Of course it is, and our view is that sustainability is consistent with and supportive of long-term profit maximization. But laissez-faire economists, including most famously Milton Friedman, say that every other duty that a business might pursue is illegitimate or a distraction from the main event of creating profits. Friedman even takes the position that corporate philanthropy is suspect because it deprives shareholders of the right to determine what to do with their money.

The skeptics' argument against sustainability was recently set forth in the distinguished international finance magazine, *The Economist,* which concluded, "The selfish pursuit of profit serves a social purpose."[3] Therefore, social responsibility is a needless, even counterproductive, concern for managers.

This is an economist's quintessential argument: bulletproof in theory, useless in reality. Even the most hard-nosed free marketer accepts the fact that there *are* social responsibilities that all businesspeople implicitly acknowledge.

Andy once had a conversation with a purchasing manager for a large telecommunications company who was adamant that social responsibility had nothing to do with his job.

"All right, then," Andy asked him, "how would you describe your job?"

"My job is to buy products for our company at the lowest price," he replied.

"And would you buy from a foreign supplier that you knew was employing ten-year-old girls and paying them sixty cents a day for their labor?"

"Oh, well, of course I wouldn't do *that*," he replied.

"Not even if they offered you the lowest prices, by far?"

"No way."

"What if child labor was legal in the supplier's home country? And what if you could somehow guarantee that no one would ever find out?"

"No, I still wouldn't buy from them. It just isn't right."

"And do you think your company would support your decision to sacrifice profit in this case?" Andy asked.

"Absolutely. I'm certain of it," said the purchasing agent.

Case closed. The purchasing manager realized that social responsibility *was* part of his job. He and his company were *already* practicing socially responsible management, even when, in the short run, it conflicted with their responsibility to maximize profits. If Andy had posed the same question about a U.S. supplier with a horrible worker safety record, or one embroiled at every turn in bitter disputes with the local community, the answer probably would have been the same. And many businesspeople behave in much the same way.

Once we accept that managers and businesses behave as if they do have responsibilities other than maximizing profit, the only questions are, How exactly do we define the other proper responsibilities of businesses? and How can businesses most effectively discharge those responsibilities? Not that these are simple questions—in effect, this entire book is devoted to trying to answer them! But they are the *real* questions on which we need to focus, rather than the red herring question as to whether businesses have any social responsibilities at all.

We aren't advocating imposing one's personal moral choices in business. The purchasing manager shouldn't quiz potential suppliers about their religious beliefs or political preferences. Such personal matters would be irrelevant in almost any business context. A distinction between private morality and the demands of sustainability needs to be drawn, and can be.

Don't business leaders and managers have a legal obligation to maximize profits? In fact, no. Harvard Law School Professor Einer Elhauge notes that although all companies need to make profits to stay in business, "no corporate statute has ever stated that the sole purpose of corporations is maximizing profits for shareholders" or even make them the top priority. Most lawyers and legal scholars agree that managers are free to pursue other objectives; and in the United States at least, thirty states have adopted laws that explicitly authorize managers to "consider non-shareholder interests, not only of employees, but also of customers, suppliers, creditors, and the community or society at large."[4]

Absent criminal conduct, fraud, or negligence, if the shareholders are dissatisfied with the company's orientation toward profits, they can exercise their rights to change the board, oust management, or sell their stock, but they can't sue. There is nothing illegal about managers' pursuing goals beyond profit.

Shouldn't social, economic and environmental issues be the government's concern? Yes. But as we have seen repeatedly—most recently in the failed response to Hurricane Katrina in 2005—business is now often better equipped to deal with certain social and environmental issues than are governments. And business is the only sector that can create meaningful economic growth.

While the strength and reach of the business sector has grown, the role of the public sector has shrunk in most countries, partly due to pressure for less regulation, lower taxes, and decreased social activism by government. Many community organizations, social activists, and environmentalists are practically giving up on government and putting extra effort on trying to get the free market—that is, business—to work its magic for the long-term benefit of society.

Some activist organizations that once dedicated themselves to limiting corporate power now seek to harness that power to serve the public interest. No matter where you draw it, the line between the responsibility of government and that of business has blurred considerably in recent years, and business is increasingly engaged on issues that were formerly thought to be the exclusive or primary domain of government.

Isn't the concept of sustainability anticompetitive or anti–free market? No. Sustainability produces financial and competitive advantages for those companies that embrace it, find the sweet spots, and make it work for them, not against them. In fact, companies and CEOs in some of the world's most competitive markets (such as autos, consumer products, and extractive industries) are the most highly engaged in pursuing sustainability. Sustainability may be the competitive differentiator in the years to come, as the evidence mounts that it is helping these companies beat the competition.

It's not surprising, therefore, that business organizations that focus on sustainability (such as the World Business Council for Sustainable Development) tend to be strong advocates of competition and free trade. They find that when markets are truly open, the result is often not a race to the bottom, as feared by some environmentalists and labor activists, but a race to the top, in which companies with safer, more productive, and more responsible business practices win in the marketplace. And sustainability advocates in the business world are seeking ways to use free-market mechanisms wherever possible, as with the new markets for trading emissions rights, which are proving to be an effective means of reducing air pollution without intrusive regulation.

In a free-market economy, however, pure competition ought to give way to limited forms of cooperation for the benefit of the broader society in some cases, and this applies to certain sustainability initiatives. Industrywide codes of conduct may be necessary, for example, when it would be unfair or unreasonable to expect some companies to do the right thing (for example, voluntarily limiting the number of fish they catch) while leaving others to profit even more by continuing to act badly.

Don't free markets incorporate social and environmental costs in product pricing? If this is so, don't markets themselves regulate the sustainability of businesses by exacting a price for nonsustainable behavior? Not yet. The idea of so-called full-cost pricing, which incorporates all the external costs of a good or service into the price paid, is an attractive one. If full-cost pricing were the norm, goods that pollute or otherwise damage society would be priced higher so as to cover the cost of repairing or eliminating the injuries caused. But in fact, full-cost pricing is rarely in effect. Many environmental and social costs remain hidden and subsidized, paid for by taxpayers or by others, rather than those who benefit directly from the manufacture or use of the products that impose the costs.

Air pollution poses a cost to the environment, for example, but so long as companies pollute within their legal limits, society bears the costs (smog, childhood asthma, and adult lung diseases), and the companies and their shareholders enjoy the profits. Similarly, Wal-Mart legally shifts health care costs to the public (and away from its customers or shareholders) when it fails to provide health insurance to a high percentage of its employees, who then turn to hospital emergency rooms and other "free" medical services, which are paid for by taxpayers, hospitals, or insured patients whose rates go up as a result.

Some of this cost shifting is now being addressed. Wal-Mart is facing state mandates to spend at least 8 percent of its payroll on employee health insurance or pay the difference into a public fund. Carbon pollution is a cost in transition, moving gradually toward full-cost pricing thanks to the new regulations established in most countries under the terms of the Kyoto Treaty.

Full-cost pricing works, at least insofar as it has been implemented by governments, mostly in Europe. Under new product "take-back" laws, computer and automobile companies must pay the costs associated with the ultimate disposal of their products or in some cases their packaging. These requirements put the financial burden on those who benefited from the creation of the product and who are in the best position to address the problem.

These mandates have caused companies to seek ways to reuse, recycle, or reduce the amount of material that must be taken back. European auto companies, for example, have competed to create design-for-disassembly programs to maximize the reuse of car parts. Computer companies are finding beneficial uses for their waste products, hoping to turn waste into revenue-generating feedstock for other products. Full-cost pricing can help the free market work by deploying economic incentives to protect the environment.

These are isolated examples. Many environmental costs to society and most social values are harder to reflect in full-cost pricing. How do you internalize the social cost of child labor or the loss of jobs in a community that has suffered a plant closing? The reality today is that full-cost pricing, although potentially an important tool for sustainability, isn't yet adequate by itself for the markets to regulate the environmental, social, or economic behavior of companies.

Isn't sustainability just a fad in the developed world that will lead to continued impoverishment of the developing world? This is a hard one. Questions abound about how to achieve greater growth in the developing world while moving the planet as a whole toward long-term sustainability. It has been estimated that in 2050, with a world population approaching nine billion, it will take the resources of five planet Earths to enable the people of China, India, and Africa to consume goods at the same rate as Americans today.

Keeping the people of the developing world poor is not an option, either morally or economically, so it seems clear that significant adjustments will be required around the globe—especially on the part of businesses and consumers in the developed world. Some responsible companies are working to address this problem, developing goods and services that will generate profits while creating economic progress in the developing world. Others are hoping for technological breakthroughs to solve the problem.

Didn't Adam Smith demonstrate that human behavior is driven primarily by self-interest, not by altruism, and that we are all better off if people and corporations just pursue their enlightened self-interest? Lee Raymond, the CEO of Exxon, liked to point to his company's stock price and financial performance (buoyed in 2005 by the current run-up in oil prices) to argue that sustainability is a waste of time and that BP and other sustainability leaders in his industry should "stick to their knitting." It seems clear-eyed and perhaps reassuring to certain investors to assert that only self-interest is a genuine, permanent, and reliable motivating factor for human beings.

But even Adam Smith did *not* endorse the caricature of human nature implied in the extreme free-market position. In addition to *The Wealth of Nations*, the great economic work that founded the free-market school of economics, Smith wrote a book titled *The Theory of the Moral Sentiments*, in which he set forth his understanding of human nature and morality. He wrote passages that the Friedmanites rarely quote, such as this one:

> The wise and virtuous man is at all times willing that his own private interest should be sacrificed to the public interest of his own particular order or society. He is at all times willing, too, that the interest of this order or society should be sacrificed to the greater interest of the state or sovereignty, of which it is only a subordinate part.[5]

We needn't agree that virtue consists in being willing "at all times" to sacrifice one's private interest to the public interest. But it's important to reject the Friedmanite position that the pursuit of private benefit is the only legitimate activity of business.

In the words of management thinker Henry Mintzberg,

> The argument that Milton Friedman and others use is that business has no business dealing with social issues—let 'em stick to business. It's a nice position for a conceptual ostrich who doesn't know what's going on in the world and is enamored with economic theory. Show

me an economist who will argue that social decisions have no economic consequences! No economist will argue that, so how can anyone argue that economic decisions have no social consequences? And if we train managers to ignore the social consequences, what kind of a society do we end up with[?] According to [Russian novelist] Aleksandr Solzhenitsyn . . . we end up with one that rests on the letter of the law, and that's a pretty deadly society.[6]

We return, for practical purposes, to the real question: *How should businesspeople carry out their responsibilities as citizens of their communities and the world so as to maximize both the long-term profits and growth of their companies and the benefits to society?* Companies that find their way to the sweet spot where sustainability and profitability meet are in a much stronger position for the long haul.

7

RENEWING THE PENOBSCOT

"A More Productive Use of Capital"

> We've come to realize the ecological costs of tapping
> nature for our purposes, and where possible we've
> started paying Mother Nature back.
> —*George E. Schuler, the Nature Conservancy*[1]

Giving a Voice to the Critters

John Banks, director of natural resources for the Penobscot Indian Nation, was worried.[2]

He was one of eight people charged with a seemingly impossible task: to find a universally acceptable solution to the decades-old problem of how to reopen one of Maine's most beautiful but most industrialized river systems to salmon and other fish that needed to use its waters as a spawning ground.

The eight were gathered around a table in the office of PPL Corporation, the utility company that managed several controversial dams that produced hydroelectric power using the waters of the Penobscot River. They included representatives of groups that had long been at odds. There were leaders of environmental organizations, officials from the U.S. Fish and Wildlife Service, sport and commercial fishermen, and Scott Hall, chief negotiator for PPL. Banks himself was there on behalf of the Penobscot Nation, the Indian tribe that had lived on the banks of the river for millennia and regarded it, along with the natural life it supported, as sacred.

The issues were deeply contentious, involving a complex mélange of property rights, tribal sovereignty, the needs of sportsmen and fishermen, concerns over pollution, the growing demand for hydroelectric power, and the future development of Maine's economy. And the odd assemblage of stakeholders around the table were unaccustomed to trusting one another, having long battled in the courts and in the news media over their differing goals for the Penobscot. Now, somehow, they had to find common ground and forge a long-term plan for the river. The only alternative was to go back to court and waste more years of effort and millions of dollars in further squabbling.

The group had been meeting regularly for weeks, gradually whittling away at areas of disagreement while leaving one huge question unresolved: Would there be any way to *remove* the most controversial dams from the Penobscot—a move that would cost PPL millions and reduce power production even as it revitalized the river? This was the knot the negotiators would somehow have to untie.

As the discussions wore on, moments of strain among the participants multiplied. People were arguing more, listening less, and having increasing trouble finding consensus. "I was getting worried," John Banks recalls. "So one day, I decided I would bring a couple of eagle feathers with me to our next meeting. Then I asked for a few minutes before we started to work. I didn't know what I was going to do exactly, but I knew the right thing would come to me. And it did."

Armed with his eagle feathers—regarded by Native Americans as sources of profound spiritual power—Banks began to circle the table, talking quietly and touching each participant on the shoulder with a feather as he reached that place at the table. "We have to take our egos out of these discussions," he said as he walked. "Remember that we're not doing this for recognition or praise or to get our names in the paper. Remember all the critters we're doing this for—the fish and bugs and otters and birds that live on the Penobscot and don't have a voice of their own. We're here for them, and they're the ones we need to think about."

In the annals of American corporate life, it was certainly one of the most unusual meetings any company had ever hosted. Did John Banks's spiritual "intervention" on behalf of the wildlife of the

Penobscot have the desired effect? "I don't know for sure," John says with a smile. "But everyone thanked me for the reminder. And we started having more productive sessions after that."

Within weeks, the logjam broke. The group came up with an unprecedented solution. Suddenly, there was hope for the Penobscot.

Who Owns the Penobscot?

Running some 240 miles from its source near the Canadian border to the Atlantic Ocean and fed by 467 lakes and ponds, the Penobscot River and its tributaries serve as a watershed for fully one-third of Maine and is the largest river system located entirely within the state. It's a beautiful river, much admired by nature-lovers and those who live along its banks. But for decades, the Penobscot has also been a center of controversy among electric power companies and other businesses, environmental groups, fishermen, the Penobscot Indian Nation, and government agencies.

For each of these groups, the Penobscot has a different meaning.

For industry, it's a source of hydroelectric power, a nonpolluting, renewable form of energy that is vital to the economic growth of New England. For the utilities with hydroelectric plants, it's a source of revenue. For environmentalists, it's the natural heart of Maine and a habitat for countless species, some of them rare or in danger of extinction. For outdoorsmen, it's a former angler's paradise that now supports only a tiny fraction of the salmon, sturgeon, shad, striped bass, alewives, and other native sea-run fish that once filled its waters. For the Penobscot Nation, it's an ancestral homeland and a sacred space rich with spiritual energy. And for the government agencies, it's a headache—a shuttlecock among warring interests, each appealing to government and the courts for support.

Each of these groups has its own legitimate claim on the resources of the Penobscot River, each views the others with suspicion and sometimes hostility, and each is prepared to fight to defend its own claims with tenacity and money. Under the circumstances, it's not surprising that the Penobscot has been the focus of bitter battles with significant economic, political, social, environmental, cultural, and even religious implications—a recipe, it seemed, for endless, irresolvable conflict.

Yet in June 2004, an unprecedented agreement concerning the future of the Penobscot was reached among all the stakeholders who'd been competing for control of the river.

This agreement launched the largest river restoration project ever undertaken east of the Mississippi. Three dams that have blocked the flow of the lower Penobscot for generations—Veazie Dam in Veazie, Maine; Great Works Dam in Old Town, seven miles upstream; and Howland Dam, at the mouth of the Piscataquis River another twenty-two miles upstream—will be sold by PPL, the energy company that owns them, to the Penobscot River Restoration Trust, a not-for-profit organization operated by the stakeholders. The trust will raise $50 million to pay PPL for the dams.

The trust will then demolish the Veazie and Great Works Dams. Howland Dam will be decommissioned, its entire flow shifted to a bypass channel that fish are able to navigate; at Milford Dam a few miles above Great Works, an elevator-like hydraulic fish lift will be installed. In addition to $50 million for the dams, PPL will have the opportunity to offset 90 percent of the power lost through increases in the generating capacity at several other dams in the Penobscot system.

These changes will vastly improve access to over five hundred miles of the Penobscot and its tributaries for the salmon and other fish that once swam far upstream to spawn. The removal of the two lower river dams will restore unimpeded access to most of the historical habitat for native sea-run species like sturgeon and striped bass, which do not travel as far upstream as salmon. Without dams slowing the current, the river's water will be colder and will flow more rapidly, providing a better environment for the salmon and flushing out pollutants that have despoiled the river.

As various species of fish return to the river, eagles, ospreys, cormorants, mergansers, gulls, and other predatory birds will flourish, having a wider array of foods to choose from, further assisting the salmon population to increase. Federal biologists now predict that, in time, the yearly Atlantic salmon runs on the Penobscot could increase thanks to the natural renaissance expected on the river.

The people of Maine will benefit too. The Penobscot Indians will be able once again to take the traditional journey by canoe from their ancestral homes to the sea, and will also enjoy their treaty-reserved sustenance fishing rights. Local anglers' clubs, forced to abandon fishing on the Penobscot in recent years, will return. New river rapids will support whitewater rafting and kayaking, promoting a resurgence of tourism. And government agencies, from the Federal Energy Regulatory Commission (FERC) to the U.S. Fish and Wildlife Service, can finally stop spending their days and evenings in endless battles over the Penobscot's future.

In a world where long-lasting conflicts often appear intractable, how did the many stakeholders of the Penobscot manage to find common ground? A crucial role, it turns out, was played by a middle manager—a Maine native named Scott Hall, who works for PPL. Hall lives with his family near the banks of the Penobscot and was determined to find a solution for a business problem that had festered for decades.

The Industrialization of the Penobscot

Since before recorded time, the Penobscot River has been home to the Indian tribe that bears its name.

Tribal lore declares that the Penobscot Indians have lived along the river's banks for ten thousand years, and archeological evidence confirms that natives were harvesting fish from its waters between 6000 and 4000 B.C.E. For millennia, the Penobscots used the river and its tributaries as a natural highway for their birch-bark canoes and as a source of shad, sturgeon, salmon, eel, and other fish that they speared, trapped in nets, or caught in stone or wooden weirs.

The coming of the Europeans 250 years ago disrupted the Indians' traditional way of life. Commercial fishermen arrived in the 1760s and immediately began harvesting salmon and other fish from the Penobscot, shipping large catches to markets in southern New England. Within two generations, logging had also become a huge industry, and the Penobscot was pressed into service as a living conveyor belt, as timbermen floated giant pine logs down the river to mills for processing and to harbors for shipping. The massive log drives produced significant pollution in the form of logs, silt, and fragments of wood and bark that clogged the river bottom.

By 1834, when Veazie Dam was constructed, the logging companies had begun to build dams on the river to power their sawmills, with sluices, or gates, to permit downstream passage for the logs. Later, more dams were built to provide power for paper mills, pulp mills, textile plants, and electricity-generating stations for Maine's growing population. In time, over a hundred dams of various sizes could be found along the Penobscot and its tributaries.

Prior to 1830, fifty thousand to seventy thousand adult salmon swam up the river every year from their habitat in the Atlantic to spawn in the headwaters near the Canadian border. Countless shad, sturgeon, and other sea-run fish filled the river and its tributaries as well. Soon thereafter, damming began to obstruct the runs. In 1869, a report by Maine's first Fisheries Commission described the effects:

> When the fish came [to Veazie Dam] in the spring they found an impassable barrier across their way; they gathered in multitudes below the dam and strove in vain to surmount it; many returned down the river, and after the usual time for spawning of shad was past they were taken in weirs to the town of Bucksport, loaded with ripe spawn they could no longer contain; a phenomenon which Mr. John C. Homer who has fished with weirs at that point for forty-three years had never observed at any other time. These were doubtless shad whose natural spawning grounds lay far up the river, and who had after long contention given up the attempt to pass the Veazie Dam. A great many shad and alewives lingered about the dam and died there, until the air was loaded with the stench.[3]

To make matters worse, newly constructed paper mills and other industrial facilities in and on the river began to produce significant pollution as chemicals used in production processes were dumped into the waters. The commercial salmon catch began to decline, falling from over ten thousand fish in 1880 to just forty fish in 1947, the last year commercial salmon fishing was permitted.

For a time, sport fishing on the Penobscot continued to thrive. In 1912, members of the Penobscot Salmon Club launched an annual tradition by delivering the spring's first salmon to President William Howard Taft at the White House. For eighty years, local anglers competed for the honor of catching the presidential salmon. In 1992, George H. W. Bush became the last president to receive one of the dwindling stocks of Penobscot salmon.

Efforts were made to revive the fish population. Starting in the 1960s, the river and its tributaries were periodically stocked with salmon and other fish, and fish ladders—mechanical bypass systems that allow the salmon and other fish to swim upstream to their spawning grounds *around* the dams—were installed in many locations. An estimated $200 million was spent on various fish revival schemes. But continued difficulties in traveling upstream for the adults, poor rates of survival for the young fish due to pollution, and commercial overfishing of salmon in the Atlantic continued to reduce the numbers of fish in the Penobscot system.

Today the Penobscot still has a few sturgeon, salmon, shad, alewives, and several other species of native sea-run fish, but all the populations are substantially diminished, and some, such as sturgeon, are extremely rare. Today only a thousand salmon appear in the lower reaches of the Penobscot every spring. Removing these endangered fish from the river is now prohibited, and the aging members of the old sport fishing clubs now gather merely to play cribbage and reminisce about their fishing exploits of a generation ago.

"We Are the Penobscot River"

As the Penobscot River changed, so did the lives of the Indians who depended on it.

When the building of dams on the Penobscot River began in the 1830s, the Penobscot Indians were in a legal no-man's-land, like most northeastern tribes. Their rights had been spelled out in treaties negotiated with the state of Massachusetts (which controlled what is now Maine until 1820), but the treaties had never been ratified by Congress. Generations of Penobscots were thus not officially recognized by the federal government.

That changed in 1975, when the Indian Self-Determination Act gave the tribes a special status as "domestic dependent sovereigns," nations within a nation with the right to manage many functions otherwise assigned to the federal government. Today the twenty-two hundred members of the Penobscot Nation have their own tribal government, not subject to state jurisdiction, headed by an elected chief and a twelve-member council. They also write their own local ordinances, which are enforced by tribal courts.

The passage of the Indian Self-Determination Act was a milestone for the Penobscots in their generations-long battle to reclaim control over lands the Indians had used for thousands of years. It led to a major land claims case against the state of Maine, in which they and other tribes sought to force the state to acknowledge its obligations under the old treaties. Under a 1980 settlement, the state formally turned over control of certain natural resources of the river to the Penobscot Nation, including the exclusive right to harvest fish, wildlife, and plants from the more than two hundred islands in the river that are part of the Penobscots' reservation. However, since 1988, the tribe has voluntarily refrained from fishing in the Penobscot, partly because of the scarcity of fish and partly because of worries about dioxin, mercury, and PCBs that pollute its waters.

Nonetheless, Indian control over the river's resources is not merely symbolic. The Penobscots harvest a wealth of plants for consumption and medicinal use. Some ignore the health warnings and eat fish they take from the river, which is one reason the Penobscots suffer from cancer rates that are double those found among the general population of Maine, according to John Banks.

The river is also more than just a provider of natural resources. As the ancestral home of the tribe, the Penobscot River is also a source of spiritual nourishment and meaning for them. John Banks puts it very simply: "We are the Penobscot River, and the Penobscot River is us." The tribe's traditional ceremonies are held on the islands, and water from the river plays a central role in the rites, as it does in the sacred sweat lodge gatherings where meditation, prayer, and fasting lead to spiritual purification. "In 2000, my wife and I were married on one of our islands," John Banks recalls, "but the river was too polluted for us to use it for drinking as prescribed in our ceremony. We had to bring water from a spring instead."

After 1980, armed with their new, more powerful legal status, the Penobscots began seeking to reclaim the river in hopes of revitalizing their old connection to its sacred waters. Through various means—litigation, publicity, and public protests—they began pushing industry to clean up the river, and they started forging more and more effective alliances with sporting groups, environmentalists, and government agencies to make this happen. Chief among their targets: the dams that had choked the river, contributed to its pollution, and decimated its fish population.

Warfare over the Penobscot

By the late 1990s, the problem of what to do with the dams on the Penobscot had been in the inbox of Scott Hall for nearly a decade.

Scott holds two degrees from the University of Maine. Motivated by a lifelong love of nature ("I used to rush home from school so I could watch *Wild Kingdom* with Marlin Perkins on TV"), he first pursued a B.S. degree in wildlife management. He then held a series of conservation-related jobs in government and with NGOs, working for the state Department of Marine Resources as an entry-level field technician ("basically, a guy who pulled up nets into a boat in the Gulf of Maine") for the state Salmon Commission, and for the nonprofit Sportsman's Alliance of Maine. Having grown frustrated over the apparent disconnect between business and the environment he observed in all these positions, he went back to school to earn a master's degree in public administration. "I wanted to develop my managerial skills," Scott says. "I knew there had to be a better way to run an organization."

As his credentials suggest, Scott straddles the worlds of environmentalism and business. His ability to speak the language of people on both sides of this divide would ultimately prove to be crucial in helping him solve the Penobscot puzzle.

In 1989 Scott went to work for Bangor Hydroelectric, the utility company that owned and operated several of the dams on the Penobscot River system. As one of their resident environmental experts, Scott manned the interface between the company, the government, and the environmental community. He dealt with compliance issues; represented the firm in its negotiations with federal and state agencies, the Penobscot Nation, and NGOs; and handled applications for operating licenses from FERC and other government offices.

These were enormous, time-consuming tasks. For example, whenever the FERC license for a hydroelectric dam comes up for renewal, the process of preparing and submitting the application, developing reports, defending the application, responding to appeals from every imaginable interest group, and, if necessary, dealing with court challenges can take up to *twenty years*. (Scott's office contains a flow chart that outlines the various steps in the FERC licensing process. Printed in type smaller than the text on this page and containing a mind-boggling network of boxes, arrows, and dotted lines, it stretches across a roll of paper that measures three feet by six feet.)

Scott and his colleagues also spent a lot of time doing independent research into the technical, biological, and environmental challenges that electric utilities face around the dams—for example, radiotelemetry studies on how fish were using the passageways that had been constructed for them to help them get past the dams on the Penobscot. This work helped Scott deepen his expertise in the realities of how living things were affected by energy technology.

Of course, despite his instincts as a naturalist, Scott was duty bound as a representative of Bangor Hydro to represent the company's best interests as defined by management. And Bangor Hydro believed in taking a tough stance. When conflicts arose over resource management issues, the company pushed its legal and regulatory rights to the limit, yielding to environmental, sporting, and Indian constituencies only when forced to do so by court rulings, government regulations, or intense public pressure. Bangor Hydro's stance provoked an equally unyielding attitude from the company's adversaries. As Hall quickly discovered, his background as an environmentalist wasn't enough to soften the hostility directed against his company. Early in his tenure, an acquaintance from Scott's environmental days told him, "Now that you work for Bangor Hydro, I can't trust any report you produce."

"Once," Scott recalls, "I attended a public hearing about some environmental issue—the same kind of meeting I'd attended many times in the past while working as an environmental advocate. This time, people's reactions to me were shockingly different. As we went around the room introducing ourselves, I said, 'Hi, I'm Scott Hall, and I'm here on behalf of Bangor Hydroelectric.' The guy sitting next to me was a lawyer representing the Atlantic Salmon Federation. His head just snapped back, and he turned and glared at me. I might just as well have said, 'Hi, I'm the spawn of the devil.'"

Bangor Hydro's toughness produced unintended consequences. For example, in some dam licensing disputes, government agencies ended up imposing unusually onerous rules concerning fish passages around the dams—"vengeance requirements," in Hall's words, because "the agencies were so angry at the company" for its uncooperative attitude. Perhaps understandably, those rulings heightened the company's sense of being beleaguered by environmentalist enemies, and Bangor Hydro dug its heels in even deeper for the next fight.

Starting in the mid-1980s, the ongoing battles about the future of Maine's rivers began to focus on a proposal by Bangor Hydro to build a major new dam at Basin Mills in the lower Penobscot. It would have been one of the largest dams in the entire system, located in the portion of the river that in the eyes of most environmentalists already had too many dams. Gordon Russell, of the U.S. Fish and

Wildlife Service, just shakes his head when asked about the Basin Mills proposal. "It would have been the death knell for the salmon, which we were desperately trying to restore at that time. And it would have effectively precluded future restoration of other species, like shad and alewives."

The various interest groups staked out their positions. State and federal fishery agencies, environmental groups, and the Penobscot Indians all opposed the new dam. But some of the nearby communities favored it. Increased power generation would produce new local tax revenues, and Bangor Hydro sweetened the proposal by promising to build recreational facilities on or near the river. Seeking a balance between economic and environmental concerns, the Fish and Wildlife Service proposed a trade-off: the agency would support building the Basin Mills Dam in exchange for removal of the Great Works Dam, located just upstream and less efficient in terms of both energy production and fish passage. This solution, which they felt at the time was the best they could hope for, would minimize the damage to the river and its denizens.

But Bangor Hydro was uninterested in compromise. Gordon Russell describes the company's combative attitude very simply: "They wanted to win, and in the process show us up." The controversy wound up in the courts, where it remained for years. Meanwhile, additional disputes brewed over the relicensing of the Veazie and Orono Dams, which Bangor Hydro had wrapped into its application for Basin Mills. Those battles became entangled in the overall war about the future of the Penobscot.

Caught in a thankless position between an intransigent company and its angry opponents, Scott Hall kept seeking a solution. Prior attempts to find a compromise on Basin Mills, including a major negotiating effort directed first by Maine's congressional delegation, then by Governor Angus King in 1996, failed primarily because of a lack of trust among the parties. When FERC denied Basin Mills a license in 1998 and everyone involved filed appeals, it became even more difficult to find a solution that all parties could accept.

Throughout the years of the Basin Mills controversy, the anti-utility forces had grown more united. The broad-based environmental groups found common cause with the local sport fishermen, recognizing their shared interest in the health and vitality of the river. They in turn began to draw support from local businesses and governments, which saw the potential for increasing tourism and the tax revenues it would produce if recreational uses of the river could be enhanced. And as the Penobscot Nation and other tribes won new recognition for their land- and water-use rights from Congress and the federal courts, they emerged as still another ally, one with tremendous legal leverage as well as popular support among millions of Americans who recognized the fairness of their ancestral claims to the land they once owned.

Change in Ownership, Change in Attitude

In 1999, Bangor Hydro sold nine dams and power plants—in fact, practically all of its power-generating assets along with some transmission-line rights—to PPL Corporation, a utility firm based in Allentown, Pennsylvania, and formerly known as Pennsylvania Power and Light. The sale was the result of utility deregulation, which required the separation of electric generation from transmission and distribution. Over time, utilities like Bangor Hydro that had controlled power from production to sale were forced to narrow their focus to distribution, divesting themselves of production facilities.

Suddenly, Scott was employed by an out-of-state corporation about which he knew very little. Perhaps, he thought, it was time for him to move on. He'd been wrestling with the environmental challenges of energy production for a long time and was fed up with the seemingly endless battles. When he heard that PPL intended to cut costs and improve efficiency in its new Maine operation, he worried that these "carpetbaggers" with their bottom-line focus might be even more rigid in their attitudes than Bangor Hydro had been.

But before Scott could decide, Jim Potter, the PPL executive who'd been put in charge of the new operation, called him. "Become part of our team," Jim urged him. "We need your knowledge, your local ties, and your links to the environmental community. There's a chance that we can make some positive breakthroughs, with your help." This is different, thought Scott, and he agreed to give the new management a chance.

To his surprise, he found that he had greater flexibility to operate at PPL Maine than he'd had at Bangor Hydro—despite the fact that PPL was a much bigger company. And the new management's emphasis on efficiency also translated into a new, more cooperative attitude toward outside stakeholders. Managers at PPL just didn't have the time or resources to waste on head-butting battles to prove a point. "Jim Potter and I agreed," Scott says, "that working to find common ground with the community rather than doing battle with them would be a better way of doing business—'a more productive use of capital,' in Jim's words. Of course, he was talking about *human* capital—time, energy, talent—which is actually the most expensive and valuable capital we control."

Notice the driving force here. PPL's shift toward stakeholder engagement wasn't motivated primarily by the desire to be corporate good guys or to save the planet but rather by the need *to protect and maximize profits*. The company sensed that a sweet spot in which both corporate and stakeholder interests could be served would be a more productive and lucrative place to do business. And the only way to find such a sweet spot would be by working with those stakeholders rather than continuing to fight them.

PPL's new attitude quickly began to yield dividends. The renewed operating license for the Milford Dam required PPL Maine to develop a plan for removing logs from the bottom of the Penobscot River. PPL developed a log removal plan and submitted it for approval to FERC. Soon, however, the Penobscot Nation announced that they weren't satisfied with the plan.

In the Bangor Hydro days, the company would probably have prepared for a protracted legal battle against the Penobscots. Instead, Scott decided to pay a call on John Banks and some other tribal leaders. "What don't you like about our log removal plan?" he asked.

"Well, we think the environmental safeguards can be improved," John told him. "But even more important, we want you to hire some members of our tribe to do the work. We know the river better than anyone, we've suffered more from its pollution than anyone, and our people need jobs. Letting us handle the assignment is the fair thing to do."

This wasn't the first time the Penobscots had lobbied for contracting work with the local utility company. Bangor Hydro had rejected similar requests, considering it a matter of principle: "We should be able to hire whoever we want, based on costs and qualifications. That's a basic rule of free enterprise." But Scott Hall and PPL Maine chose a different approach, figuring, "The best use of our people is to keep the turbines running—not to litigate."

PPL agreed to hire tribal members to remove the logs. The job was done on time and on budget, and suddenly the lines of communication between the power company and the tribe were just a little more open. It was a hopeful sign.

Swimming Upstream Together

Scott and the others at PPL Maine were determined to use the new atmosphere as an opportunity to work out a long-term plan for the future of the Penobscot. With advice and consent from Jim Potter and PPL corporate chieftains in Pennsylvania, Scott and his colleague Dick Fennelly developed a detailed proposal to settle many outstanding issues related to damming, energy production, the environment, and economic use of the river system. It included a provision that PPL would give up on its Basin Mills proposal (whose rejection by FERC the company still had the legal right to appeal). The company was also open to the possibility of decommissioning Howland Dam, rather far upriver. In return, PPL wanted the environmentalists and their supporters to agree to cooperate with the company in its upcoming dam relicensing efforts.

In October 1999, Scott invited the various Penobscot stakeholder groups to attend a meeting at PPL. Twenty-five people participated, representing all the key stakeholders, including the Penobscot Nation, the Atlantic Salmon Federation, Maine Audubon, the Natural Resources Council of Maine, Trout Unlimited, American Rivers, and an array of federal and state agencies. Individual points of view around the table ranged from the moderate to the radical, though all were suspicious, to some degree, of the goals and motives of PPL Maine. Scott greeted the assembled crowd and laid out the settlement proposal he'd labored over.

That proposal was quickly rejected. But the effort to gather everyone around the same table had not been wasted. The meeting had launched a long-term process for working out a solution to the riddle of the Penobscot that all the stakeholders could accept.

The first step was to reduce the size of the working group. Encouraged by PPL, the various environmental NGOs met with the agencies and tribal leaders over the next several months, identifying shared priorities (improved water quality, reopened fish habitats), goals (dam removals on the lower Penobscot), and assumptions (the need to minimize economic disruption for PPL and the local economies). (As a strategy, PPL's approach was the opposite of "divide and conquer." The company encouraged cooperation among its erstwhile adversaries, hoping to build a broad consensus behind some ultimate solution.)

In 2000, the leading NGOs formed a coalition called Penobscot Partners. It was now possible to convene manageable, productive working sessions involving just seven or eight people: Scott Hall and Dick Fennelly from PPL; Laura Rose Day, representative of Penobscot Partners; John Banks or another Penobscot Nation leader; one or two representatives of the federal government; and leaders from the natural resources agencies of the State of Maine. Nevertheless, it would take more than four years of negotiations for a workable solution to emerge.

Hammering Out Consensus

Removal of Edwards Dam from the Kennebec River in 1999 helped unite the stakeholders around a vision of what could be done, and the Penobscot Partners began to focus on dam removal as the most practical long-term solution to the problems faced by the fish populations of the Penobscot. But the idea posed serious financial challenges for PPL. Finally, at one meeting, a mildly frustrated Scott Hall declared, "Look, guys. If you expect us to remove dams, you'll have to pay for them. These are valuable assets, and our company can't eliminate them for nothing." He didn't regard this as a proposal, just a candid description of economic reality.

To his surprise, at the next meeting, Laura Rose Day, the chief spokesman for Penobscot Partners and point person for all the groups not at the table, asked, "Remember what you said about us paying you to remove the dams? If we can raise the money, would you actually consider it?"

"Sure," Scott answered, "if the price were right." Suddenly a basis for a settlement began to take shape.

The Penobscot Partners hired experts to analyze the economic issues involved with purchasing the dams. PPL discovered that dam removal was more financially feasible in this case than in many others. The lower Penobscot River included twin channels, the smaller back channel known as the Stillwater River itself the site of a dam. This provided the opportunity to shift power generation away from the main stem of the river, which would thereby be freed up for fish passage.

PPL and its stakeholders began to explore the business and environmental effects of reopening the lower Penobscot by removing Veazie and Great Works Dams and increasing energy production at other locations in the river complex. As the numbers rolled in from the experts, it became clear that dams could be removed without significantly reducing PPL's generating capacity, so long as a series of modest energy enhancements could be agreed to and implemented without substantial environmental studies or other regulatory requirements.

The parties now had a concept around which they could all rally. The difficulty of hammering out the specific details of an agreement, paragraph by paragraph came next. All the negotiators were involved. "Whoever squawked the loudest about a particular clause was given the job of rewriting it," Scott Hall recalls.

Of course, throughout the process, Scott and Dick needed approval from PPL's top brass for any major business commitment. They stayed in contact by phone continually, and every few months visited Allentown to explain the current status of negotiations to the corporation's executive leadership. PPL Corporation's attitude toward PPL Maine was consistent: as long as you can make the numbers work, we're open to any environmental solution you think is appropriate. This flexibility gave Scott the leverage he needed to forge a practical agreement.

In exchange for the sale of the lower two mainstream dams on the Penobscot and the Howland Dam on the Piscataquis River tributary, the environmental coalition agreed not to contest PPL's efforts to relicense its six other dams. PPL would be able to increase power-generating capacity at those dams by raising water levels and adding or renovating turbines, thereby replacing fully 90 percent of the eighteen-megawatt capacity and revenues of the dams to be sold.

The final agreement filed with FERC was signed on June 25, 2004, by PPL Corporation; the Fish and Wildlife Service, the Bureau of Indian Affairs, and the National Park Service, all agencies of the U.S. Department of Interior; four natural resource agencies of the State of Maine; the Penobscot Indian Nation; American Rivers; the Atlantic Salmon Federation; Maine Audubon; the Natural Resources Council of Maine; Trout Unlimited; and the Penobscot River Restoration Trust.

Although the deal was a monumental breakthrough and a gigantic step forward, the road ahead is not necessarily an easy one. The coalition must raise some $50 million needed to purchase and demolish the dams, and its members are using their leverage and contacts in pursuit of this ambitious goal. For example, the Penobscots have been working with a tribe that runs a casino that specializes in fundraising for environmental groups. They have also been using their leverage with the federal government in support of requests for government funds. So far, a $1 million grant has been received from the National Oceanic and Atmospheric Administration in the Department of Commerce. The Fish and Wildlife Service has provided another $2 million. Maine's governor John Balducci has pledged $3 million to $5 million in state funds for community development efforts that are expected to help offset decreased tax revenues from the lost power production. A private fundraising firm has been engaged to seek further money from foundations, corporations, and private donors.

What happens if the necessary $50 million can't be raised? Under the terms of the agreement, the PPL dams will remain, but state-of-the-art fish passage facilities will have to be installed. Design of those passages has already been approved by PPL, which would preclude a return to the kind of prolonged battles over such facilities that once seemed unavoidable. However, the stakeholders would retain the right to contest the still-pending licensing of the Great Works and Howland Dams—and it's likely they would do so. Scott Hall and his stakeholder partners still have plenty of work to do.

Lessons of the Penobscot Partnership

The story of the Penobscot is, admittedly, extraordinary. But let's see what lessons we can glean for other organizations faced with seemingly intractable sustainability challenges.

Embracing accountability can unlock significant gain. Bangor Hydro thought battling its adversaries was the best way to protect the bottom line. PPL realized that a better way to maximize profits was to bring its historical adversaries inside the tent. In fact, it was the stakeholders, not PPL, who initially advanced the ideas that allowed PPL to emerge in a far stronger financial and community relations position.

But credit PPL for being willing to engage. As a result, the company created millions of dollars of extra shareholder value. Start with the $50 million purchase price for the dams, which might well have been denied new permits and shut down without compensation. Then consider that the company will get to keep 90 percent of the lost revenues from the sold dams by increasing water flow over its remaining dams. Consider the time and money saved by obtaining the preapproval of various licenses and technologies. Then esti-mate the money PPL saved in terms of litigation, consultants, PR firms, and the like. PPL's calculable financial gains were all due to embracing its accountabilities to nonfinancial stakeholders.

PPL Corporation's financial performance has been very strong. Since 1999, PPL's stock has more than tripled the performance of the S&P 500 Index.[4] It's clear that operating in a sustainable manner has not only enhanced the company's financial and nonfinancial performance and its credibility, but enriched its investors as well.

The contrast between PPL and Hershey could not be more stark: Hershey blew a $12 billion deal, lost share value, wasted mil-lions in legal and consulting fees, alienated its employees and the community, and got the kind of publicity you can never live down. There might well have been an outcome that would have worked for both Hershey and the stakeholders, but Hershey never gave itself the chance to find out.

Search high and low for the sweet spot. Scott Hall and PPL reached a sweet spot for the company—a way to continue to oper-ate its hydroelectric dams without compromising the broader inter-ests of society. The likelihood of reaching any such sweet spot given Bangor Hydro's reputation for intransigence and the phalanx of his-torically antagonistic stakeholders seemed remote. But as we noted in Chapter Five, shareholder and stakeholder demands that appear to be in conflict can often be reconciled. PPL proved this despite a four-year struggle and many false starts.

By comparison, Hershey faced far fewer obstacles and enjoyed more numerous options than PPL. But PPL embraced accountabil-ity and found the sweet spot, whereas Hershey chose to hide behind a wall.

Focus on mutual gain, not on short-term profits. Sustainability is about creating long-term shareholder value. The Penobscot solution required four years of engagement, and the payout to the company for the dams could take years more. Getting to the sustainability sweet spot would have been impossible if PPL's focus had been solely on the next quarter's numbers. By focusing on the long-term problem facing the company and the stakeholders, Scott Hall was able to create millions of dollars in extra value for PPL.

Corporate culture makes a difference. One can imagine that Bangor Hydro would have stormed out of any meeting in which the idea of dam removal was being entertained. But the new attitude of stakeholder engagement and acceptance of accountability that PPL brought to the former Bangor Hydro created an opportunity for everyone to gain, including the shareholders. By contrast, Hershey's long-standing penchant for secrecy and isolation worked against the company's own financial interests.

Political skills matter. Scott Hall proved to be a skilled politician in the best sense of that word. He invested extraordinary time and effort in developing and facilitating a process of active engagement. He brought all the key stakeholders to the table, established an atmosphere of mutual trust and respect, and remained open to the kinds of unorthodox ideas that proved to be crucial to the solution. He engaged PPL's non-financial stakeholders in every way possible. The result was a win for everybody, including PPL's shareholders.

Middle managers can make it happen. No one at PPL fired a sustainability starting gun. Scott Hall wanted to solve a difficult environmental problem for his company, and he did it pretty much on his own. You don't need a budget, a staff, or a detailed executive mandate to get moving on sustainability. Scott's support consisted of a go-ahead from corporate headquarters, an admonition to make sure the numbers worked, and a commitment to support him if they did. Beyond that, the executives stayed out of his way. By contrast, at Hershey, decisions about the sale and how to handle it stayed at the highest levels of the company, with no involvement by mid-level employees. Perhaps Hershey would have seen the issues more clearly had middle managers been consulted.

PPL and its stakeholder partners created more than a win-win solution. They created a win-win-win-win-win solution, in which virtually every stakeholder in the complexly interwoven world of the Penobscot came out ahead—including, of course, the company's shareholders. It's a testament to what creative managers can do when they are determined to keep looking for the sweet spot and refuse to give up no matter how great the challenges may appear.

Part Two

HOW SUSTAINABILITY CAN WORK FOR YOU

8

WHERE DO YOU STAND TODAY?

Your Self-Assessment

Nothing is as difficult as not deceiving oneself.
—*Ludwig Wittgenstein*, Culture and Value

Dealing with an Immediate Crisis

When speaking about the challenges of corporate responsibility, Dennis E. Welch of Northeast Utilities (NU) used to say, "If you want to transform your company, it helps to have a crisis."[1]

Welch should know. He was given the job of transforming NU from the inside after it found itself the subject of a massive criminal investigation by the U.S. Environmental Protection Agency and the Connecticut Department of Environmental Protection. Welch is no masochist, but he recognizes that at many companies, transformational change begins with the pain of an ad hoc response to an immediate crisis.

So if your company is facing external criticism, internal rebellion, a government investigation, or potential lawsuits over such issues as the environment, community relations, employment policies, or worker safety, you should view the painful reality as an opportunity in disguise. Start your company on the path to sustainability by addressing the immediate crisis. Then use the atmosphere of heightened awareness and sensitivity as a basis for anticipating and responding to tomorrow's issues today. That's how Welch worked with CEO Mike Morris to transform NU from an environmental felon to a model corporate citizen.

Sustainability Jujitsu: Turning Crises into Opportunities

The sooner you can create a big-picture vision to give context to today's problem, the sooner you can begin transforming crises into opportunities—a practice we like to call *sustainability jujitsu*.

Nike learned sustainability jujitsu the hard way.[2] The use of child labor in outsourced manufacturing plants by suppliers of clothing, shoes, and sporting goods was a festering issue among social advocates throughout the 1980s and 1990s. But most American companies that marketed or retailed those goods did little to address the problem until it burst into the news in 1996. Prompted by suggestions from Pakistani human rights activists, veteran journalist Sydney H. Schanberg traveled to South Asia to investigate charges that children were being exploited to produce products for the global market. The resulting story, titled "Six Cents an Hour," appeared in the June 1996 issue of *Life* magazine. It was illustrated with a photograph of a twelve-year-old boy named Tariq surrounded by the pieces of a Nike soccer ball that he would spend most of a day stitching together. His pay for the work: about sixty cents. The unspoken contrast with the millions being paid by Nike in endorsement fees to athletes like Michael Jordan struck many as morally repugnant.

In a matter of weeks, activists all across Canada and the United States were standing in front of Nike retail outlets, holding up Tariq's photo and urging customers not to purchase Nike products. In a movie he was shooting at the time (*The Big One*), satirist Michael Moore tried to film Nike CEO Phil Knight accepting a free airline ticket to Indonesia to witness firsthand the conditions at another substandard supplier factory. And in the popular *Doonesbury* comic strip, outraged activist Kim declared, "Do you know if you *doubled* the salaries of Nike's 30,000 employees here [in Vietnam], the annual payroll would be about what the company pays Michael Jordan?" Doonesbury disagreed, pointing out that if Nike *did* increase its factory workers' salaries, "Michael would want more. He's *very* competitive."[3]

The storm of protest over labor policies in the developing world produced business headaches for Nike and for many others in the apparel industry, including Kathy Lee Gifford and Wal-Mart. Nike's immediate response made it worse. Phil Knight took a combative stance, admitting only that "we've made mistakes in the sense that we haven't been perfect," and calling criticism of Nike "a growth industry" consisting of people who "have sort of their own reasons for the business that they're in."[4]

But the pressure mounted, and in the long run, Knight and Nike showed a willingness to learn from the crisis. Nike eventually launched a six-point reform effort, which included requirements that all new employees in factories making Nike products be at least sixteen years old, that free middle school and high school classes be provided to workers, and that independent NGOs be permitted to monitor working conditions at Nike factories. Over the next several years, the reform effort expanded to include development of a detailed code of conduct for Nike suppliers, creation of a trained team of internal monitors to check factory conditions, and support for development of a common monitoring platform for the entire sportswear industry. In its 2004 corporate responsibility report, Nike took the unprecedented step of disclosing the names and locations of *all* its outside suppliers, in effect saying, "We are doing everything we can, and you're invited to check."[5]

Nike suffered some setbacks along the way. The company stumbled in 2001 when a social activist and attorney disputed Nike's claim that its wage and labor policies were not only fair but exceeded business standards for Asian companies.[6] Nike wound up paying $1.5 million to settle a false claims lawsuit and suffered enormous additional damage to its reputation and credibility. (The case is discussed in more detail in Chapter Twelve.) But Nike has continued to push forward, spending tens of millions both to improve its image and make substantive changes in its suppliers' practices.

Nike has a critical business reason to improve its labor record. It's called protecting the brand. Most of Nike's net worth reflects the value of its brand. Any of Nike's many competitors—Reebok,

Adidas, Keds, New Balance, Saucony—can make and sell athletic shoes virtually identical to Nike's. But they can't command the same premium prices because they don't have nearly the same brand strength as Nike. They don't have that "swoosh" logo and what it stands for in the minds of consumers: Michael "Air" Jordan, Niketown, and the hope that they too can "Just Do It." Nike spends tens of millions of dollars each year to promote the status, the image, the glamour of owning a pair of Nikes, all of which is embodied in that swoosh. But if the swoosh starts to bring Tariq to mind, rather than Michael . . . Nike is a goner.

But the swoosh survived, and today Nike is regarded as a model by many in the sustainability movement (although its image may still lag among the general public, which takes much longer to catch up on such issues). Having spent the money to improve its labor practices, Nike is trying to recoup its investment by gaining competitive advantage from it. Nike can now enhance the swoosh by portraying itself as the industry leader on child labor and social causes generally, forcing its competitors to make the kinds of costly investments in practices and processes that Nike has already made. In response, Reebok, Adidas, and others have created the Fair Factory Clearinghouse, a coalition to spread the costs and pressure of trying to catch up to Nike.

Nike is engaged in sustainability jujitsu—flipping an oncoming risk into an opportunity. Shell, whose executives now frankly admit they "got religion" during the Brent Spar incident, did the same thing. So did NU (Dennis Welch's company), which leveraged its employees' focus on the federal environmental investigation to establish a corporation-wide environmental management system as well as a new attitude about compliance. The result: tighter management in almost every area.

The fast-food industry is currently trying hard to employ jujitsu with charges that its products are a major cause of obesity. The National Institutes of Health issued new guidelines in 1998 which suggested that more than half of Americans were overweight;[7]

Surgeon General David Satcher said in the same year that childhood obesity had become "an epidemic" in the United States;[8] in late 1999, the U.S. Centers for Disease Control and Prevention cited the "growth of the fast food industry" as contributing to a dramatic rise in calorie intake by Americans;[9] and later media exposés, such as Eric Schlosser's best-selling book *Fast Food Nation: The Dark Side of the All-American Meal* (2002) and Morgan Spurlock's documentary *Super Size Me* (2004) pointed to fast food as *the* culprit.

The companies responded by changing their menus and providing more accessible nutrition labeling, but did so far too late to discourage the lawsuits, protests, and additional reports that are now in the works. Snack foods are being banned from school lunchrooms across the country, and the movement is spreading to Europe.

The food companies have taken very different approaches to the obesity "crisis," depending on where they stand. The Whole Foods grocery chain has turned the issue on its head, offering its customers fresh produce and organic foods (and rewarding investors with a 31 percent increase in net income from 2003 to 2004). Wendy's has played the contrarian, offering an enormous, health-defying, twenty-ounce bacon cheeseburger as a way to differentiate itself from the competition. PepsiCo has chosen a middle ground, offering a wider range of healthier snacking choices and using small green dots ("Smart Spots") to label products that meet criteria based on statements from the U.S. Food and Drug Administration and the National Academy of Sciences. Kraft has followed suit with its own program.

Determining Where You Stand

A crisis often motivates a company to embrace sustainability. But a crisis can carry you only so far. What's the next step? Regardless of your position—whether you are the CEO, a department head, or a plant manager—you should begin by looking at where your organization stands today: its strengths, weaknesses, opportunities, and risks in relation to the sustainability imperative.

We suggest looking at four areas of activity:

1. *What your company says:* its reported policies and performance in regard to the environment, labor, health and safety concerns, and other sustainability issues, and what it is saying and measuring internally

2. *How your company operates:* the environmental and social impacts of the company's practices and processes on employees, as well as up and down the supply chain and in the communities where the company operates

3. *The nature of your company's business:* the impact of the products and services the company offers as well as its business and profit models

4. *How sustainability applies to your industry:* the particular ways in which sustainability is being defined in your industry in terms of specific performance or reporting issues

A companywide self-assessment is a healthy step for any organization newly focused on sustainability, and firms like PricewaterhouseCoopers that specialize in such reviews can help you with the process. But even if your company as a whole is not involved in a formal self-diagnosis, you can review the company or the performance of a single department or division. You can gain knowledge quickly by reading reports or scanning the Internet, and acquire additional insight over the course of several hours spent brainstorming with one or two sympathetic colleagues.

Middle managers are in a good position to make or assist with a sustainability assessment. They know from firsthand experience how to evaluate what the company is saying and doing. They are in regular contact with stakeholders and so can serve as sources for the best information about stakeholder concerns. And they certainly know what's going on within their own departments.

In the remainder of this chapter, we'll outline the kinds of questions you need to consider when conducting a sustainability self-diagnosis.

What Your Company Says

Many companies, especially larger ones, have already planted a flag in the ground on sustainability, making a public commitment to responsible behavior, setting forth a broad strategic vision, or issuing guidelines for corporate activity. Some companies that have not yet embraced the overarching concept of sustainability have established objectives in specific areas—environmental impacts, worker safety, diversity, or community relations. So the easiest way to begin an analysis is to look closely at what your company has already said about sustainability and at the available information about its past and current practices and future objectives.

If your company currently issues a sustainability or environmental report, start by reading it. Perhaps your firm is one of the hundreds that are using the sustainability reporting guidelines issued by the Global Reporting Initiative (GRI) or some other reporting standard.

Study whatever reports your company has issued. Look at the vision statement, the goals and objectives, and the prescribed behaviors (such as a corporate code of conduct) to see what kind of environmental, social, or economic performance your company is committed to achieving. Then determine progress by comparing the goals to the actual performance as described in the reports. Are there gaps? If so, are the gaps shrinking over time? Have company policies been adjusted as necessary to improve performance consistently from one year to the next? Answers to questions like these will help you determine how seriously your company takes sustainability.

The lack of a company report on social responsibility or environmental commitment may imply a lack of awareness or concern. We find it telling, for example, that Hershey Foods currently offers *no* company report on any aspect of sustainability, unlike most of its competitors.

Your self-assessment shouldn't be based solely on your company's say-so. You need to delve into the reality that doesn't appear in the reports. Some companies create "birds and bunnies reports" filled with image-boosting photographs and stories that mask a lack of real commitment. So if your company's environmental report is short on data but long on pictures of the flannel-shirted CEO standing next to a waterfall or shots of employees and their children frolicking on the beach—or if it devotes five pages to describing the environmental or community awards it has received without mentioning the fine it paid the EPA—you may begin to question the seriousness of the company's dedication to sustainability.

A meaningful sustainability report is balanced, providing bad news as well as good. No company can do everything right all the time, but many companies like to report that they can. Look at the written materials: Has the company met or exceeded *every* target? Are *all* the trends moving in the right direction? Does *every* story shine a favorable light on the company? Does the company insist on calling every problem "an opportunity"? Such a report strains credulity and leads the sophisticated reader to ask, "What *aren't* they telling me?"

This kind of corporate image-laundering in regard to the environment is called *greenwashing*. A newer term, *bluewashing*, refers to a similar spin game that companies sometimes play in terms of their social commitment. We'll explain more in Chapter Thirteen about how to make sure the reports your company issues are credible and balanced. For now, when it comes to assessing where your company stands, you need to read your company's reports with your eyes wide open.

The clearest sign that your company means business is the presence of *specific* objectives, targets, and performance indicators related to sustainability, with measurement of progress based on reliable data. If expectations are explicitly described and progress toward them objectively measured and honestly reported, then the company's commitment to sustainability is likely to be real.

You may already have a general understanding of your company's or department's major social or environmental impacts. Check to see whether there are specific performance measures in those areas—for example, targets for reducing pollution or unnecessary packaging, goals for worker training, or percentages of raw materials to be purchased from small or local suppliers. That's a quick and easy way to see whether your company is walking the talk.

Finally, take a look at your competitors' reports and public statements to see what they are saying, doing, and measuring, and how you compare. You are likely to find wide discrepancies between reports from companies in your industry. You can probably get a quick overview by visiting your competitor's website or that of the GRI, where you can access over seven hundred reports sorted by geographical location, name, or industry.[10]

If your company, like Hershey Foods, does not publish any kind of sustainability or environmental report, you may want to find out why not. Or simply begin the job of developing the relevant information for your part of the organization.

How Your Company Operates

How you run your business may be more or less sustainable. Does your company or department look for the sustainability sweet spot, or does it focus solely on the narrowly defined business interest of the moment? Think about such issues as

- How you handle chemicals in the manufacturing of your products, whether as ingredients, as waste materials, or as by-products
- Whether and how you test your products on animals
- What pollution you generate in the process of creating your products or performing your services, either directly (such as

wastes emitted into groundwater by your factory) or indirectly (such as air pollution generated by the power company from which you buy your electricity or by vehicles that deliver supplies to your facilities)

- Whether labor or human rights issues exist in or around your company or its suppliers, from mandatory overtime or inadequate health insurance to child or forced labor

- The strength of your relationships with your employees and the communities in which you operate, and whether and how you take their interests into account when making key decisions that might affect them

Seeing how your company deals with existing rules and regulations is an essential part of your diagnosis. Is your company generally in compliance with laws and regulations? How often has the company been subject to fines or sanctions, and for what? Do you and your colleagues roll your eyes in frustration at the mention of regulators, or do you embrace the value of being in compliance? And does the company strive to hold itself to an even higher, beyond-compliance standard?

Of course, complying with laws governing pollution, labor rights, and other practices is important. But most responsible companies recognize the value of going beyond compliance, further along the sustainability path. And this value isn't just moral—it's financial as well. For example, some companies continued to dump hazardous wastes after the environmental and health hazards they posed were obvious, waiting until the law forced them to stop. They were legally within their rights to do so. But Congress eventually passed the Superfund law, which created retroactive liability for the damages caused. Thus companies that insisted on their legal right to pollute not only hurt the environment but also ultimately hurt themselves and their shareholders as well.

By contrast, BP's beyond-compliance mind-set has helped the company identify risks and reduce them before problems arise. In 2004, BP fired 252 employees as part of an internal drive against bribery and corruption, without facing any front-page scandal itself.[11] (CEO Lord Browne explained the crackdown with the words, "Human ingenuity will always find something to get up to. It is our job to track it down.") BP followed up by introducing a companywide code of conduct that includes requirement of disclosure of any gifts worth more than $50. All of this in the absence of any specific legal requirements, simply because BP prudently wants to do *more* than the law demands.

PepsiCo too has gone far beyond compliance, with a pilot program that requires proposed capital expenditures to pass through a sustainability analysis (designed with help from PricewaterhouseCoopers) alongside the traditional return on investment (ROI) calculation. When any project over $10 million—a new product line, a new plant, a renovated facility—is evaluated for ROI by the company's capital management committee, the project's impact on the Triple Bottom Line is also considered.

This TBL review empowers project proponents to look into the future on a whole range of issues that had not previously been systematically considered and to make appropriate adjustments to the expected rate of return. Thus PepsiCo might choose to lower the financial hurdle rate for a project with a measurable community benefit or raise it for one with a quantifiable environmental risk. The new requirement also strongly encourages proponents to work consciously to move their projects toward the northeast corner of the Sustainability Map (Chapter Two).

When examining how your company operates in terms of the Triple Bottom Line, don't overlook your economic impacts on the community, including job creation; monetary flows (where money comes from and to whom it goes); local contracts generated; and local, state, and federal taxes. These can be at least as important as environmental and social impacts. As one senior manager at PepsiCo notes, "You cannot imagine the tangible financial benefits that accrue to a plant with a twenty-year history of good relations with the town. A plant that runs smoothly year in and year out is worth its weight in gold."[12]

Sometimes the best way to evaluate how your company does business is by turning to outside sources of information.

If you suspect that your company is engaged in green- or blue-washing, you can begin to test its commitment and performance by checking out what others are saying about you and comparing these outside evaluations with your own knowledge. Over two hundred websites, most maintained by NGOs, actively monitor and report on corporate behavior in regard to the environment, social issues, and other sustainability concerns. Not all of these websites are credible, and many offer one-sided views, but you can often piece together the most accurate picture by evaluating what everyone is saying, both inside and outside the company.

Some of the best sources are the websites of CSR Wire, maintained by a consortium of companies, NGOs, agencies, and organizations interested in corporate citizenship, sustainability, and social responsibility; Business for Social Responsibility, a member organization with corporate and not-for-profit members that provides information, tools, training, and advisory services to help companies make CSR an integral part of their business operations and strategies; and the Interfaith Center on Corporate Responsibility, an association of 275 faith-based institutional investors that advocates socially and environmentally responsible business policies, monitors company behaviors, and encourages shareholder resolutions on major social and environmental issues.[13]

The Nature of Your Company's Business

We've just described some ways to assess the "how" of your business—the practices, procedures, and policies that your company uses in carrying out its activities. Now let's look at the "what": the goods and services you produce, which are the central reason you are in business. How sustainable is your product or service itself? This is perhaps the most challenging question any company can address.

Answering it begins by considering whether or not the goods and services you offer fill a societal need. Of course, a company will quickly go out of business if it fails to produce a product or service that customers want to buy. But even a product or service that many customers buy may conflict in specific ways with societal needs or even with those of the customers themselves.

Think about home insulation made with asbestos, gasoline or paint containing lead additives, or, more recently, perhaps, drugs with allegedly undisclosed side effects. Though these products were willingly purchased by customers who believed they met a need, they are now known to be harmful to health. They've harmed millions of people and cost society billions of dollars due to hospitalizations, lost income, and premature deaths. In retrospect, society's interests were harmed rather than helped by the development and sale of these goods.

Some health professionals are now predicting the same for parabens, a group of synthetic preservatives used in some cosmetics, shampoos, deodorants, and other beauty products that may cause cancer and disrupt the production of endocrines in the body.[14] Others contend that the manufacture and sale of handguns cause grave harm to society; still others consider gambling and alcohol inherently harmful. And cigarettes are still being sold and smoked all over the world. All these products raise serious sustainability issues.

In still other cases, goods and services that are in themselves benign have harmful secondary impacts or side effects. Most people would agree that personal computers and telephones are pretty handy to have around, but not the estimated two million tons of electronic trash they create every year. We can't live without electricity, but we certainly could live without the pollution and climate change caused by today's power-generating technology.

Examining your business through the lens of sustainability can have a profoundly disruptive effect. In 1999, Ford Motor Company's first corporate citizenship report included an interview between chairman Bill Ford Jr. and sustainability expert John Elkington in which Ford expressed doubts over the long-term sustainability of the gas-guzzling SUV—a major source of Ford's profits.[15] The result was a firestorm of controversy that even included a rebuke of Bill Ford by his own board of directors. Perhaps the young chairman was injudicious in his language. But he was right to initiate a conversation about the kind of change that ultimately Ford and other car companies will have to undertake.

Today, as Ford predicted, SUVs are facing a backlash. According to a recent poll, 92 percent of Americans are worried about our dependence on foreign oil, and 93 percent want government to mandate better gas mileage from cars and trucks.[16] U.S. sales of SUVs have slowed because of gas prices and environmental concerns. And in the burgeoning Chinese car market, tough fuel economy standards have recently been introduced—particularly targeting the SUV.[17]

Evaluating the long-term sustainability of your product or service isn't easy. Judgment calls are inevitable. Some socially responsible investors consider the manufacture and sale of military weapons irresponsible, and screen out military contractors from their portfolios. No one wants war. But what if the presence of weapons can be shown to deter wars or limit their severity? The development and use of certain kinds of modern weaponry that significantly reduce collateral damage ("smart bombs," for example) strikes us as being socially responsible, if not sustainable.

There is no line that marks whether your company or its products are sustainable. Sustainability is an area (the sweet spot) toward which responsible businesses move in search of long-term profitability and success. Assessing the current situation of your company or your department is an eye-opening first step when you're ready to embark on this journey.

How Sustainability Applies to Your Industry

Many sustainability issues are highly industry specific. Pharmaceutical companies, for instance, face different kinds of social and environmental issues than automobile manufacturers, banks, mining companies, or retailers. (see Figure 8.1). Your self-assessment should include a look at where your industry stands, the driving forces affecting sustainability in your industry, and the position of your company in relation to industry-specific issues.

Figure 8.1. Key Sustainability Issues
in Selected Industries

Industry	Sustainability Issues
Pharmaceuticals	Demand for new business models to make medicines affordable and accessible in the developing world
Agriculture and biotech	Need for measures in response to criticism and fears surrounding genetic modification of seeds and food organisms, and water scarcity
Pulp and paper	Creation of certification programs designed to guarantee environmentally friendly means of harvesting timber products
Computers and telecommunications	Need to narrow the "digital divide" through philanthropy and development of bottom-of-the-pyramid products, and electronic trash
Apparel	Demand for intensified scrutiny of supply-chain labor and environmental practices
Automotive	Backlash against SUVs and other vehicles with major environmental footprint and high energy costs
Energy	Concern over environmental impact of drilling and of fossil fuels on global warming
Banks and finance	Need for systematic and credible evaluation of the environmental, economic, and social impacts of development projects to which financial support is given
Mining and other extractive industries	Concern over environmental damage; pressure to disclose payments to corrupt or abusive governments
Food	Need to address consumer and regulatory pressures related to obesity

One place to start looking for insights into your industry is the GRI, which provides industry-specific guidelines for the automotive, financial services, mining and metals, tour operator, and telecommunications sectors. These guidelines, though focused on reporting, provide insight into significant industry-based issues and were developed with industry participation. Your industry trade association will also know if there are any sustainability initiatives going on in your sector.

Several major industries are exploring what sustainability means to them and issuing reports on their conclusions. Much of this activity is taking place in Europe under the auspices of the World Business Council for Sustainable Development, which currently has five such projects under way, focused on cement, electricity, forest products, mining and minerals, and mobility (that is, transportation). Some of these projects appear likely to lead to permanent cooperative agreements.

Cooperation among competing companies is sometimes an essential element of sustainable management. As with maintaining profitable fishing stocks or eliminating questionable payments to corrupt regimes for the rights to natural resources, only joint action can solve the problem. These are situations in which the unfettered workings of competition can't solve the problem without additional help.

If you're active in an industry where this type of collaboration is needed to protect some vital sustainability interest or create a new and valuable sweet spot, you must either strive to enlighten the managers of competing firms in hopes of creating industrywide consensus, or lobby some supraindustry body—such as a national government or an international regulatory body—to impose necessary regulations. In such cases, your competitors can also be important and valuable stakeholders.

9

SHAPING YOUR SUSTAINABILITY STRATEGY

> Paradoxically, the language of shareholder value may
> hinder companies from maximizing shareholder
> value. . . . Practiced as an unthinking mantra, it can
> lead managers to focus . . . on improving the short-
> term performance of their business, neglecting . . .
> longer-term opportunities and issues.
>
> —*Ian Davis, managing director,*
> *McKinsey & Company*[1]

Strategic Sustainability in Action

You've analyzed the current sustainability status of your company or business unit and developed a general sense of its strengths and weaknesses. Now it's time to translate these strengths and weaknesses into *business opportunities*.

Your strengths, of course, are something to build on—skill sets, material resources, cultural advantages, and stakeholder connections you can leverage to make your operation bigger, stronger, more profitable, and more sustainable in the future. Your strengths present business opportunities that may be fairly obvious, as they are natural outgrowths of what you are already doing well.

Your weaknesses are dangers that you must identify and remedy—missing skills, resource depletions, cultural blind spots, and stakeholder relationships that have soured or simply vanished and whose implications you need to examine and address before they cause real damage. But even your weaknesses may point the way to business opportunities. If you can tackle and fix one or two of the weaknesses that have held you back, you may find that opportunities to create new products, open new markets, or develop new relationships that once appeared out of reach are suddenly attainable.

In this chapter, we'll look at some of the strategies that the best-run companies and savviest managers have developed in pursuit of sustainability.

Finding the Sweet Spot: Starting with Your Corporate Strategy

One way to begin to develop a sustainability program is to examine your overall corporate strategy in order to identify the sweet spot where strategy and sustainability meet. This makes sense because, as we've stressed, your sustainability approach and your overall business plan must ultimately be one and the same, not two separate programs working in parallel. If you take a close look at the specific strategic directions your department or company has chosen to pursue—the business models, product and service categories, and customer markets your company has identified as being ripe for growth—you will probably find that there is a recognizable sustainability component to each: an intersection between your business strategy and the interests of the wider world.

The key to finding the sweet spot, then, is simple: *always be on the lookout for the overlap between profit and the public good*. That's where opportunities lie.

Consider the global strategy being pursued by Unilever, the $48 billion consumer products corporation known for its food, home care, and personal care products, marketed around the world under such familiar brand names as Dove, Hellman's, Lux, All, Lipton, Birds Eye, Skippy, and many others. As defined by the company's executive leaders, Unilever's current corporate strategy focuses on four top "priorities for growth."[2] Let's look at these and the rationale behind each:

1. *Developing and emerging markets.* Why? Because the markets of Asia, Africa, and Latin America represent the greatest growth opportunity for the near future. Unilever estimates that 95 percent of the world's population increase between today and 2010 will occur in the developing world, which is also growing rapidly in terms of per capita income. With 35 percent of Unilever revenues already coming from the developing world, the region is one in which the company has a strong foothold that can be the basis for enormous growth in the years to come.

2. *Personal care*—that is, soaps, deodorants, hair care products, and the like. Why? Because this product category exhibits above-average rates of growth, is a relatively fragmented market, and is characterized by a strong personal connection between the consumer and his or her favorite products—all of which create great opportunities for a company like Unilever with a strong portfolio of globally recognized and respected brands.

3. *Vitality innovation*—that is, products that offer health benefits and increased energy, such as Lipton teas containing antioxidants, drinks and spreads made with low-cholesterol, high-protein, and high-vitamin ingredients, and so on. Why? Because of a worldwide trend toward growing consumer interest in the healthfulness of the products they use, which portends a continued shift toward such products and away from products perceived as unhealthy.

4. *Winning with customers*—that is, creating stronger bonds both with consumers and with the retailers and distributors who help bring Unilever products to market. Why? Because Unilever's brand strength as well as its "reach across the store"—its presence in many aisles of the typical supermarket, drug store, and convenience store—give the company special "shopper insight," creating opportunities for future sales growth.

This, then, is a summary of Unilever's current corporate strategy. But where is the sweet spot? How do Unilever's four strategic keys overlap with sustainability?

Let's start with the focus on developing markets. In this case, identifying the sweet spot isn't difficult. Selling more products in the developing world would clearly be a win for Unilever. Those sales will not only provide immediate benefits in the form of increased revenues but also help build a base of customer loyalty that should lead to sustained growth, as the countries of the developing world gradually emerge from poverty and achieve higher levels of disposable income.

Increased sales in the developing world will also be a win for society, because anything that helps improve the standard of living for millions of the world's poorest people is clearly a socially responsible thing to do. Unilever is one of many companies that are deeply engaged in figuring out how to make their goods and services accessible and affordable to people living on less than $2 a day. Even better, many of the business activities driven by this process also spur economic growth and provide opportunities for the poor. Profits retained by local businesses, such as retailers and distributors, will help promote growth, create jobs, and launch a continuing spiral of economic benefits that can help increase the market for consumer goods and lift entire regions out of poverty.

Of course, *identifying* the sweet spot in relation to this strategy is easier than *occupying* it. Many companies have written off the developing world as a market, believing that the relatively low incomes of most people there and the significant business risks involved make it a bad business bet. But Unilever is addressing this issue directly.

Unilever has discovered that it's usually not practical to try to sell the same products that are popular in the developed world when seeking breakthroughs in the developing world. The products themselves as well as the packaging, advertising, marketing, distribution, and pricing strategies must all be tailored to the needs of the regional and local communities.

Although rural villagers in countries like India or Kenya with modest cash incomes may be attracted by some of the same brand promises Westerners respond to, they can't afford the full-size cartons of food or health care products that Americans or Europeans are accustomed to buying. Unilever has therefore developed alternative forms of packaging and pricing designed to be suitable for developing-world customers. In Asia and Africa, Unilever sells single-use shampoo and hair care sachets (marketed under the Sunsilk brand); small, discount-priced bars of soap (Lifebuoy); and single-serving packets of soup seasoning cubes (Knorr Cubitos). All these products can be purchased one at a time for just a few cents, which may be all the spending money that an African housewife has at a given time.

Unilever constantly surveys comparative economic conditions in the eighty-two countries that represent 90 percent of the company's business to make certain that its marketing approach fits local needs as closely as possible. According to company studies (2004), Unilever's lowest-priced home, personal care, and food products were priced at less than 5 percent of the minimum daily wage in fifty of those eighty-two countries.[3]

In Nigeria, for instance, sales from small product packets priced at the equivalent of ten cents or less made up over 35 percent of Unilever's total in-country sales. Making products of developed-world quality available to customers in the developing world represents a growing portion of Unilever's profitability, as well as a contribution to the well-being of a less advantaged portion of humankind—a sweet spot bull's-eye for the company and its stakeholders.

The overlap between Unilever's business strategy and the needs and interests of society can be identified in relation to each of the company's other key "priorities for growth" as well. Unilever has targeted personal care products as a growth opportunity. Because of the health benefits derived from the use of products like soap, shampoo, toothpaste, and detergent, the sweet spot here is fairly obvious: if Unilever can expand the use of its personal care products around the world, populations will live longer and healthier lives at the same time that Unilever will enjoy increased sales and profits.

In an effort to occupy and expand this sweet spot, Unilever is partnering with such NGOs as the London School of Hygiene and

Tropical Medicine and the International Scientific Forum on Home Hygiene to develop programs that encourage better personal hygiene practices around the world. In India, Unilever has launched a program known as *Swasthya Chetna* ("health awakening"), which is working with teachers, community leaders, and government agencies to educate two hundred million people about such basic health practices as washing hands daily with soap. If the program succeeds, it will help prevent the spread of such ailments as diarrhea, which is a leading cause of infant mortality—as well as encouraging greater sales of Unilever products.

"Winning with customers" (that is, building on Unilever's unusual knowledge of and connection with consumers), the company's fourth strategic key, offers another sustainability foothold. Unilever's Project Shakti is providing training in sales, marketing, and entrepreneurship to over thirteen thousand women in India, giving them the skills they need to sell Unilever products to a potential market of over seventy million rural customers. As of 2004, Shakti distributors were active in fifty thousand villages covering twelve Indian states. These women were, on average, *doubling* their families' annual incomes through their efforts . . . at the same as they expanded Unilever's market penetration in India.

It's clear that Unilever's strategic growth targets offer enormous areas of overlap with their stakeholders' natural agenda for economic, social, or environmental prosperity. Other companies employ similar strategies. GE's Ecomagination initiative is focused on identifying business opportunities derived from the growing need to protect the natural environment through improved energy efficiency and reduction of waste and pollution. To the same purpose, American Electric Power (AEP), the midwestern energy conglomerate, is rebalancing its business portfolio to include a large and growing collection of wind farms and other renewable energy sources.

Unilever, GE, and AEP all illustrate the same crucial principle of sustainability management: start by examining your company's overall business strategy. What are the key strategic drivers of future growth that your company has already identified? What are the drivers in *your* part of the business? Then ask, Where is the potential overlap between these drivers and the environmental, social, and economic needs of society or our current stakeholders? That overlap is your sweet spot—the greatest future source of gain for your company or department. Your next job is to develop strategies that will take advantage of that overlap.

Minimization and Optimization

A fruitful way to think strategically about your business's sweet spot is to think in terms of *minimization* and *optimization*.

For our purposes, minimization means reducing the size of your footprint, in terms of the adverse environmental, social, and economic impacts of your activities. Minimization is aimed at reducing ecological damage, reducing employee accidents, and decreasing harm to the community. In normative terms, minimization is "being less bad."

Optimization is "being more good." We use the term to mean producing positive benefits in the three areas of environmental, social, and economic impact. Optimization can take you far beyond minimization. Optimization aims not just to reduce pollution, but to restore the environment; not just to eliminate employee accidents, but to create a healthier, happier workforce; not just to decrease harm to the community, but to revitalize it (see Figure 9.1).

The yin and yang of minimization and optimization come together in the elegant and visionary formulation of architect William McDonough, who urges a gradual redesign of all human industrial processes such that every waste stream becomes someone else's feedstock. The idea is simple: first you minimize your waste streams, then you optimize them, creating biological or technical nutrients that go into new products. The ultimate in eco-effectiveness, McDonough's vision of endless reuse suggests an "ecology of abundance" in which the more things we produce, the more we have.[4]

Figure 9.1. Minimization and Optimization

Business Function	Minimization	Optimization
Worker health and safety	Reduce workplace accidents.	Create a healthy and happy workforce.
Environmental protection	Clean up hazardous wastes.	Use waste as a feedstock for other products.
Energy use	Reduce the use of fossil fuels.	Shift most energy use to solar power.
Product packaging	Reduce the use of needless packaging.	Create packaging that biodegrades and contains seeds or fertilizer.
Customer service	Respond more quickly to customer complaints.	Work with complaining customers to develop new and better products.

Minimization: Pursuing Sustainability by Being Less Bad

Thinking about minimization and optimization can help you discover sustainability strategies that you can use immediately to assist your company or department.

A company that pursues a minimization strategy is buffing its credentials as a good corporation and as a desirable neighbor and partner for the communities in which it operates. And like all sustainable pathways, minimization offers distinct economic benefits as well. Think of minimization as part of a strategy to *reduce cost and risk*. Minimization can cut costs (by trimming waste), reduce debt (by making your capital expenditures more efficient), lower the potential for losses (from lawsuits, regulatory and legal restrictions, and public relations disasters), and increase profit margins (by all of the above). Thus, by reducing the risks and costs associated with doing business, minimization can enhance your company's ability to consistently reach or exceed its profitability targets.

A few examples among the many that could be cited will show how minimization strategies can generate both financial and non-financial benefits.

Waste reduction is a simple form of minimization. 3M is a leader in this area through its thirty-year-old program known as Pollution Prevention Pays (3P). Launched in 1975 by Dr. Joseph Ling, a Chinese-born sanitary engineer who headed environmental responsibility for 3M's worldwide operations, 3P encourages and rewards employees who create breakthrough ideas to eliminate pollution at the source (rather than cleaning it up after the fact) and that also produce a financial payoff for 3M.[5]

Here's an illustration. 3M uses solvents in the manufacture of its products (films, fiber optics, and fuel cells, as well as the tapes and adhesives found in virtually every home and office). These solvents create hazardous air pollution when they evaporate. In 1987, the company had to spend over $200 million to reduce the emissions coming from these solvents, without addressing their source.

New technologies developed under 3P have reduced or eliminated the use of many solvents at 3M. The famous Scotch brand tape is now made using water-based (rather than solvent-based) adhesives, and 3M surgical tapes are manufactured using a patented hot-melt process that eliminates the use of highly toxic solvents. All told, 3M employees have generated over fifty-six hundred projects in the 3P program. Together they've prevented the creation of more than 2.2 billion pounds of pollutants and generated savings of nearly $1 billion for 3M, counting only the first-year savings from each project.

3P is more than just a collection of projects. It establishes companywide targets for minimization, which currently include five-year objectives to cut energy use by 20 percent, waste by 25 percent, and volatile organic air emissions by 25 percent. The program is expanding to include life cycle management (LCM), which anticipates environmental, health, and safety issues as part of the conception and design of products, enabling the company to eliminate problems and excess costs from the beginning. LCM is now a standard part of

3M's new product development process, and by 2010, LCM reviews of all *existing* 3M products should be complete.

Minimization can also produce large financial benefits when applied to reducing workplace injuries and accidents. Manufacturers and distributors have long understood that as injuries go down, so do lost work days, workers' compensation claims, employee grievances, lawsuits, operational slowdowns, and other costs. Even accounting firms and other professional service providers see the financial value of reducing employee distress. Internal PricewaterhouseCoopers (PwC) studies indicate that it costs the firm from two to three times annual salary to replace a manager when the full costs of recruitment, hiring, and training and of work disruption are considered.[6] Thus, whenever a manager leaves, it's as if PwC continues to pay that salary for at least two years. So the company's excellent work-life balance, employee wellness, and partner-employee connectivity programs, all of which improve employee retention, serve to boost the firm's profitability and the quality of client service while being recognized as responsible corporate behavior.

Minimization can also be a strategy for reducing negative qualities in your products. As we've already seen, public awareness of obesity has mushroomed in recent years, posing an enormous business risk for fast-food companies like McDonald's. One of McDonald's competitors, the Subway chain of franchised sandwich shops, has devised a minimization strategy around the obesity issue. Using a series of memorable television commercials featuring Jared Fogle, a real-life customer who lost 245 pounds while eating exclusively at Subway, the company deliberately draws a sharp contrast between its most popular product, the hero sandwich stuffed with cold cuts, cheese, lettuce, tomatoes, and other fresh ingredients, and McDonald's best-known menu items, which contain far more grams of fat. Thus Subway is practicing both minimization and sustainability jujitsu, making its offerings less bad and thereby flipping a business risk into an opportunity.[7]

So far, the strategy seems to be working. Since Subway began showcasing the comparative health benefits of its products in 2000, revenues have surged from $5.1 billion to $7.75 billion. For the past three years, Subway has been expanding faster than any other fast-food chain. Today Subway has 19,500 stores in over seventy countries (including more U.S. stores than McDonald's) and expects to reach 30,000 within five years.

Here are some ways to look for minimization opportunities that can help your company no matter what business you are in:

- *Look for processes and procedures that generate waste.* Are raw materials, energy, water, or other physical resources being discarded, spoiled, or going unused? (If you don't know, you should. Creating a program to measure, monitor, and track your inputs and outputs in all these areas is an essential first step.) What about the time, energy, and talent of your employees—are these being wasted? Chances are good that an operation that generates waste can be transformed into a source of savings for your company and move you toward the northeast corner of the Sustainability Map.

- *Look for areas of stakeholder conflict.* Think of complaints or objections as gifts: they pinpoint areas where you must improve to meet your objectives or the needs of your stakeholders. So take persistent, good-faith complaints seriously, whether they come from employees, customers, suppliers, distributors, neighbors, community groups, or any other stakeholders. Identify the cause of the friction and reduce it to save your company or department time and money and to create other benefits in the form of goodwill, improved morale, and enhanced reputation.

- *Benchmark your company against others.* Investigate how your competitors are finding and reducing waste and compare your performance. You can often find out simply by visiting their websites or reading their environmental reports. Companies tend not to view minimization as a core part of what they do and therefore are relatively free with this information—even when it offers a competitive edge.

From Minimization to Optimization: The Sustainable Path to New Profits, New Products, and New Markets

As we've explained, optimization goes beyond minimization. Moving from minimization to optimization can pay rich rewards. What begins for many companies as an attempt to minimize a problem may gradually evolve into an effort to optimize by creating new and valuable solutions.

The so-called brownfields movement in the United States is a fascinating example of a phenomenon that began as minimization and evolved into optimization.[8]

During the 1980s, an estimated 450,000 despoiled and abandoned industrial locations around the United States were identified, assessed, and slated for cleanup under the federal Superfund program or similar state-based schemes. These toxic sites, usually in urban areas and often near rivers and other environmentally sensitive areas, became a nightmare for governments, businesses, and the communities in which they were located. Total estimated cleanup costs for the corporations held responsible ran into the *trillions* of dollars.

The Superfund law created unintended results. The high costs of cleaning the sites and the draconian legal liability for anyone who owned one caused developers to run at the first sign of contamination. So polluted sites, "brownfields," languished while developers rushed to pave "greenfields"—tracts of untouched land in outlying areas—ironically exacerbating problems of congestion and pollution, and contributing to unsightly exurban sprawl.

That was not what environmentalists had intended when they lobbied for the Superfund program. "We would prefer to have development occur in cities where infrastructure already exists . . . because it helps to protect green spaces, which we would like to retain as green spaces," explained Ed Hopkins, director of the Sierra Club.

Seeking a solution, environmentalists began to work in concert with real estate and business lobbyists to push for changes that would relax the liabilities of brownfield owners, offer tax breaks to make developing brownfields more profitable, and create environ-mental insurance that would help pay for the cleanups.

As these reforms were enacted, the minimization approach to brownfields gave way to optimization. Polluted tracts once seen as huge headaches to be avoided were now sought after as sites for office buildings, supermarkets, housing developments, and parks. As the movement has flourished, over $6.5 billion has been invested by pub-lic and private enterprises in brownfield cleanup and development, creating some twenty-five thousand new jobs. As a result, thousands of communities are gaining new economic and environmental life.

Jacoby Development Company, an Atlanta-based builder that focuses almost exclusively on brownfield sites, is codeveloper of Atlantic Station, a $2 billion project located on the heavily pol-luted 138-acre site of an old steel mill near Atlanta. A national model for smart growth, by 2015, Atlantic Station is expected to include 6 million square feet of office space and 1.5 million square feet of retail and entertainment space, including the first Ikea in the Southeast; eleven acres of public parks; three thousand to five thou-sand rental apartments and condos; and one thousand hotel rooms.

By evolving from minimization to optimization, the brownfields movement has created an enormous sweet spot into which builders, businesses, and communities have rushed. Developers are cleaning the environment, saving greenfields, moving abandoned properties back onto the tax rolls, and helping create economic development in depressed areas, making millions of dollars in the process.

DuPont has leveraged technology and marketing to move beyond minimization toward optimization. DuPont's "Safety, Health, & Environmental Commitment" outlines several specific targets, most of them clearly linked to minimization:

- Zero injuries, illnesses, and incidents
- Zero waste and emissions
- Conservation of energy and natural resources, and habitat enhancements

Yet as the concept of sustainability has permeated DuPont's culture over the past two decades, the company has moved toward more ambitious optimization goals.

For example, DuPont paints cars for Ford at an assembly plant in Oakville, Ontario.[9] By altering its contract with Ford so as to get paid based on the number of cars painted rather than on the quantity of paint used, DuPont realigned its goals with those of its customer while creating a financial incentive for its workforce to operate more efficiently. As a result of the change, hydrocarbon emissions from the plant have dropped by 50 percent.

Optimization was just a short step away. DuPont created a recycling program called the DuPont Carpet Reclamation Program, which (before it was recently sold) recycled and reused over sixty million pounds of carpet for manufacturing floor tiles, carpet cushion, auto parts, and other products. DuPont actively seeks new product lines and markets that do not rely on unsustainable processes or nonrenewable resources—investing, for example, in agribusinesses that specialize in seed, soy protein, and crop protection products as well as in West African research aimed at developing new and safer insecticides for use in cotton growing. DuPont has also developed a technique for manufacturing a critical ingredient for a polyester-like polymer using a fermentation process based on renewable corn sugar rather than petrochemicals.

Thus minimization and the new mind-set it fosters are leading naturally toward optimization, both in terms of promising new products and in more efficient processes.

Optimization can also be about discovering or creating new markets. Unilever's effort to sell low-cost products in the developing world is one example. But similar discoveries are waiting to be made even in supposedly mature markets, such as the United States.

In May 2005, the *Wall Street Journal* reported that the hottest new growth market for insurance was to be found among the forty-five million Americans who lacked health insurance due to the rising costs and narrowing eligibility rules imposed by traditional employer benefit plans.[10] Companies such as UnitedHealth Group,

Aetna, and Blue Cross have developed low-cost health insurance plans with specially tailored menus of benefits designed to appeal to college students, part-time workers, the self-employed, and other underserved groups. Smart marketing? Yes—and an optimization strategy that offers an important social benefit at a time when the health insurance safety net that Americans once relied on has developed more than a few holes.

Here are some insights to consider when your company is ready to pursue the benefits of optimization:

- *Push minimization efforts toward optimization.* When you focus time, energy, and creativity on new ways to reduce your company's footprint (whether in environmental, social, or economic terms), the process of innovation that is unleashed is likely to stimulate ideas that can lead to increased productivity, improved efficiency, and other breakthroughs.

- *Look for new product and service ideas that grow out of your sustainability efforts.* Follow the examples of DuPont and of GE's Ecomagination, which are building new businesses and expanding old ones based on innovative ideas developed in the course of pursuing minimization or optimization strategies.

- *Look for new markets that are "hidden in plain sight," in the margins of the more obvious, traditional markets.* The developing markets of Asia, Africa, and Latin America offer surprising opportunities, as companies are demonstrating. But underserved markets can be identified even in the developed world, as illustrated by the large market for low-cost health insurance in the United States. Discovering such markets can be the outgrowth of an optimization strategy that starts by identifying social and economic needs that are going unmet, then seeks to develop a business strategy to address those needs profitably.

Optimization is a powerful form of sustainability jujitsu—transforming a problem into a solution by looking for the hidden opportunity. Today's most successful companies are shifting from defense to offense on sustainability, moving from "How can we minimize this problem?" to "How can we gain from it?" That shift in thinking will represent the difference between success and failure for an increasing number of companies in the decades to come.

The New Realities of Risk

Risk management is a critical component of any business strategy. But today's sustainability challenges are creating new forms of risk that most business leaders and investors have yet to comprehend fully.

When low rainfall in Kerala, India, caused a water shortage in 2002, political activists staged protests against both the Coca-Cola and Pepsi plants in the city, blaming the beverage companies for withdrawing too much water from the local acquifers.[11] Pepsi's hydrogeologists proved that their plant drew water from a *separate* deep-well aquifer, one that had no connection to the city's water source. But this failed to stop the protests, and Pepsi's managers quickly recognized that thirsty people couldn't care less about the science—that bottling water and soft drinks in the plant while people nearby lacked water for their homes and their families was unacceptable to the community and presented a significant business risk.

Using technical information that had been gathered when Pepsi built its plant, the company improved the community well, thereby restoring water to Kerala, and began a program to build community wells in other areas. At the same time, aggressive water management procedures were established at the Pepsi plant, including the creation of ponds on the plant premises to increase the recharge of the acquifer.

Meanwhile, protests continued against Coca-Cola, and the Coke plant was shut down in early 2004 by the local government. With the Coke plant shut, political activists driven by anti-U.S. sentiments turned their attention to Pepsi. Bowing to political pressure, the Kerala government ordered the Pepsi plant closed, but with no local support the protests failed and the plant reopened almost immediately. In fact, when political activists tried to shut the Pepsi plant down again in late 2005, they were stopped by the local villagers.

The Pepsi story illustrates three important truths. First, most companies today are running risks that don't appear on traditional radar screens. Second, they can often reduce or eliminate those risks if they can identify them. Third, fostering community support and involvement—when done responsibly—can prove to be a powerful risk-management tool. Before building its Kerala plant, Pepsi had performed its usual risk analysis of the area's water supply, which determined that the plant's aquifer held enough water to produce Pepsi beverages. But it never occurred to the company that its operation might be at risk because the town would run out of water from a separate supply. Now Pepsi realizes that the well-being of the community is part of the company's responsibility. "We are beginning to understand risk in a totally new way," says a senior Pepsi executive.

In our newly interconnected world, risks are greater than ever before, and they are everywhere. Outside-the-box thinking is fine, but it must be accompanied by robust, systematic, outside-the-*company* thinking.

Media firms like Disney, Time Warner, Viacom, and GE (which owns the NBC television network) might easily have assumed that the decades-long controversy over the health risk of tobacco posed no risk to them.[12] But those companies are currently being targeted in a campaign launched by the University of California-San Francisco Center for Tobacco Control Research and Education and endorsed by the World Health Organization, the American Medical Association, and other public health groups. The objective: to force media companies to eliminate from movies, especially those rated PG and G, any images that glamorize or promote smoking.

Stories like these can be told about many companies. But when considering emerging risks that their companies face, many managers simply think, "Not me," and set sail blindly, armed like early seafarers with maps that described the far reaches of the globe with the words "Here Be Monsters." A systematic approach to sustainability and stakeholder engagement will enable forward-looking companies and managers to see beyond the horizon and recognize new forms of risks before they strike.

10

LAUNCHING YOUR SUSTAINABILITY PROGRAM

> Begin somewhere. You cannot build a reputation on
> what you intend to do.
>
> —*Liz Smith*

Low-Hanging Fruit

There's no single correct starting point for your sustainability program. Starting with strategy is an excellent approach, but not the only way to begin. If there's one thing that a lifetime in business teaches, it's that you have to be opportunistic—and that applies to sustainability, too. So what's the *easiest* first step to take down the path of sustainability?

For many companies, the answer is to go after the low-hanging fruit: to start by grabbing a few early victories with projects that are easy and obvious, that meet an established need, such as customer demand or a requirement to cut costs.

The first step is often taken by a division, department, or plant led by a manager who sees a compelling business need and understands the potential value of sustainability earlier than others. If the benefits are real, it's not long before someone recognizes the value of a more comprehensive approach, obtains senior sponsorship, and leverages the effort throughout the organization.

Middle managers can and often do play a critical role in the early stages of a sustainability program. 3M's Pollution Prevention Pays was driven first at the departmental level, by the head of environmental quality, then by managers and engineers who identified minimization opportunities within their domains to create immediate savings. The company adroitly fostered this entrepreneurial spirit, spread the word (and the incentives), and ultimately produced the momentum that changed the direction of the entire organization.

We recommend that you start small. Do not make a big announcement or convene a task force, draw up a sustainability vision or strategy, then fail to follow through. A false start creates many problems, including employee cynicism that the effort is a publicity stunt or simply a "program du jour" that will soon disappear. That attitude will be hard to overcome later when you decide to get more serious about the issue.

Here are some ways to identify some early wins in your business unit:

- *Look at your customer's needs.* Look for sustainability issues that will resonate with your customers—a great way to find sweet spots. Do your customers have environmental, social, or economic needs you can fulfill or concerns you can address, as GE is doing with climate change? Do your company's products or services have undesirable side effects you can reduce? Can your products be made easier to reuse or recycle? Can you productively use anything your customers discard? Do you know how to tackle an environmental or social issue that might be confounding your customers? Volvo followed this approach when it made auto safety a differentiating factor and a sales strategy in the 1980s. It recognized that a significant subset of the automobile marketplace was especially concerned with safety, felt that its needs were ignored by the major automakers, and would pay a premium for features like airbags. In the words of one auto research analyst, "American automakers were fighting it [enhanced safety] tooth and nail. Volvo got people to pay for it."[1]

- *Work with your supply chain.* Next, think of your company or department as the customer. What could your suppliers do that would make your operation more sustainable? Examine your supplier code of conduct or individual contracts to see what requirements are already in place and whether it makes sense to tweak them. Look for ways to partner with your suppliers, as Nike partnered with Delta. In exchange for becoming Nike's exclusive airline, Delta agreed to offset all carbon associated with Nike employees' flights either by becoming more fuel efficient or by purchasing carbon reductions elsewhere through planting trees and the like.

- *Leverage your current position.* If you've already moved forward in one area, create additional competitive advantage by pressuring the competition to follow suit as Nike is doing with human rights and child labor. Electric companies in the northeastern United States that are required by local governments to install scrubbers and move to low-sulfur coal are using the legislative process to pressure their midwestern competitors to do the same.

- *Start with your current skill set.* Don't try to be all things to all people. You will get better, more meaningful results sooner if you focus your efforts around what you do and know best. If you manage a product line at a food company, the best use of your resources would probably be to assist in addressing hunger or nutrition or to deal with obesity, rather than trying to lead the way on energy conservation or the digital divide. If you have a strong supply chain, think about how to leverage it by working with suppliers to improve environmental or social performance for the extended enterprise.

- *Anticipate an impending change.* If you can foresee where you or your customers are about to get squeezed, you may see new sweet spot opportunities. Toyota anticipated rising gas prices and developed hybrid technology years before Ford and GM. After Brent Spar, Shell understood that stakeholders would be increasingly important to its industry, and decided to master the art of scenario planning and other engagement techniques that have helped it stay ahead of the competition.

- *Empower individuals*. Scott Hall's efforts on the Penobscot River illustrate how just one motivated manager can make a difference. His bosses set some basic ground rules (that is, "make the numbers work and check with us before you make a deal") but gave him the flexibility and support he needed to get the job done. He succeeded where governors and members of Congress had failed.

Making Sustainability Operational: Goals, Processes, and Key Performance Indicators

Whether you start in response to a crisis or by harvesting some low-hanging fruit, you'll eventually want to develop a structure for your efforts so as to leverage your work, give your efforts visibility, or just measure the results. You may decide to create a formal sustainability organization, appoint a champion, or operate a network of committed managers on an ad hoc basis.

Regardless of which way you choose to go, it will be helpful to build certain foundational program elements. These include specific goals to which you are committed, defined processes to help you achieve those goals, and key performance indicators (KPIs) that will allow you to measure your progress toward the goals.

Your ultimate objective should be to incorporate the sustainability mind-set into the operational decisions being made daily by employees. Not that sustainability will be the deciding factor in every decision, but the economic, environmental, and social dimensions should always be considered, just as return on investment, strategic fit, and resource constraints are considered in every important business decision.

Setting Goals

You'll need to define specific goals for your sustainability program or project, both to establish what you're trying to accomplish and to make it possible to measure whether you're getting there. In theory, goals should be defined with reference to your strategy. However, in the real world, you may simply be handed a goal, or you will choose one that seems to fit with where you are already headed.

One easy way to get some traction on sustainability is to consider how sustainability could be built into your existing business goals. For example, suppose your business unit has a cost reduction goal. An energy conservation or employee retention program would further that goal. Suppose your goal is a defined increase in customer satisfaction. Perhaps you can assist your customers with health and safety issues or waste disposal costs related to your product.

For the CFO at Hershey Foods, a business goal for 2002 was evidently to sell the company so as to maximize the return to shareholders. A highly compatible social goal would have been to manage the sale in a way that would have been minimally disruptive or even advantageous to employees and to the town of Hershey. Had that objective been established, the sale might have had a better chance of success.

As you establish your goals, think also about the specific procedures and performance indicators you will need in order to reach each one. You will save yourself a lot of time and aggravation if you know these in advance. Many companies have had to retract or modify goals that later proved too expensive or difficult to implement or measure.

Defining Procedures and Key Performance Indicators

To reach your goals, you'll need procedures and KPIs that will allow you to reach them. How, for example, do you implement the goal of "no child labor" when many countries define that phrase in different ways? Without specific plans, the goal is almost meaningless and even dangerous, as you are bound to encounter situations you are not prepared to handle.

Developing sustainability policies and procedures is sometimes fairly straightforward. Health and safety experts are skilled at writing procedures designed to reduce accidents, for example. But developing procedures for some areas of sustainability requires a wide range of talents, backgrounds, and skills.

As we suggested with goals, try to integrate new requirements into existing ones. Amend your human resources policies and procedures to address child labor issues; amend your standard contracting language to require suppliers to avoid child labor.

If you must develop entirely new procedures, test their workability before you roll them out. Understand who the stakeholders are and involve them in developing or reviewing the policy. Try implementing procedures on a pilot basis to work out the kinks in advance.

KPIs are critical tools that can, like the gauges on a car's dashboard, help you determine whether you're likely to reach your destination.

Successful companies often use *leading indicators* to measure their progress. For example, energy companies hold safety training sessions prior to any dangerous job. These have proved to be effective in reducing accidents, but they are often skipped or shortened by impatient workers. So a leading indicator of workplace safety might be the percentage of times the safety sessions are successfully carried out. *Lagging indicators*, by contrast, tell you about what has already happened. Monies spent on workers' compensation claims would be a lagging indicator of safety.

Many books have been written about how to establish sustainability goals, procedures, and KPIs (we recommend some of the best in Appendix B). And the topic of defining sustainability metrics for reporting purposes is one we'll address in more detail in Chapter Thirteen. But here we want to stress a few overarching points:

- *Establish goals that further the primary objectives of your business.* Some commercial banks, for example, have invested heavily in water and waste conservation programs or paper recycling, but do not conduct robust due diligence on the community or environmental impacts of their loans.
- *Strive for simplicity.* Keep the number of goals small and mutually reinforcing. Reducing water use and eliminating your

pollution of the river near your factory, for example, may be mutually reinforcing goals, as both might involve redesigning processes to minimize the flow of water through the plant. But such goals as eliminating worker accidents, reducing carbon emissions, and simplifying product packaging have little tendency to support one another. Consider tackling these in sequence rather than simultaneously.

- *Make sure the goals are clear and understandable.* A goal like "no child labor" is too vague. You need to determine specific age limits; decide whether to make exceptions for part-time, after-school, or summer employment or for children who are supporting others; decide what do about local laws or customs that conflict with your policies; and determine how you'll monitor and enforce the program and how you'll handle violations.

- *Integrate goals with goals, procedures with procedures, and KPIs with KPIs.* If your operation already has existing goals, procedures, and KPIs, look to add environmental or social aspects into them. Rather than crafting a separate set of environmental procedures for a plant, incorporate environmental procedures into the general operating manual, wherever possible.

- *Develop clear, consistent definitions of every term and measurement unit included in your goals, procedures, and KPIs.* Don't assume that employees in different departments or locations around the world use the same words to mean the same thing.

- *Strive to define every goal and KPI in terms of a number.* Qualitative goals are inherently subjective and therefore almost impossible to verify. Only when your progress is quantifiable can you guarantee that everyone will understand and accept the validity of your analysis, results, and self-assessment.

Getting Organized

By now we hope you have a good understanding of how sustainability might affect your job and of how to get started within your own department or domain. As with pollution prevention at 3M, many of the most successful corporate programs began by leveraging the efforts of one department or individual within the company. But most companies eventually look to expand those efforts because of the enormous power of these ideas at the strategic level. In the pages that follow, we'll offer some advice and discussion about which individuals, groups, departments, or teams within the company are typically best positioned to tackle companywide sustainability challenges.

Because of the wide range and interdisciplinary nature of activities that fall under the rubric of sustainability, many companies start by creating a *task force* to define and drive their efforts. A task force includes operational managers, key department heads and divisional representatives, and people with the power and responsibility to determine how to structure and define the effort and move it forward on a permanent basis. It also includes, or has direct access to, technical experts such as environmental or supply chain specialists.

The task force may ultimately be supplanted by or evolve into a permanent sustainability department, or at least a position within the organization that is charged with pushing the program forward—a *sustainability champion* in the form of a team or an individual executive who is personally committed to sustainability and has the knowledge, clout, and prestige necessary to make the effort significant.

In some companies, the champion's role is clearly played by the CEO. Chad Holliday, CEO and chairman of DuPont, has chaired the World Business Council for Sustainable Development and written books and articles on the subject. His personal commitment to sustainability is unmistakable, and this sends a message to the rest of the organization that no one can ignore.

The following are among the many important functions served by the sustainability champion; this person or team

- Organizes staff support, technical resources, and information on sustainability for the rest of the organization

- Facilitates and encourages communication among the various parts of the corporation around sustainability, so that innovations and solutions developed in one division are quickly spread to others

- Oversees and drives corporation-wide systems for measuring, reporting, and incentivizing sustainability efforts, so that there is uniformity and fairness in all these systems

- Represents or supports the corporation in its dealings with other companies, the government, and the various stakeholder communities where broad sustainability issues are concerned

Alcan, the aluminum company giant, uses multiple champions. Recently retired CEO Travis Engen personally championed sustainability at the top, working with a director of sustainability and the head of corporate communications, whose efforts are aided by champions within each of Alcan's business units. Designated sustainability champions in key business units who are trained to assist others in identifying the sweet spots and operationalizing sustainability within their unit bring the effort closer to ground level, which is where sustainability must take hold to create the greatest value.

A *sustainability department* can be an important resource for managers throughout the company, offering expertise, resources, connections, and coordination. But locating sustainability in its own department risks isolating it as an "add-on" to core business processes. Staffers in a sustainability department often end up fighting uphill battles with production managers, R&D departments, financial officers, and human resource personnel who speak different languages, have different objectives, and see the organization and the world from different points of view. Trapped in "sustainability land," they spend most of their time figuring out how to build bridges to other people in the organization.

In the long run, integrating sustainability into operations is the only way to go. Like quality, sustainability must be built in, not added on. Sustainability can be the specialized province of a handful of experts, but it's far more effective to educate your operating managers about sustainability and let them apply this knowledge to their own goals and strategies.

Under Sony's Green Management 2005 program, employees from virtually every area of the corporation—R&D, procurement, product design, production, marketing, customer service, and many others—are expected to integrate environmental objectives into their jobs. Each department is required to contribute to corporation-wide environmental goals, which are defined in specific, quantitative terms—for example, a 20 percent increase in recycled materials used by product weight, or a 30 percent reduction in total waste generation at each business site. Managers and business units are supported in these efforts by companywide educational programs, workshops, and an annual conference devoted to information sharing. But it's clear that the managers themselves are committed to the environmental targets, and their job performance is judged, in part, on their success in achieving those goals.[2]

The Virtual Sustainability Department

For many companies, the ideal solution to the structural dilemma may be to create a *virtual sustainability department*. This means linking together many employees from various departments to share ideas, insights, and tools related to sustainability. It also involves permitting managers to seek additional support from outside sources—consultants, NGOs, business partners, suppliers, customers, and others who can contribute to the effort.

We call this a *virtual* department for several reasons. First of all, it's not a department in the traditional sense. It doesn't appear on any corporate organizational chart, it controls no budgets, and there are no employees assigned to work full time for it. Second, the people who participate are often linked electronically, using all the modern communication means at their disposal—email, blogs, internal and external websites, telephone, fax, satellite video—to share ideas around sustainability. Third, this virtual department is in constant flux. New people are continually joining the network while others are dropping out (at least for a time) as projects begin and end.

The notion of the virtual sustainability department puts a high premium on networking inside and outside the company, so knowledge management methodologies, especially in a global organization, can be either a big stumbling block or a powerful lever. At DuPont, for example, engineers report wasting hours looking for environmental data or a key regulation needed before they can make a decision that takes just thirty seconds once the information is available. And in the early stages of "going sustainable," the challenges can be especially acute.

Innovative technology can be enormously helpful here.[3] For example, newly developed software search programs can scan people's emails to find a particular word or phrase—let's say *carbon* or *climate change*—to identify who in the company knows about a certain topic. This makes it possible to communicate quickly and easily with everyone in the company who is concerned about a given issue. Such applications as ActiveNet, Collaboration and Expertise Networks, and Verify K2 Enterprise are already being used at such companies as Morgan Stanley, Northrop Grumman, and ABB Group, and even by the U.S. State Department to facilitate networking around shared concerns. These new electronic systems are a far cry from older attempts at building companywide knowledge management systems, which tended to be clumsy, time-consuming, and slow. Tailored to ways the human mind actually works (as opposed to arbitrary methods of sorting concepts to which people are expected to conform), these new systems are drawing enthusiastic participation and producing real results. At Shell, a global Web-based bulletin board has saved $200 million per year, generating and sharing far more useful information than the company's 1990s-era document management system ever did. (Of course, you have to be careful how you use knowledge management software, lest you violate employee privacy—which would *not* be a positive step toward greater corporate responsibility!)

How do you launch a virtual sustainability department? How does it operate? Here are some ideas.

- *Start with personal networks.* To identify those who ought to be included in the department, get together with two or three key people who have already indicated their interest in and commitment to the concept of sustainable management. Then spend time brainstorming the names of people from throughout the organization who ought to be invited to participate. Think about whom you know in research and development, marketing, operations, human resources, finance, and other departments that may be interested in sustainability and may "own" needed resources or expertise within your enterprise.

- *Survey the organization.* Augment your list of names with a general survey of the organization. Send a questionnaire via email or inbox soliciting interest. Specify the key areas of focus (pollution reduction, improved worker safety, ethical management of the supply chain, sustainable package design, and so on) and ask employees to indicate their areas of interest and relevant background. Keep the questionnaire brief; if it takes longer than five minutes to fill out, the response rate will plummet.

- *Look for every kind of diversity.* When drawing up your final invitation list, strive to make it reflect the diversity of the company—not just in demographic terms (gender, age, ethnicity, sexual orientation, politics) but also in business and professional terms. Be sure to include both line and staff employees, company veterans and relative newcomers, technical experts and communications specialists, "numbers" people and "people" people. Consider the various resources that you might need, and try to engage at least one person that can help deliver each kind. And if possible, strive to ensure that every major area of your business—in terms of geography, product line, target market, and profit center—is represented.

- *Put someone in charge.* Someone must accept responsibility for monitoring, guiding, stimulating, and controlling the activities of the department. If possible, work with senior management to write this task into his or her job description, include it in any annual list of objectives and incentives, and give it a significant chunk of assigned time (50 percent or more).

- *Use technology to help establish your virtual community.* One of the key roles of the virtual sustainability department will be to provide a forum in which employees can address questions, challenges, problems, and opportunities; share ideas; and raise concerns. Work with your company's IT team to create knowledge management systems to facilitate the kind of interaction you need. At PepsiCo, the communications department has set up an electronic bulletin board and e-room devoted to CSR, which facilitates internal communication and helps further the sustainability education and involvement of key managers. The department also produces electronic presentations on specific topics that are housed on a website and can be used by managers throughout the company for discussion and brainstorming with their employees.

- *Have periodic face-to-face meetings.* Electronic communication should be supplemented with live communication. Some topics can't be discussed in sufficient depth via email or blog, and communication is often livelier in the context of an informal get-together or structured workshop. These meetings needn't be elaborate or very frequent; they might be scheduled once a quarter or twice a year, and might vary in length from half a day to a full day. If you can meet off-campus in a convenient hotel or other conference setting, so much the better; this helps reduce the chance that people will be called away to put out fires or attend other meetings.

- *Publicize your results.* On a regular basis, spread the word throughout the company about what the department has achieved. (This is especially important when the department is virtual, as it doesn't appear on the traditional organization charts and therefore may be overlooked in the usual internal reports.) You can use existing communications media (the company newsletter or weekly email bulletin) or create a new venue of your own. Share bad news as well as good. Don't merely recite the awards you've won or the favorable press coverage you've received. Your credibility within the company will be enormously enhanced if you announce, "Last year, we fell short of our goal to reduce workplace injuries. Here are the details, as well as our plans to reverse the trend next year."

- *Refresh the team as needed.* Like any working group, the virtual sustainability department will need fresh blood from time to time. Be on the lookout for new employees to add to the team, and when necessary retire others whose interest has waned or whose job descriptions have changed.

Whether you end up using a task force, champion, multiple champions, a virtual or real sustainability department, an existing department, or some other organizational model, try to move quickly to embed sustainability planning and goals in the working processes of key departments in the company. Then expect to reexamine your program at least once a year. Determine what's working and what isn't, and make adjustments as needed. Like other business issues, the sustainability challenge continually evolves, and your organization must evolve with it.

11

MANAGING STAKEHOLDER ENGAGEMENT

With whom will we be partners, and with whom just friends?

—*Bjorn Stigson, president, World Business Council for Sustainable Development*[1]

Seeing Through Your Stakeholders' Eyes

Taking a fresh view of yourself and your company is one of the many concrete benefits you can derive from stakeholder engagement—provided that you enjoy *real* rather than sham engagement. It's not about *pretending* to listen to your stakeholders, holding occasional conversations with a couple of the more tractable activists who follow your industry, making a donation or two to a worthy cause, and issuing press releases to claim credit. It starts with *active, empathic* listening: trying to understand and accept the viewpoint of even your worst enemies and experiencing your business as they do. This is a difficult challenge.

One of the hardest aspects of accepting your opponents' point of view is bearing with a degree of tunnel vision on their part. Many advocacy groups feel that they are trying to save the world, and they view their favored issue as being of paramount importance to that salvation. This often leads to a narrow viewpoint that can be hard to appreciate or fully understand. Furthermore, no matter how closely outsiders track your company or your industry, they almost never know the details as well as you do from an insider's perspective. So some of the criticisms you'll hear from stakeholders will strike you as

uninformed and unfair. You'll find yourself saying (or at least thinking) things like these:

- "I can't believe they're still attacking *us* for that environmental damage. That mess was made by prior management, and
  we've been working hard to set it right." (Mistaken assumption: that you get the benefit of the doubt because you're new
  management. In reality, activist stakeholders don't care; you
  are still the polluting corporation.)

- "Give me a break. What does HIV/AIDS have to do with us?
  It's a tragedy, surely, but obviously not of our making. We give
  generously to the AIDS Fund and provide awareness programs
  and condoms for our employees. What else do they expect?"
  (Mistaken assumption: that your business interest begins and
  ends with your employees and does not extend to their families,
  your customers, and the community in which you operate.)

- "Sure, our health and safety record isn't great. But it's better
  than it was last year and the year before that. Don't we get any
  credit for improvement?" (Mistaken assumption: that you
  should get an A for progress. In sustainability as in other fields,
  only excellence earns an A. And if other companies, especially
  your competitors, achieve at higher levels, why can't you?)

- "So one of our suppliers used child labor. We have a code of
  conduct our suppliers are supposed to follow; we can't control
  them." (Mistaken assumption: that your suppliers and vendors
  are separate from you and operate according to different standards. In fact, your suppliers work for you; they depend for
  their livelihood on meeting numerous requirements that you
  impose—regarding quality of goods, timeliness of delivery,
  price, and so on. You can also enforce strict requirements on
  child labor.)

Your responses may be fair, reasonable, and justified. And when
you engage with NGOs, community groups, government agencies,

and other stakeholders, you should always present your side of the issues frankly and nondefensively, just as Scott Hall did on behalf of PPL. You may receive an understanding reception, just as Scott did.

But you may not. Most stakeholders have a view of the world that is different from yours. Your stockholders and investors don't agree with you all the time, so it's unrealistic to expect 100 percent agreement from your nonfinancial stakeholders.

And even when environmentalists, labor activists, and community groups understand and sympathize with your point of view, they have their own reasons for doing what they do. Just as you have shareholders and a board of directors to whom you must answer, they have donors, members, and boards of their own. When they raise funds or seek other forms of support, they need to show results, just as you do. If they can't get a clear win from their encounter with you, they will at least need to show that they held your feet to the fire. The sooner you accept this, the better. Once you do, you can transform your engagements with stakeholders, making them more open and mutually beneficial.

When you sit down with your adversaries, make the central agenda item (spoken or unspoken), "How can we both get something positive out of our disagreement—something we can each bring back to our stakeholders and that will benefit everybody involved?" See it as a business deal. And as with any business deal, don't assume that you know what's in your adversaries' best interest. Figuratively join your adversaries on their side of the table, looking at your business operations through their eyes, and find ways to modify your operations to respond to their legitimate concerns.

Who *Are* Your Stakeholders, Anyhow?

Stakeholder mapping, a technique for identifying and prioritizing your stakeholders, is a powerful diagnostic tool. It helps you identify your current position in relation to the various interest groups, community organizations, economic and financial interests, government agencies, and others who take an interest in or can affect your activities. It is important to note that not only does the company have stakeholders, but so does every division, department, business unit, plant, and facility. And understanding who they are and what they want is a prerequisite to effective stakeholder engagement.

An easy way to start is by putting your stakeholders in three categories: those within the company (internal), those with whom you do business (value chain), and those outside the company (external). This type of stakeholder mapping is often called a *target analysis*, simply because it resembles an archery target with your organization at the center (see Figure 11.1). Most stakeholders will fall neatly into one or another of the three circles shown on this diagram. On occasion, however, a particular stakeholder may fit into two or even three categories (for example, by being both a shareholder and a community activist), which would typically give this individual or group greater impact on your organization.

To start mapping, make a list of individuals and organizations in each category. The more specific you can be, the more effective the mapping. Name names and take time to brainstorm these lists; some stakeholders who may be important may not be immediately obvious—for example, the local newspaper.

Figure 11.1. Categories of Stakeholders: Target Analysis

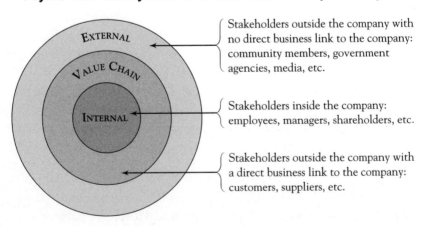

Stakeholders outside the company with no direct business link to the company: community members, government agencies, media, etc.

Stakeholders inside the company: employees, managers, shareholders, etc.

Stakeholders outside the company with a direct business link to the company: customers, suppliers, etc.

Identifying and segmenting your company's (or your department's) stakeholders will generate further insights into how you
interact with them and how they perceive your current sustainability status, all of which can easily become part of your self-assessment
(see Chapter Eight). For each stakeholder, consider these questions:

- How do we communicate with this stakeholder? Do we have
  open lines of communication that permit both sides to express
  needs, concerns, and problems easily and honestly?

- What are the stakeholder's interests as they affect our company?
  How are we addressing those areas of concern?

- What are the major conflicts between the needs of the stakeholder and those of our company? How are those conflicts
  being managed? Are we moving toward a mutually satisfactory
  resolution of those conflicts? Are we headed toward a sweet
  spot? If not, can we find one and head in that direction?

- Who within our company is responsible for this stakeholder
  relationship? What policies, procedures, and principles are in
  place for guiding the relationship? What objectives, explicit
  or implicit, has the company set, and what incentives are in
  place that affect the management of this relationship?

What Do Your Stakeholders Care About?

A second technique for stakeholder mapping is known as an *impact
chart* (see Figure 11.2). It's an easy way to organize your insights into
how specific sustainability issues affect particular stakeholders.

To create this type of chart, draw up a table in which every possible stakeholder group is listed in its own row. (The list shown in the
sample chart is illustrative only; your own list is likely to be much
more detailed and specific.) In the vertical columns, list the key
issues, or impacts, relevant to your company. Then examine each
cell in the chart and ask, Does this group of stakeholders have an

interest in and an impact on our activities in relation to this issue? If so, put a check mark in that cell. In some cases, the stakeholders will be connected to issues that are not on your list, and these too should be recorded. The resulting pattern of checked and empty cells will help you answer such questions as the following:

- Which issues or impacts affect the broadest array of stakeholder groups? (It's likely that these issues will present the most complex challenges for stakeholder relations.)

- Which stakeholder groups have an impact on the largest number of relevant issues? (These are groups that deserve the most consistent and thoughtful nurturing by managers from within your organization.)

- Specifically how do our impacts and the interests of this stakeholder overlap? (This will identify either sweet spot opportunities or areas of conflict.)

Figure 11.2. Impact Chart

Stakeholders	Issues and Impacts					
	Human Rights	Technology Implementation	Lobbying and Proposed Legislation	Economic Effects	Safety Impact	Environmental Effects
Customers	✓		✓		✓	
Community	✓	✓		✓	✓	✓
Environmentalists		✓	✓			✓
Regulators	✓	✓	✓			✓
Unions	✓			✓	✓	
Employees	✓	✓			✓	✓
Media	✓		✓		✓	✓
Competitors			✓			

How Do You Prioritize Your Stakeholders?

A third way to look at your stakeholders is to prioritize the many individuals and groups vying for your attention, interest, and resources in terms of their potential impact on your organization. To do this, you can create what we call a *priority table* (see Figure 11.3).

Like the impact chart, the priority table begins with a list of all your key stakeholder groups. (Again, the list shown in the sample table is illustrative only.) For each stakeholder, estimate its possible impact: its ability to help or harm your company in whatever way it might act—lobbying, making statements to the media, purchasing your product or boycotting it, contacting other influential third parties, or other actions. Rate help and harm, each on a scale of 1 to 5, with 5 being the greatest ability to help or harm, 1 the least.

These ratings for each stakeholder will depend entirely on your company's current situation and challenges. Suppose your company is facing a financial crisis due, in part, to costly commitments for employees' future retirement benefits. Your financial health may depend on whether you can negotiate a reduction in those liabilities with the leaders of the employees' unions. The ability of the unions to help or harm you right now would be unusually high, possibly critical to your company's future, whereas at some other time your ratings for the unions might have been much lower. Environmentalists or customers would not rate as high, in terms of their ability either to help or harm you, at the moment.

The third column in the table is labeled Likelihood of Acting, and it should contain decimal fractions ranging between 0 and 1. A rating of 0, of course, would reflect *no* possibility that a particular stakeholder will take action to influence your company; a rating of 1 would reflect the *absolute certainty* of stakeholder action. In the example, the unions are shown as most likely to act, with a rating of 0.8 (the equivalent of 80 percent likely), whereas the customers are least likely to act, rated at just 0.3 (30 percent).

To determine the relative priorities, you'll add up the two help-or-hurt columns to come up with a total, which will range between

Figure 11.3. Priority Table

	Ability to Help Us	Ability to Hurt Us	Likelihood of Acting	Overall Priority
Customers	4	1	0.3	1.5
Community	2	3	0.5	2.5
Environmentalists	1	3	0.7	2.8
Regulators	1	4	0.6	3.0
Unions	4	5	0.8	7.2
Employees	3	4	0.5	3.5
Media	1	3	0.4	1.6
Competitors	1	2	0.6	1.8

2 (least) and 10 (most). Then multiply this total by the rating for likelihood of acting. The resulting numbers serve as a guide in prioritizing your stakeholders. Those individuals and groups with the highest total scores are the ones that demand the most immediate and focused attention from your organization.

Using each of the three systems we've illustrated in the last few pages, you should be able, at any given time, to sketch an accurate map of your most important stakeholders. If you can do this, it means that you can identify the most influential people in the life of your organization and have at least a broad-brush strategy for managing your relationships with them.

Advanced Stakeholder Strategy

We've looked at who your stakeholders are, what they care about, and which ones might be the most important in terms of their ability to affect your agenda and their likelihood of doing so. The question now is, What do you do about it?

You can use all the information you've acquired (and laboriously mapped) as a means of developing strategies for managing a specific program or initiative, such as a plan to expand your factory in an environmentally sensitive region. One way to plot strategy is by creating an *influence grid* (see Figure 11.4).

Figure 11.4. Influence Grid

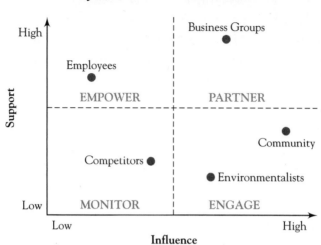

This grid consists of a vertical axis representing the degree of support for the particular program or initiative, and a horizontal axis representing the degree of influence each of various stakeholders might have on your initiative. This grid is just a more highly focused version of the priority table, created in the same way.

Having created the influence grid, you then map each of your key stakeholders. You can begin to develop your strategy according to where each stakeholder group falls on the grid:

- With stakeholders whose support for you is high but whose influence is low (as with Employees in the sample grid shown in Figure 11.4), your strategy should be to *empower* them. Work with these stakeholders to enhance their influence by supporting their efforts to attract members, communicate through the media, and spread their message to the larger world.

- With stakeholders whose support for you is low and whose influence is also low (as with Competitors in the sample grid), your strategy should be to *monitor* them. Under normal circumstances, you should have little to fear from these stakeholders. But you should track their behavior and communications so that if the dynamic should change such that these stakeholders gain greater influence, you will be prepared to work with them or oppose them, as necessary.

- With stakeholders whose support for you is high and whose influence is high (as with Business Groups in the sample grid), your strategy should be to *partner* with them. Look for opportunities to work together in support of your shared goals, thereby augmenting your own influence and increasing the chance of achieving your goals.

- With stakeholders whose support for you is low but whose influence is high (as with Environmentalists and the Community in the sample grid), your strategy, in our view, should be to *engage* them. Keep the lines of communication open, seek areas of agreement (however minor these may appear), and look for ways to influence their thinking to be more favorable toward you (or at least less intensely negative).

The utility of an influence grid and especially the importance of ensuring its accuracy can be illustrated by contemplating what might have happened if the board of the Hershey Trust had attempted to map their own stakeholders onto such a grid before announcing their plan to sell Hershey Foods.

Figure 11.5 shows how the board apparently viewed the attitudes and influence of their key stakeholders. In the upper right-hand corner of the grid, we see two stakeholders the board probably viewed as significant: potential buyers of Hershey Foods (such as Nestlé, Cadbury Schweppes, and Wrigley) and the office of the Pennsylvania attorney general (as represented by Deputy Attorney General Mark Pacella).

As of August 2002 (prior to the sale announcement), the Hershey Trust would have considered both of these stakeholders highly influential. Potential buyers were influential because their readiness to make attractive offers for the company was critical to any sale, and the attorney general would be influential because, under state law, the actions of trusts are overseen by his office.

Figure 11.5. Influence Grid as Mapped by the Board of the Hershey Trust (August 2002)

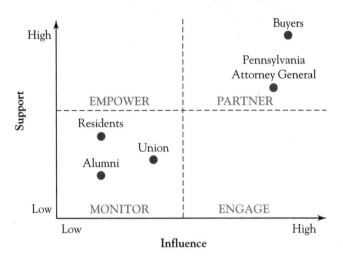

The board also had reason to believe that both would be supportive of the possible sale: buyers, because of the opportunity to expand their market base and sales by snapping up a major competitor; and the attorney general, because the board believed that his office favored greater diversification of the trust's assets, which, in their view, mandated a sale of their Hershey Foods stock holdings.

We place three other stakeholders in the lower left-hand corner: the residents of Hershey, Pennsylvania; the union representing Hershey Foods employees; and the alumni of the Milton Hershey School. The board assumed that local residents and the union would have negative attitudes toward the proposed sale because of the uncertainty it would introduce concerning the economic future of the town. And the board could well have assumed that at least some of the school's alumni would vehemently oppose any action that would alter the ninety-plus year relationship between the trust, the company, and the school.

But the board would also have believed that these three groups had minimal influence over any sale. Community and worker protests are common when corporations are put on the block, but they rarely manage to derail a sale. And, as Hershey resident Kathy Taylor pointed out, history suggested that any protests would probably be muted: "There wasn't much outcry in town when the discount drug store was taken away or they shut down the junior college. So the board must have figured there would be no outcry when they decided to sell the company."[2]

Unfortunately for the board, it badly misgauged the realities on the ground.

As we've seen, soon after the proposed sale was announced, protests erupted from many quarters. Within weeks, it became obvious that the actual attitudes and degree of influence of several of the key players in the Hershey drama were quite different from what the board had assumed (see Figure 11.6).

The influence of the attorney general *was* high; indeed, he turned out to be the most important stakeholder of all, as revealed by his ability to win a court order temporarily halting the sale altogether. But his supposed approval of the sale, if it had ever existed, had evaporated. Attorney General Mike Fisher claims that the board of the trust misinterpreted his deputy's recommendation

Figure 11.6. Corrected Influence Grid as Revealed During the Hershey Controversy (September 2002)

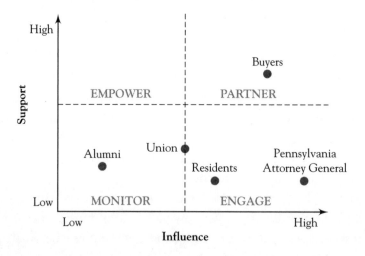

about diversifying the fund's holdings; Fisher would have favored a partial sale of Hershey stock, but not sale of a controlling interest. Had the board members understood this, they could have engaged the attorney general in a discussion about how to accomplish their objectives without crossing swords with him.

Most crucially, the residents of Hershey (and to a lesser extent the union) proved to be far more influential than the board anticipated. Not only did they mount far stronger protests than they had over previous unpopular steps, but they succeeded in mobilizing public opinion around the country behind them, making skillful use of the town's image as America's beloved Chocolatetown in their public relations campaign. By presenting the board's actions as callous and ill-considered, they probably reduced the eagerness of potential buyers to make generous offers for the company (which is why we've moved the Buyers circle slightly south in the revised influence grid). Even more important, the residents helped motivate the attorney general to take his strong legal and political stance against the sale. The confluence of forces that the residents helped put in motion (supported by the union and the Hershey School alumni) ultimately doomed the sale. Again, engagement with the town and the employees would have been a much more promising course of action than the steamroller strategy that the company tried to employ.

The moral? Before launching any major corporate initiative, gather the people who are most deeply knowledgeable about your key stakeholders and work on developing a timely and accurate influence grid that maps those stakeholders' positions in your world. If you perform this exercise with skill and care, it may save you and your company a world of grief.

12

DEALING WITH SPECIAL STAKEHOLDER CHALLENGES

We can either dance with you, or dance on you.

—*Greenpeace slogan*

You're Responsible for Your Value Chain

Sustainability involves issues of communication, shared vision, and the balancing of interests with all your company's stakeholders, both inside and outside your company. Among the most crucial of your stakeholder relations—and the most challenging to manage—are those with the other companies in your value chain. These include companies both upstream (those who supply you with raw materials, finished products, skilled or unskilled labor, and services of all kinds) and downstream (distributors, marketers, retailers, middlemen, and others who help you deliver goods and services to customers).

Managing these value-chain relationships may seem very straightforward. They are generally traditional business relationships, in which each party is primarily focused on profit and in which shared objectives, obligations, time frames, incentives, rewards, and penalties are spelled out in contracts or established in the course of dealing. The terms of engagement are negotiated by the parties, with each side seeking its own best interests and with the comparative bargaining power of the organizations playing a major role in determining which side will enjoy more favorable treatment. Thus, when a powerful retailer like Wal-Mart is negotiating with suppliers, the retailer holds the upper hand and can usually dictate terms; when a supplier like the DeBeers Consolidated Mines has near-monopoly control of a valued commodity—in this case, diamonds—the supplier can dictate terms to retailers.

But once sustainability is on the agenda, the nature of the relationship changes. Now profit may no longer be the defining consideration in mapping out contract terms. Thus, when Nike, newly focused on sustainability issues, negotiates contracts with supplier factories in Asia or Latin America, the discussions are not solely focused on increasing profit margins, reducing costs, improving efficiency, and guaranteeing quality. Now Nike also pushes its suppliers on such issues as worker safety, factory conditions, overtime wages, and, of course, child labor and human rights.

Nike's commitment to sustainability is thus transmitted to its supply chain almost like a beneficial virus. Policies, procedures, and guidelines that Nike has developed to govern its own behaviors become part of the management systems of Nike suppliers, which are required to share the TBL responsibilities Nike has assumed. Even Nike's corporate commitment to transparency is being shared by its suppliers: Nike's 2004 sustainability report listed all its suppliers—the first time any major company in the shoe or apparel industry had made this information public.[1] Nike has in effect opened its supply chain to global scrutiny, inviting NGOs and interested members of the public to examine every link in the process by which Nike products are designed and manufactured, whether those links are technically inside or outside the company.

It may seem arbitrary and even unfair for a company to impose its own TBL commitments on its suppliers. But in today's interconnected world, it's probably inevitable. Stakeholders and the general public no longer recognize strict lines of separation among closely linked businesses. In the eyes of the world, if you're making a profit from a particular product or service, you're responsible for its creation, distribution, sale, and even, in some cases, its ultimate disposal. You can't disavow responsibility for a product or package that bears your logo just because it spends most of its lifetime outside your direct control.

When companies try to distance themselves from a problem they participated in creating—no matter how fair or unfair it may be to blame them for the problem—the public quickly recognizes that buck-passing is taking place, and soon *every* involved party ends up with a soiled reputation. Both Ford and Goodyear looked bad during several months of public debate over which was responsible for rollover accidents in Ford Explorers.

You cannot hope that downstream or upstream problems will go unnoticed or remain unlinked to your company. The public, the media, government agencies, and advocacy organizations are now accustomed to following the value chain to uncover the ultimate sources of problems that threaten the environment, public health, or community interests. So, for example, when mad cow disease was first diagnosed, unsanitary and unsafe practices in meat processing plants were discovered almost immediately.[2]

Complexities of Responsible Value-Chain Management

It would be easy if value-chain management was simply a matter of applying your company's internal policies up and down the chain. The reality is complicated by a range of factors, including the following:

Varying legal and regulatory regimes. Laws covering environmental protection, labor rights, worker safety, child labor, and other issues vary widely from one country to another. Many companies that adhere to local laws have been harshly criticized when those laws permit them (or their suppliers) to pollute or to maintain factory conditions that would not be tolerated in their home countries. Even progressive companies have been criticized for offering different pension or health benefits to similar workers in different countries, charged with valuing employees in one country more highly than those in another. Finding the right balance among business realities, political and PR pressures, and the desire to "do the right thing" can be difficult and complicated, all the more so in a global economy.

Social and cultural differences. In certain countries, bribery is a traditional cost of doing business, but most companies refuse to pay, and prohibit their suppliers from asking for or soliciting bribes. Many companies have been flummoxed by cultural restrictions in the Arab world concerning women. P&G's commitment to diversity and women's rights was tested in 2000 when the company hired four women for its office in Jeddah, Saudi Arabia. Local regulations, clearly discriminatory by Western standards, required that the women be designated as contractors, paid less than males, and given offices in a separate building. P&G pursued the responsible path, exerting constant, low-key pressure to lessen the restrictions. Eventually the women became official P&G employees with strong career-path management positions, and, as P&G proudly notes in its 2004 sustainability report, "Progress this year has been so great that the four women attended a major strategy meeting in the same room with the men." This is a small step, but a significant one, especially for the women involved.[3]

Difficulties of enforcement. Many companies are unwilling to impose requirements on their suppliers that they know they can't enforce. Some have established rigorous auditing programs, paid for by the suppliers themselves, as a contract condition, under which independent verifiers make scheduled and unscheduled inspection visits to factories. Others rely on self-certification or a simple commitment to meet their requirements. But almost every company complains about the difficulty of enforcing against suppliers who are intent on evading the rules.

Because of these and other constraints, pushing your entire value chain toward greater sustainability can be a tricky balancing act. Today, for example, Levi's has considered phasing out operations in China because of that country's human rights record.[4] In other countries where child labor provides a family's only income and where human rights are protected, Levi's pays contractors to keep the children in school to age fourteen. Levi's is trying to adjust to differing circumstances, varying its tactics to address human and labor rights issues as they arise in different situations.

The Many Faces of NGOs

Managing companies in your value chain is challenging, but you have a direct financial relationship with them that gives you some leverage and control. If conflicts become unmanageable, you can usually stop dealing with them and find new business partners. That option isn't available when it comes to dealing with most other stakeholders, and certainly not with the advocacy organizations often referred to as nongovernmental organizations (NGOs).

NGOs are the stakeholder groups that many business people misunderstand and mismanage, often with painful results. They include a wide range of lobbying organizations, citizens' interests groups, environmentalists, labor and human rights activists, and many other organizations that sometimes operate as if making life difficult for your business were their only objective.

Business leaders who assume that NGOs are all fundamentally hostile to business are making a big mistake, however. NGOs are as varied as corporations themselves, and almost as numerous: an estimated sixty thousand NGOs are operating today around the world. Recognizing the many and sometimes subtle differences among them is crucial for any business that wants to forge a mutually beneficial relationship with an NGO or simply get the NGO out of its hair. The attitudes and approaches taken by NGOs toward business have been evolving rapidly in recent years, and savvy businesspeople are altering their thinking and behavior to suit.

We find it helpful to think about NGOs in three categories, based on their primary area of focus:

1. *Company focused.* These NGOs often take a skeptical or aggressive attitude toward business and can be hostile if provoked. Their goals vary widely, but they generally want to limit the influence of business. They seek legal, regulatory, and moral restrictions on certain corporate activities and, in some cases, try to reform business. Some NGOs in this category explicitly position themselves in opposition to specific companies or

industry groups; others are organized around the corporate role on certain issues, such as the environment, labor or human rights, public health, HIV/AIDS, or worker safety, and focus on particular companies or industries that are identified as especially bad actors on the issue. *Examples:* Greenpeace, Human Rights Watch, Transparency International, the Coalition for Environmentally Responsible Economies (CERES), People for the Ethical Treatment of Animals (PETA), Rainforest Action Network.

2. *Policy focused.* These NGOs are devoted to influencing government policy either directly, as special-interest lobbying groups working to support specific forms of legislation and regulation, or indirectly, using financial and opinion-shaping influence to try to sway elected or agency officials. Corporations are, in a sense, an indirect target of these groups, who seek policies that are designed to change corporate behavior, among other things. Consequently, policy-focused NGOs are usually less directly confrontational than company-focused NGOs— except when they perceive their interests as colliding with those of a specific business. *Examples:* Audubon Society, IUCN (International Union for the Conservation of Nature and Natural Resources, commonly known as The World Conservation Union), International Union of Concerned Scientists, Amnesty International.

3. *Issue focused.* These NGOs are devoted to solving specific environmental, social, or economic problems. They are interested in businesses and governmental organizations that affect progress on their issue. They will work with businesses or government agencies if they believe synergies are possible that may advance the cause. *Examples:* CARE, the International Red Cross.

The lines between these categories are not hard and fast, and not every NGO fits neatly into a box. Environmental Defense (formerly known as the Environmental Defense Fund), for example, is company, policy, *and* issue focused. It sues companies over environmental depredations; its think tank works with other companies on projects (such as a program with MeadWestvaco to protect the cockaded woodpecker on company-owned lands); its lobbyists fight for and against legislation (for example, in relation to global warming); and its staff also works on specific initiatives (such as a current drive to preserve and restore the famous Hetch Hetchy Valley in Yosemite National Park).

Policy- or issue-focused NGOs may target certain companies as a way of making their point or when they can't get what they want by other means. Although most companies tend to pay closer attention to those NGOs that are aiming directly at them, policy- or issue-focused NGOs may also either cause problems for business or be helpful. It's all a question of whether they consider your company friend or foe.

When businesspeople are scanning their environment to evaluate stakeholders that may have an impact on their companies in the years to come, they need to understand the *kinds* of NGOs that are out there and the specific organizations they are dealing with, and approach each engagement accordingly.

When dealing with a high-priority NGO that is likely to turn aggressive (or become "riled," as Greenpeace says), proceed with caution. Stakeholder mapping and analysis are called for, as is a consultation with those in your organization whose activities might be targeted. Also speak with your attorneys and your PR professionals. Before pursuing any strategy, triple-check the accuracy and completeness of every document you file and every public statement you release, and leverage all your resources of goodwill, media connections, and social support to publicize your side of every controversy in order to stay off the defensive.

Avoid the temptation to "go negative" on an adversarial NGO. You may be convinced that your opponents are misguided, politically motivated, even venal or corrupt. But coming from *you*, such charges will generally ring false and may even backfire. Most people generally assume that any controversy pitting business against an NGO is a David-and-Goliath battle, with business as the powerful bully and the NGO as the heroic underdog.

Under these circumstances, the best media strategy is to appear statesmanlike, while being honest and responsive. Spend time, energy, and money presenting your side of the argument in a positive light. And when it's plain that you are *wrong* on a particular point, don't dig in your heels. Concede the issue promptly and completely, if possible going *beyond* what your adversaries demand in offering transparency, reparations, and an appropriate change in policy. If you take this approach, what could have been a weeks-long drip-drip-drip of negative news will be transformed into a short-lived story that few people will notice or remember. And if you move quickly to admit and fix the problem, you might even come out a winner, as did Northeast Utilities in addressing its environmental issues at the Millstone nuclear power plant.

Conflicts with policy-focused NGOs take place primarily in the lobbies of Congress and state legislatures, in the offices of elected officials, in hearing rooms of federal and state agencies, and in the sphere of electoral politics. If you work for a large corporation, you probably have a lobbying presence in the relevant state capitals as well as in Washington, D.C.; if your company is a smaller one, you may participate in politics through associations organized by industry, region, or special interest. Whether you are a large or small business, it is important to keep lines of direct communication open with those NGOs that are focused on policies that could affect you. You ought to be meeting with them periodically to explore areas of mutual concern; to discuss each other's views, positions, and reasoning; and to seek common ground.

Forging Partnerships with NGOs

For various reasons, all three types of NGOs are more open to cooperation with business today than ever before. One reason is a shift in attitude on the part of the NGOs themselves. More and more NGOs have come to see the power of the free market as a source of energy for improving our world. Many NGOs are largely giving up on government regulation as *the* solution to environmental, social, and economic problems and instead are working directly with companies and consumers to find sustainability sweet spots in the form of market-based win-win solutions. George Carpenter, director of corporate sustainable development for P&G, describes his work in leveraging stakeholder connections as being about "corporate social *opportunity*," and the phrase expresses the potential for positive leverage that exists when businesses and NGOs can find common ground.[5]

Greenpeace is often considered a classic business-focused NGO—a radical environmental group that is reflexively hostile to growth and business interests. This image is badly outdated, as dramatically demonstrated at the 2002 World Summit on Sustainable Development, in Johannesburg, South Africa. This once-a-decade confab brought activists and businesses together from around the globe. Hundreds of businesspeople attended, including about fifty CEOs from some of the world's largest companies, under the general auspices of the World Business Council for Sustainable Development (WBCSD).

Jeff Ball, an energy and environment reporter for the *Wall Street Journal*, was speaking with one of the authors during the summit when his cell phone rang. "Gotta go! Greenpeace and the WBCSD are making a joint announcement on climate change!" Ball ran off, and later reported, along with the rest of world's media, the startling news that the WBCSD and Greenpeace had stood side by side to call for a global warming framework. It was like witnessing a joint press conference by Custer and the Indians.

This was just part of a new stage of evolution for NGOs and business. Since the 2002 summit (whose theme, appropriately enough, was "Partnerships"), Greenpeace, the Rainforest Alliance, PETA, the Sierra Club, and other globally prominent advocacy organizations once considered antibusiness have embarked on partnerships and alliances with a number of global corporations. In the words of Stephen Tyndale, executive director of Greenpeace, "We need companies because companies are in a position to deliver the solutions. And when they engage, they can move faster and be more dynamic and creative than government. With the right company, it enables you to get things done that you could never possibly do on your own."[6] Hence Greenpeace's partnership with Unilever to develop environmentally friendly refrigeration technology and the Sierra Club's assistance to Ford in helping market its new hybrid vehicles.

The Rainforest Alliance is also working cooperatively with business. Its mission is to preserve the rain forest along with the diverse strains of plant, insect, animal, and human life that depend on it. In the past, the Alliance has clashed with many businesses that sought profit through activities that harmed the rain forest.

Today the Alliance is emphasizing market-based activities that can both protect the rain forest and facilitate the search for profit. Working with companies like Chiquita that have been heavily criticized for poor environmental practices and human rights abuses, the Alliance has developed certification programs that assess the way companies are growing crops and timber or how tourism is being managed. The organization uses market-based conservation mechanisms, and conducts audits that track some two hundred criteria to verify that coffee growers, banana farmers, and pulp and paper companies are operating sustainably.

Managing Partnerships with NGOs and Other Stakeholders

Partnerships with NGOs and other external stakeholders can provide enormous business benefits when properly managed. What are the keys to managing partnerships for maximum corporate benefit? Here are some important tips:

- *Do your homework.* Use the stakeholder mapping techniques described in Chapter Eleven to identify and prioritize opportunities for collaboration and partnership. Note that the "environmental community" or the "social justice community" is not monolithic. Nuclear energy has long been anathema to environmental groups, for example, and many still strongly oppose it. Yet concern about global warming has caused a rift on this issue, because nuclear power doesn't add to greenhouse pollution. British scientist James Lovelock, who helped found the European Green movement, is now pronuclear.[7]

- *Study potential partnerships to determine the likelihood of success.* Part of your homework is to look at how the NGO connects with other organizations. How does it spend its money? More important, from whom does the NGO raise it? What are its objectives in general and in working with you specifically? The specific personalities of NGO leaders can make a big difference in your ability to work with them. It helps greatly to have the right personal chemistry, as Scott Hall of PPL had with the environmental and Indian leaders in their negotiations over the Penobscot River dams.

- *Create a network of stakeholder organizations.* Use your networking skills to link from one NGO leader or organization into other groups with related interests. P&G is masterful at working though NGOs to get access to communities and to community-based groups it might otherwise not be able to contact.

- *Focus on the long haul and be prepared for continuing challenges.* Most NGOs that are willing to work with business are looking for marriage partners, not one-night stands. You build credibility and trust with advocates only over the long haul. Envision what a long-term relationship would look like and where it might lead. And don't assume that working closely with a group in one area makes you immune from criticism by the same group elsewhere. Thus Greenpeace criticized Unilever for creating mercury pollution in India at the same time that it was working with the company to develop a climate-neutral refrigerator.

- *NGOs can be marketplace allies or marketplace adversaries.* Some NGOs have become increasingly sophisticated at using the marketplace to inflict pain. You may face direct action from a disaffected NGO—for example, a forty-foot banner that denounces your company flying over your headquarters.

But you are just as likely to hear about an action aimed at your customers, suppliers, or investors. "We attack the weakest link in the company's value chain," says Kert Davies of Greenpeace.[8]

- *Set specific expectations, then lower them.* Partnerships with NGOs and other stakeholders may be highly formal, with memoranda of understanding that define all the terms of engagement: the purpose, scope, duration of the project, and how disputes are to be resolved. Or they may be based on handshake agreements, shaped and maintained on an informal basis. In either case, the best way to ensure success is to clarify expectations from the beginning and avoid overly ambitious goals. Partnerships with NGOs are usually harder to manage, more costly, and more time-consuming than expected, and it helps if everyone understands and acknowledges that reality.

- *Have an exit strategy.* Just as with commercial partnerships, NGO partnerships can fail or fall apart. Some NGOs will react badly and seek to retaliate. The best way to avoid that is to acknowledge the possibility of failure at the beginning and agree on how it will be handled by all sides. This discussion will serve the added benefit of lowering expectations appropriately and increasing trust.

Most companies see stakeholder engagement as a sideline, relegated to someone as a fourth job if he or she can get around to it. That is a big mistake. Stakeholder engagement should be an explicit part of your strategy and receive all the resources and attention it requires. Pfizer, for example, provides funding to its local operations groups that are trying to develop NGO relationships. Alcoa establishes key performance indicators that it uses to measure the progress of its managers toward achieving important goals related to stakeholder engagement. And Anglo-American, the global mining and natural resource conglomerate, monitors its success at stakeholder engagement by having the relationships scrutinized, analyzed, and reported on by the same outside auditors who examine the company's other sustainability practices.

Creating Your Own Stakeholders

It's sometimes advisable, even necessary, to *create* stakeholders—to encourage or facilitate the formation of a group of company stakeholders to provide a forum in which issues can be raised, discussed, and, one hopes, resolved. We aren't suggesting that you foster conflict where none exists; we are advocating for an open channel for dialogue through which existing concerns can be managed constructively.

Nike used this technique to get back on its feet after allegedly failing to follow through on its own labor rights promises.[9] In the midst of a campaign to repair its public image, Nike was sued by lawyer and activist Marc Kasky for false advertising over its claims in press releases and letters to customers that the company was now enforcing strict workers' rights policies at supplier firms. (The legal battle that ensued turned primarily on the question of whether or not Nike's statements constituted "commercial speech," which is less fully entitled to First Amendment protection than other forms of speech.) When the U.S. Supreme Court refused to hear the case in 2003, tacitly upholding a California Supreme Court ruling in favor of Kasky, Nike was forced to settle, agreeing to pay Kasky's workers' rights organization $1.5 million.

The company had issued a TBL report in 2001, but had been in a bunker during the lawsuit, refusing to issue another report and therefore failing to address the still troubling issue of child labor.

However, Nike had joined CERES, a dynamic and highly effective advocacy organization of investment funds and environmental and public interest groups that originated the Global Reporting Initiative (GRI) and works with companies in support of sustainability. Nike asked CERES to create an independent review panel to assess and, where necessary, challenge Nike's sustainability reporting policies and evaluate its next report.

The review panel was designed to represent many of Nike's key stakeholder groups. Members included Neal Kearney, general secretary of the International Textile, Garment and Leather Workers Federation; Vidette Bullock-Mixon, director of corporate relations and social concerns for the investment board of the United Methodist Church; and Liz Cook, director of the Sustainer Enterprise Program of the World Resources Institute.

The assessment was time-consuming and in some ways risky for the company, but it led to a positive result. According to the panel's unedited public statement, which appears as a three-page insert in Nike's 2004 corporate responsibility report, the company made "significant improvements" after the first critical review of the report. The panel praises the company for its candor, especially its willingness to disclose the names and addresses of all its contracted manufacturing facilities around the world. The panel also lists eight ways in which the report could be substantially improved.

Nike thus preempted the possibility of another effective attack on its practices by engaging with some of its harshest critics and by agreeing to an open and uncensored collaborative process. In today's interdependent world, the way to gain control of a difficult situation involving stakeholders is often by giving up some control to them, working cooperatively rather than trying to dominate.

Other companies have set up similar independent review programs. Faced with community anger over safety and air pollution issues around its crude oil refinery and chemical plant in Norco, Louisiana, the local Shell subsidiary established the "Good Neighbor Initiative" to work collaboratively with community representatives and technical experts to improve environmental performance and establish an independent monitoring organization.[10] In 2002, this group began measuring air quality and other environmental conditions around the facility using guidelines established by the EPA; it published the data on its own website and in Shell's annual sustainability report, describing the project, the progress made in reducing pollution, and continuing problems at Norco. This created credibility for the company and provided an ongoing forum for discussing issues and resolving disputes.

Creating stakeholder groups to provide independent views or to work with you on initiatives or projects can be a powerful way of transforming hostility into positive energy for change. But it can backfire if not handled with a high degree of attention and integrity. Here are some important dos and don'ts to remember if you plan to try this strategy:

- *Do* seek stakeholder partners with real credibility and strong credentials, whose independence and integrity are unquestioned in the stakeholder communities you are trying to reach.
- *Do* give the stakeholder organizations you create or work with genuine independence, allowing them to set up their own policies and procedures and giving them the opportunity to communicate with the outside world freely and without censorship.
- *Do* offer the stakeholder groups as much corporate transparency as possible, giving them open access to company records, employees, and facilities as consistent with genuine issues of legal liability, privacy, and trade secrets.
- *Do* involve your own key leaders who are in a position to make and keep commitments on behalf of the company.
- *Don't* create an "Astroturf" organization—a phony grassroots group that masquerades as an independent NGO while secretly serving your corporate interests.
- *Do* be up-front about your role in helping create and, if necessary, fund a stakeholder group; if the connection is exposed against your wishes due to investigative work by the media, it will seriously damage both your credibility and that of any stakeholders involved.
- *Don't* renege on any commitments you make; the damage to your company's reputation will be doubly serious if you first boast about, then try to eliminate, any moves toward dialogue and partnership with outside stakeholders.

Developing Radar

Close relationships with a wide and varied array of stakeholders can enhance your ability to envision problems before they emerge in the public consciousness, which can be a huge competitive advantage. If you know where to look and keep your ear to the ground, or, better yet, have an ongoing dialogue with your stakeholders, you'll have advance warning about the problems you or your industry will be wrestling with tomorrow. It's simply smart risk management.

Ian Davis of the well-known McKinsey & Company strategic consulting firm puts it this way:

> Businesses need to introduce explicit processes to make sure that social issues and emerging social forces are discussed at the highest levels as part of strategic planning. . . . The risk that stakeholders— including governments, consumer groups, lawyers and the media— will mobilize around particular issues can be roughly estimated based on the known agendas and interest of these groups.[11]

According to Davis, the fast-food industry should have anticipated the current furor over its role in obesity, considering such leading indicators as the growing interest of government agencies in the link between obesity and disease, the increasing media focus on obesity, and the natural interest of trial lawyers in finding a new target for class-action litigation comparable to that brought against the tobacco industry. Even the publication of the best-selling exposé *Fast Food Nation*, which appears to have caused a tipping point on the issue, could have been anticipated (because, as is true of most nonfiction books, its publication was announced many months before the book actually appeared in stores).

Davis's instincts on this issue are correct. A director who works with McDonald's Active Issues Management (AIM) program, which focuses on analyzing PR issues and identifying effective strategies for handling them, told one of the authors that AIM *did* anticipate the obesity issue, but senior executives refused to allocate the resources to deal with it because they didn't believe it would affect the company and thought it better to wait until forced to respond in any event.[12]

Anticipating tomorrow's crises involves more than just being engaged with stakeholders. You need to keep many sets of antennae tuned in to a wide variety of signals: read the newspapers (and not just the business pages) and trade publications; track television, movies, and other forms of popular culture; periodically search the Internet for relevant facts and opinions via Google and other search engines; devote a few hours a month to the blogosphere; scan regular reports about the most common, most intense, and most unusual customer comments and complaints received in your service department; and stay in touch with advanced research in academic and scientific fields related to your business. All this information provides valuable advance warning about a problem most people in your industry won't see coming until it hits them.

But above all, getting to know the interests, objectives, and motivations of stakeholders who are active in and around your industry can give you important advance notice of the issues that are likely to explode next. And the most effective way of hearing about and understanding those stakeholders is by engaging in continual, open dialogue with them.

Adroitly managed, stakeholder engagement is like having radar that other companies don't, which can enable you to be prepared for tomorrow's crises today.

13

MEASURING AND REPORTING YOUR PROGRESS

It takes twenty years to build a reputation, and five minutes to ruin it.

—*Warren E. Buffett,*
chairman and CEO, Berkshire Hathaway Inc.

Sustainability Metrics—
The Unacknowledged Driver

The classic question from high school, "Is this going to be on the exam?" continues to shape the psychology of most people long after they've graduated and joined the world of work. When people know that their behavior is being observed, measured, recorded, and published, they change that behavior to meet the expectations, whether those expectations are expressed or implied. When they know (or believe) that their behavior is *not* being measured, they tend to slack off. Hence the well-known rule of organizational behavior, What gets measured, gets done.

No wonder that the burgeoning movement to observe, measure, record, and publish data on companies' behavior in regard to corporate social responsibility has become a key driver—though often an unacknowledged one—of progress toward sustainable business. The very establishment of a reporting mechanism—the Triple Bottom Line—creates pressure on companies to improve their behavior.

It may seem odd, perhaps even counterintuitive, that the pressure on companies to *report* should be one of the key drivers in making them want to *perform*. But in fact, the sustainability metrics movement is simply an outgrowth of the stakeholder rights movement and the critical lessons learned by environmentalists during the pollution-control era.

Perhaps the simplest and most effective environmental law ever passed in the United States was the "Right to Know" (RTK) provision of the 1980 Comprehensive Environmental Response, Compensation, and Liability Act, commonly referred to as Superfund. Added in 1986 as Title III of Superfund and technically known as the Emergency Planning and Community Right-to-Know Act, RTK simply requires companies to report annually on the amount of hazardous chemicals they have within each company-owned facility. Nothing in the law required *removal* of these dangerous materials, but companies suddenly faced with the simple disclosure requirement immediately began to take dramatic, unprecedented steps to redesign their processes to eliminate the need for these chemicals at all. No CEO or manager wanted to have to explain to the neighbors or employees or, worst of all, his children why his company was on the year's "Dirty Dozen" list of the worst polluters.

Between 1988 and 2003, the RTK law drove a 59 percent reduction in the amount of hazardous chemicals stored on-site by U.S. companies, by far the most dramatic voluntary environmental improvement in history—all because of a simple disclosure requirement.[1]

It's not surprising that environmental and other advocates seized upon sustainability reporting as a tool for promoting socially responsible management. In 2003, the number of shareholder resolutions calling for sustainability reporting nearly tripled. From the advocates' perspective, a disclosure requirement is often the fastest way to get a company to clean up its act.

Call it the tail wagging the dog, but one company after another is now finding that the pressure to report is driving them to create sustainability programs simply to have something *positive* to report. Wal-Mart's newfound interest in sustainability appears to be driven in part by recent demands from some of the company's shareholders, including the United Methodist Board of Pension and Health Benefits, that the company issue a sustainability report.[2] Similarly, PepsiCo's sustainability initiative started with a shareholder resolution by the New York City Comptroller (who votes the thousands of PepsiCo shares held in the city's five public pension funds), asking the company to start using the GRI guidelines for sustainability reporting.

We are firmly opposed to dog-wagging. If you've decided *not* to pursue sustainability, then don't let yourself get pushed into publishing a TBL report. If you don't care what you weigh, don't waste your money on a bathroom scale. But if you do care, then you need a scale to measure how you are doing.

As with every aspect of sustainability, the business case should drive and define your reporting effort. What kinds of information will be useful to your business in pursuing its strategic goals? What data will help your company enhance efficiency, spark innovation and increase productivity? Which information do you need to know in order to reduce waste and minimize the risks from lawsuits, regulatory run-ins, and PR disasters? What sustainability information do investors want, and what information will they be seeking in the near future? Questions like these should determine what you report and how you report it.

Knowing what to report and how to report it poses a number of practical challenges, especially considering that the most widely used sustainability reporting framework, the GRI, includes 146 individual data headings, not all of which are equally relevant to every business. Your choices should be dictated by business considerations after identifying the data that are most relevant to making your business more efficient, profitable, and sustainable.

The Global Reporting Initiative

More than three thousand corporations now issue a periodic environmental or social responsibility report, and over seven hundred and fifty voluntarily use the reporting guidelines issued under the auspices of the GRI. The GRI has clearly become the world's leading benchmark for measuring, monitoring, and reporting corporate sustainability efforts. Whether or not your company opts to use the GRI system, you need to understand it, as GRI's reporting categories and terminology are now the lingua franca of sustainability reporting around the world.

The GRI initiative was conceived by CERES in 1997 and developed in close cooperation with the Tellus Institute, a not-for-profit research center in Boston, Massachusetts. Cosponsored by the United Nations Environment Program during the lengthy development process, the guidelines were officially released at the 2002 World Summit on Sustainable Development in Johannesburg, South Africa. CERES continues to be a driving force behind the GRI, representing a large number of socially responsible investment groups and funds, many of which were using different, home-grown systems for measuring sustainable business practices. Those investors wanted a shared set of universal protocols, so that each new fund wouldn't have to keep reinventing the wheel.

CERES and Tellus understood the power and logic of making corporate reporting of nonfinancial information widely available and comparable from company to company. These organizations correctly predicted that both companies and investors would begin to change their behaviors as comparable, objective information became available. The GRI was thus modeled after GAAP—generally accepted accounting principles—which were established as a way of codifying, simplifying, and unifying disparate and occasionally conflicting accounting methodologies. The GRI attempts to put environmental, social, and economic reporting on the same plane as financial reporting in terms of rigor, clarity, accuracy, usefulness, comparability, and influence with investors.

Hence the idea of the Triple Bottom Line. For many, the ultimate goal is to merge GRI and GAAP information so that companies eventually issue one integrated report containing all the financial and nonfinancial information that investors need and want to know.

The GRI guidelines set forth eleven reporting principles that are described as "essential to producing a balanced and reasonable" TBL report. The principles are enumerated primarily to ensure credibility and comparability, and include completeness, relevance, auditability, accuracy, neutrality, clarity, and timeliness. Relevance is to the GRI what materiality is to financial reporting, the chief difference being that relevance extends not just to investors but to all stakeholders.[3]

The 146 indicators currently included in the GRI framework are grouped in categories to reflect the three parts of the Triple Bottom Line—environmental, social, and economic. Within each category, a series of "aspects" is outlined, with specific indicators grouped by relevant aspects. For example, within the environmental category, the following aspects are listed:

- Materials
- Energy
- Water
- Biodiversity
- Emissions, effluents, and waste
- Suppliers
- Products and services
- Compliance
- Transport
- Overall

If we drill down into one of these aspects—say, energy—we find the following five indicators listed:

Direct energy use segmented by primary source

Indirect energy use

Initiatives to use renewable energy sources and to increase energy efficiency

Energy consumption footprint (i.e., annualized lifetime energy requirements) of major products

Other indirect (upstream/downstream) energy use and implications, such as organizational travel, product life cycle management, and use of energy-intensive materials

Where relevant, each indicator includes specific details on what should be measured and how it should be reported. For example, the indicator "direct energy use segmented by primary source" includes this explanation:

Report on all energy sources used by the reporting organization for its own operations as well as for the production and delivery of energy products (e.g., electricity or heat) to other organizations. Report in joules.

The social category includes twenty-one aspects, ranging from labor/management relations, health and safety, disciplinary practices, and indigenous rights (the last referring to the rights of "native" peoples who may be affected by the activities of the corporation) to bribery and corruption, consumer health and safety, and respect for privacy.

The economic category includes five aspects pertaining to stakeholders who may be subject to the economic impact of the company: customers, suppliers, employees, providers of capital, and the public sector.

Roughly half the GRI indicators are quantitative and can be answered with a number; half are qualitative, requiring a description of policies, procedures, or impacts. Direct energy use, total sum of taxes of all types paid broken down by country (under the public sector aspect of the economic category), and average hours of training per year per employee by category of employee (under the training and education aspect of the social category) are all quantitative indicators seeking numerical answers.

The quantitative indicators present technical hurdles, such as defining, gathering, and checking the data and making sure that information drawn from facilities, divisions, and departments in various geographical areas can be rolled up into one number for the entire enterprise. In large companies, GRI information may be found in over forty different corporate departments, from investor relations to human resources, from the supply chain to the office of the CFO. A great deal of information must also be generated by field operations.

The qualitative indicators seek verbal responses that may be more subjective. In the economic category, for example, the aspect referred to as "the organization's indirect economic impacts," asks companies to "identify major externalities associated with the reporting organization's products and services." In the environmental category, under the biodiversity aspect, companies must describe "the major impacts on biodiversity associated with activities and/or products and services in terrestrial, freshwater, and marine environments." The qualitative indicators demand careful thought, an effort to define your company's relevant activities clearly and consistently, and, above all, a high degree of what the guidelines call "neutrality"—objective information that presents an unbiased and honest view. In other words, you shouldn't try to spin your answers to the qualitative questions. It's far better to report unvarnished information.

Developing a sustainability report that follows the GRI guidelines is challenging, especially for any company that is new to the process. However, the GRI offers a great deal of flexibility and can be adapted to your industry or to your company's strategic or management needs. Under the guidelines, you can choose which indicators to report, how to define the scope of your operations for reporting purposes, the degree of accuracy and reliability of the information, and any plans you have for future reporting. The guidelines also define an "incremental approach" that your company can use to begin. Because GRI reporting is largely about disclosure and stakeholder engagement, transparency is the key. As long as you are clear about what and how you are doing it, and can manage stakeholder expectations accordingly, the guidelines provide the best framework for capturing and reporting your Triple Bottom Line.

You can describe your company as "in accordance" with the GRI guidelines if you provide information for all the indicators or explain any omissions. Such companies as Shell, Novartis, and P&G are among 140 companies that claim this status. Approximately 650 companies say they are "using" the guidelines without being in accordance with them. Such companies often take a flexible and incremental approach to the GRI, especially in the early years of reporting. They may choose to cover specific subsets of indicators that they view as most relevant to their industries or business, or they track data they find easiest to compile.

The GRI guidelines offer many benefits to businesses. One is the availability of a uniform set of indicators that define how sustainability should be measured by companies around the world and is widely accepted by the global advocacy community. A reasonably well prepared report following GRI guidelines is a valuable document to use when explaining or defending your sustainability efforts.

Studying the GRI reports developed by companies you admire— especially those in your own industry or in related industries—is an effective way to identify your sustainability strengths and weaknesses and to create performance benchmarks. Even if you choose *not* to use the GRI indicators as a basis for your own reporting, you ought to use them as a valuable tool for assessing risk—to identify potential problem areas your company ought to be examining before a problem arises. At a minimum, the GRI and its continuing evolution should be part of your corporate radar (as discussed at the end of Chapter Twelve).

If your company is thinking about sustainability reporting, we urge you to use the GRI guidelines. If the entire package strikes you as too ambitious, complex, or costly, take an incremental approach.

Identify the most important GRI indicators for *you*—the ones that drive *your* business—and work on developing accurate, up-to-date reporting on those. Note that the GRI secretariat has issued sector-specific guidelines for some industries, and technical protocols for some of the indicators; a look at those should be part of your initial scoping.

Then see what kind of data you already have. If your management and information systems are well designed, you should have access to most of the necessary information already—provided that the indicators you select are as vital as you believe. It is perfectly acceptable to start by reporting only the information to which you already have ready access, as long as you are open about what you are doing. You want to make sure that your report is not misleading, and the best way to ensure that is to disclose all the limitations on the information, whether that information is partially complete, somewhat inaccurate, or reliant on outside sources. It's also a good idea to report on your plans for improving the quality of the data in subsequent reports.

Ultimately, you may decide that the complete GRI framework is useful and necessary for your company. But remember, your reporting practices should be driven by your business needs, not vice versa. Don't think of the GRI as an inquisitor's rod; instead, look on it as a tool for running your business more effectively.

The Costs and Benefits of Reporting

Some internal advocates for sustainability reporting have encountered serious pushback in their companies because of the costs and difficulties of collecting and analyzing the data needed to issue a credible report. Perhaps this is understandable. Public companies have traditionally devoted serious time, energy, and money to gathering and reporting financial, managerial, and other data for the benefit of investors. More recently, the Sarbanes-Oxley law (2002) has dramatically increased the reporting burden, requiring companies to report additional details on the quality of their financial and antifraud controls, whistleblower protection, code of conduct, and other programs to identify and control financial malfeasance and fraud. Various tax and regulatory regimes impose further obligations to report data; in the case of a large corporation, this includes rules from numerous state, national, and international regulatory bodies. It's not surprising that most companies resist calls for yet another set of complex and costly reports to satisfy yet another constituency. "With all the reporting we have to do," they say, "when are we supposed to get any actual work done?"

TBL reporting can be difficult and expensive, but it is easy to overestimate the time and cost involved. Most publicly traded companies are *already* gathering and disclosing enormous amounts of information related to the Triple Bottom Line in a largely uncoordinated fashion. If you were to survey your company and list all the various kinds of accounts, surveys, questionnaires, and other reports you already create for stakeholders—customers, business partners, banks, insurers, industry organizations, government agencies, employees, and shareholders—you would probably find that much of the data you need in order to create a comprehensive report on your sustainability efforts exists right now, somewhere within your company. It's time to organize this vast array of chaotic information and make it work for you.

Most companies face the immediate challenge of obtaining global information rolled up on an enterprise-wide basis. This can be difficult even when money is the only common denominator. With TBL reporting, it takes time and resources to develop metrics for dozens of different denominators—from water use to HIV/AIDS data to community development impacts—that are uniform across company divisions and geographies while also flexible enough to make business sense when applied to widely varying operations. Very few companies have written procedures on data collection and roll-up outside the financial area. And the sheer effort of requesting information in language that everyone understands, collecting that information, verifying its accuracy, and compiling and publishing reports that convey it in a meaningful fashion can be costly.

Furthermore, at this early stage of sustainability reporting, most companies are unfamiliar with the array of new measures, especially for social and economic impacts. In the absence of technical guidance from the GRI or elsewhere, they are left on their own to figure out what some indicators mean and how to translate them into meaningful information.

Yet most companies have found the benefits to be worth the effort. When driven by business imperatives, reporting often leads quickly to better management and enhanced value creation. Knowing the total amount of fuel your company consumes, the number of accidents your workers experience, or the level of government subsidies you receive enables you to recognize trends, problems, and opportunities, and puts you in a position to develop and strive for long-range, enterprise-wide goals. Simple, shared goals and measurements motivate employees and trigger conversations across divisions, departments, and business functions, leveraging best practices and promoting the spread of valuable ideas and innovations.

TBL reporting is also a way to organize a vast amount of internal and incoming information about a variety of risks and opportunities. If properly and aggressively used along with stakeholder engagement, the GRI can enable you to spot emerging economic, social, and environmental issues before they become crises.

Finally, being able to communicate with the world about your sustainability efforts has enormous business benefits. Companies that don't identify or capitalize on their sustainability activities are leaving value on the table, a serious mistake in today's hypercompetitive business marketplace. An environmental cleanup at one of your older manufacturing sites is of interest not only to the community and the real estate industry but also to other stakeholders, including environmentalists, your investors, and possibly your insurance providers. If the company doesn't capture those benefits by spreading the news, it has neglected an opportunity to create valuable social capital.

Furthermore, in today's wired world it's likely that most of what you are doing is going to come out eventually. When *you* report, choosing your own time, place, manner, and style of disclosure, you build credibility and reduce negative feedback.

A TBL report will assist you in expected and unexpected ways with the advocacy community. If the report is credible, it defines you as a company that "gets it," that takes its responsibilities to society seriously. This can sometimes provide a protective aura that deflects negative attention elsewhere.

Andy was recently working with a company that had agreed six months earlier to publish a report using the GRI guidelines. The company now faced a shareholder resolution from a religious pension fund that sought a report on the impact of HIV/AIDS on the company's business. The company responded that it had just signed up to use the GRI and intended to use the GRI performance indicator to report on its HIV/AIDS programs (which presented far less of a reporting challenge). The pension fund withdrew its resolution.

The Hidden Risks of Sustainability Reporting

Costs and benefits aside, sustainability reporting presents some risks that many companies do not see or evaluate until they are into the process. These risks can be minimized or eliminated if you proceed with your eyes open.

Sustainability activists and socially responsible investors share one trait with the general public: they've learned to be highly skeptical about corporate claims of virtue. Trust in business remains low—a fact of life in today's world. Credible reporting is part of the trust rebuilding process, and you should therefore expect your sustainability reports to be challenged—particularly if they paint a rosy image of your company. Certainly any prose that smacks of greenwash or bluewash is likely to hurt your credibility unless you are able to back up your claims with irrefutable evidence. And you may come under pressure to do so from a shareholder resolution, a lawsuit (as Nike did), or some other challenge.

Interestingly, any *negative* news you report is always accepted at face value, even by antagonistic groups and individuals who normally treat every word your company utters as a falsehood. Hence this paradox: bad news is good news. One of the best ways to improve your company's image and its credibility among activist stakeholders and the public is to publicize your mistakes and failures—along with the corrective steps you are taking, of course. Don't report only your environmental and diversity awards or the fact that you've been named a "Best Company to Work For." You should also report that you fired a dozen employees for taking bribes, shut down a plant because of its terrible pollution record, and are working to improve the monitoring of your suppliers' unsatisfactory labor practices.

This may sound like unnecessary risk taking, but it's more like money in the bank—an investment in credibility that will more than compensate for any short-term criticism you may receive. Any criticism that does come will be muted (and media interest dampened) by the simple fact that you are the one breaking the news. In the long run, you'll win respect for your honesty—and the next time you have good news to report, the skepticism will be just a little less intense.

Since the early 1980s, when a few pioneering companies started issuing substantive environmental reports, two methods have emerged for obtaining independent verification. First, accounting firms and environmental consultancies have developed programs for checking the information and claims contained in company reports. These have the formality and feel of *attestation*, which in the world of financial reporting means that the information contained in the report (whether quantitative or not) is "fairly presented." Many energy companies, in particular Shell and Sun Oil, provide actual attest reports, but they are in a distinct minority: less than one-quarter of reporting companies provide this highly rigorous type of independent verification.

As we discussed in Chapter Eleven, a new form of verification has recently developed. Companies like Nike and Shell have taken to inviting critics—from environmental leaders to community and animal rights activists—to evaluate their sustainability efforts and comment on them in the companies' own reports, thus providing readers with a gut-check level of accountability, and the company with stakeholder engagement on the quality of its report.

A large part of the pressure for accuracy is coming from inside companies themselves. In the Sarbanes-Oxley era, many managers and executives want to be sure that any number that goes outside the company is bulletproof. Advocates for TBL reporting within companies have encountered highly concerned CFOs and finance managers who worry about the legal and reputational risks if an environmental or social report has a wrong number in it.

Although the focus on accuracy is to be applauded, an excessive concern with exactness can impede forward progress on reporting or result in an excessively expensive, belt-and-suspenders approach that, although possibly appropriate for Sarbanes-Oxley purposes, is simply unnecessary for today's TBL reporting.

Managers should understand, as most responsible advocates certainly do, that if you are in the early stages of sustainability reporting, obtaining an exact number for global water or energy use, employee accidents, or government subsidies may be impossible and, in most cases, unnecessary. The cure for slightly inaccurate or incomplete information is disclosure. In its 2004 sustainability report, for example, Coca-Cola states that its water and energy data cover only 68 percent of the company's operations—that's the best the company can do right now.[4] Of course, such partial reporting would be unacceptable for financial data and, ten years from now, might also be considered unacceptable for natural resource use. But transparency will cover most shortcomings in your TBL data.

You do face a serious risk if you fail to follow through on the claims, commitments, promises, and programs you set forth in your sustainability reports. To borrow from Nike, if you've promised stakeholders that you will do something, *just do it*. The Kasky lawsuit against Nike (see Chapter Twelve), which resulted in payment of $1.5 million to a workers' rights organization and the cessation of reporting by the company for three years, was sparked by the company's failure to follow through on claims it had made related to workers' rights at its supplier firms.

The Kasky lawsuit appeared to be a setback for corporate social reporting. Many said it would have a "chilling effect" on what companies would and would not say about their sustainability efforts. Fortunately, it was only a temporary setback that seems in the long run to have propelled social reporting further forward. But the $1.5 million settlement and, more significant, the years of negative publicity generated by the suit underscore an important lesson: before you publicly identify a particular area of sustainability as important to you, be certain you're prepared to mount a real effort to improve it, to measure and report your progress, and to substantiate your claims.

Kasky is a cautionary tale about making certain that the claims and commitments you make in your reports are true and verifiable. As a practical matter, the risks are far greater in being wrong about your policies and practices than in being wrong about how many gallons of water you consumed in FY 2005. So, for example, you need to be precise when you describe your "policy and procedures involving information, consultation, and negotiation with employees over changes in the reporting organization's operations (such as restructuring)" and live up to whatever your policy says. But when it comes to most of the quantifiable data requested by GRI, the perfect is the enemy of the good: Publish the most reliable information you have, disclose its shortcomings, and pledge to do better next year.

Finally, you run the risk of being disappointed if you assume that doing a conscientious job of launching a sustainability program, measuring and monitoring progress, and reporting it honestly will earn you universal accolades and support from your stakeholders. Eventually, if you keep at it, you will gain credibility and win their trust. But in some cases, in the short run, the transparent, responsible company suffers while a secretive and stakeholder-unfriendly rival benefits.

Talisman Energy, Inc., Canada's largest independent oil company, got caught up in the tragic civil war in the Sudan. Over two million people have been killed in this war since 1983, which pits the northern-based, largely Arab government against rebel groups from the predominantly non-Arab southern part of the country. The Greater Nile Petroleum Operating Company, one-quarter of which was owned by Talisman (in partnership with government-controlled companies from China, Malaysia, and Sudan), was producing oil extraction fees of up to a million dollars a day in 2001 for the Sudanese government.[5]

Outraged that a Canadian firm was helping support a murderous government, church and public pension funds (such as the influential California pension fund known as CALPERS) divested from Talisman, and Presbyterian, Episcopal, and Catholic groups began demanding that Talisman sell its interests in Sudan. In a public relations nightmare, groups of nuns began showing up at Talisman's facilities in the Sudan to demonstrate, accusing the company of supporting genocide.

Talisman responded by following all the rules of stakeholder engagement, transparency, and reporting. They sent officials to attend the Sudan Catholic Bishops' Conference, met with refugee groups and NGOs, and issued detailed sustainability reports (prepared with assistance from PricewaterhouseCoopers) highlighting how their operations in Sudan were benefiting the country's people and especially their own Sudanese employees, all of whom received health and educational benefits as well as wages far higher than the national average. The company was also vocal in advocating for better human rights policies on the part of the government.

Talisman's efforts at engagement and reporting were to no avail. The nuns kept on the attack, demanding that Talisman stop paying extraction fees to the government or get out of the Sudan entirely. As a result of the constant, negative publicity, Talisman's stock price tanked, suffering what internal and Wall Street analysts began to refer to as "the Sudanese discount," an estimated 10 percent reduction off what the company's value should have been. In October 2002, after years of unfailing efforts to be responsible, Talisman succumbed to the pressure, selling its stake in the Sudan oil operation to an oil company owned by the Chinese government.

Did the transfer of ownership improve the lot of the Sudanese people? It probably made matters worse: a company trying to do the right thing was replaced by one far less committed to human rights, labor rights, employee issues, and government reform, and far less vulnerable to political pressure from the nuns.

Some businesspeople may conclude, on the basis of this story and others like it, that sustainability reporting—even the idea of sustainable business itself—is a futile delusion, and that trying to communicate and reason with stakeholders is a waste of time, money, and energy.

It's true that a strategy of transparency and stakeholder engagement offers no guarantee of success, either for your business or for society. But what business strategy does? The challenge is to find an approach that will improve your odds of victory—and the overwhelming evidence is that transparency and stakeholder engagement do just that. For every Talisman, there's a case in which a long-term commitment to sustainability has carried a company over a crisis, as in the case of J&J and the Tylenol poisonings, or Shell's misstatement of its oil reserves.

Looking Ahead: Integrated Reporting on the Triple Bottom Line

The quantity of information contained in company financial reports has grown dramatically over the past few decades, especially since Sarbanes-Oxley. Now the calls for more comprehensive disclosure on the financial bottom line have clearly spilled over to the Triple Bottom Line. Stock exchanges in Scandinavia, France, Britain, South Africa, and other countries now require listed companies to publish TBL reports. Under SEC rules established in 2003, mutual funds must now disclose how they vote their billions of shares on shareholder resolutions—many of which are about additional disclosure. And with more and more companies moving to online, real-time reporting, the quantity and detail of information in corporate reporting are likely to increase.

Perhaps most important, mainstream investors and financial auditors are calling for far broader disclosure, suggesting that the information available today is not sufficient for investors to make fully informed decisions. PricewaterhouseCoopers, led by its global chairman Samuel DiPiazza, has issued a call for "value reporting." In his groundbreaking book, *Rebuilding Public Trust*, DiPiazza calls for more transparency, not only from companies but from what he calls the entire "reporting supply chain," and cites the GRI as part of the movement to rectify this information shortfall.[6]

All these trends point to one natural outcome: in time, most or all businesses are likely to integrate the Triple Bottom Line into their basic performance reporting, tracking environmental and social impacts alongside economic and financial results in the same quarterly and annual reports that all investors scrutinize. Companies will eventually cease to issue separate environmental or sustainability reports and will instead integrate all material and relevant data in one form that presents the complete package of information that a prudent investor or other stakeholder would want to know.

This new reporting paradigm is already taking shape. Open PepsiCo's annual report for 2004, and you find the standard table of contents for a financial report opposite the table of contents for the company's GRI report. PepsiCo is among the first U.S.-based companies to include TBL data alongside their financial information in the annual report. Some companies in Europe, such as Novo Nordisk, the Danish biotechnology group, have begun to drop the distinction entirely, moving from incorporation of TBL data to full integration. As GRI cofounder Allen L. White says, "Why even bother to distinguish between what is financial information, and what is nonfinancial information? It's all information. Ultimately, the important distinction is whether it is something a reasonable investor or other stakeholder would want to know."[7]

The implication: today's Triple Bottom Line may simply be a transitional phase from an older to a newer theory of how business works. We'll look at this possibility in more detail in the Epilogue to this book.

14

CREATING A CULTURE OF SUSTAINABILITY

Things don't change. You change your way of
looking, that's all.

—*Carlos Castaneda*

Choosing a New Point of View

By now you've probably begun thinking differently about how your business intersects with society and are looking to find ways to improve your profitability while doing the right thing for your stakeholders. That's a great start. But becoming a sustainable enterprise isn't just a matter of placing an overlay on top of your conventional business thinking. It entails making a shift from an old way of thinking to a new one—a new mind-set that subtly or dramatically alters everything you see and do.

Here's an analogy. At a certain point in the last two decades, many managers learned to see fellow employees as their customers. One day, your colleague was bothering you for something he needed to do his job, not yours; the next, that same person's satisfaction with you was part of your performance evaluation—so meeting his needs became part of your job, and rightly so.

This change in viewpoint was a foundation of the quality movement, a transformation that vastly improved efficiencies within companies. In a similar way, the sustainability movement is now changing the way that managers relate to their environment and to those inside and outside the organization, with consequences that will be even more far reaching.

Sustainability seems to flourish in corporations that have four crucial traits: vision, honest self-awareness, strong leadership, and long-term thinking. These characteristics have appeared in the stories we've shared, but they're important enough to bear further emphasis and explanation.

A Vision of What Sustainability Means to Your Organization

Having a vision of sustainability means seeing how the corporate world—and your industry and company in particular—works within the larger social and natural world. This is big-picture thinking: How is the world enriched or diminished by your products or services? What are your major impacts on society, and how does your overall business strategy reflect those impacts? How are stakeholders included in your decision making, and how are the costs and benefits of what you do shared among them? How do you take into account the needs of society and of future generations? Leaders of sustainable businesses will be able to answer questions like these.

Many companies find it useful to articulate a sustainability vision or mission, often summarized in a sentence or two. DuPont's is "creating shareholder and societal value, while reducing our footprint throughout the value chain"; PepsiCo's is to "continually improve all aspects of the world in which we operate—environmental, social, economic—creating a better tomorrow than today."

It's valuable to put your vision down on paper. A brief, well-crafted statement creates clarity and provides employees and stakeholders with a set of broadly stated principles against which your efforts can be measured and that can be used to develop more specific guidelines, including your strategy, goals, and key performance indicators.

But a sustainability vision is more than catchy words. It requires you to see how to incorporate the Triple Bottom Line and its emphasis on environmental, social, and economic prosperity into every decision made throughout the organization, to think about how it takes hold at the operating level. Having a vision means constantly seeking answers to questions like these: What resources does your business take from the environment? How are those resources replenished? What are the biggest economic and social issues you face? How do you interact with the community?

It may sound as if we are advocating that businesspeople become part-time philosophers. In a way, we are. As we've emphasized throughout this book, all of us are living in a time of transition. An older vision of business, in which financial performance is seen as the *only* way to evaluate your actions, is being exposed as inadequate to the demands of an interdependent world and, in the long run, self-defeating. A new vision, still in its formative stages, is taking hold, and no consensus has yet emerged on many of the important details.

Under these circumstances, upper- and mid-level managers who aspire to leadership roles in business *must* be part-time philosophers, even visionaries. Along with all their other roles (as strategists, managers, marketers, financiers, psychologists, product designers, and so on), executives today must take the time to think hard about the social, economic, political, environmental, and cultural transformation that business is undergoing and to decide how they and their companies will participate. If they don't, they will misunderstand or be blindsided by some of the most powerful trends and changes affecting their industry, their business, and their job. As a result, they may lose control of their company or find themselves left behind in new marketplaces, where the terms of competition are quite different than in the past.

Honest Self-Awareness

Anyone who has spent time working inside corporations with executives at various levels (as most consultants have) will confirm that leaders at many companies, especially managers on the way up, find it hard to be clear eyed about their own company. Often very insightful about the financial situation of the company, they can be unrealistic or out of touch when it comes to the company's nonfinancial performance. We find this especially true at consumer product companies with big brands. It's as if the relentlessly upbeat, happy-talk attitude that pervades their consumer advertising and marketing somehow seeps back into the corporation itself, making optimism mandatory and realism suspect.

An exaggerated concern about legal liability may also play a part: managers have possibly imbibed the notion that any acknowledgment, public or private, that they or their company may have made a mistake could somehow come back to haunt them. In fact, many companies refuse even to use the word "mistake" or "problem," at least in public. They edit out all such negatives and insist on calling problems "issues," "challenges," or even "opportunities" (as in, "The discovery that we've been paying bribes to officials in the Sudan provides us with an opportunity to improve our internal compliance programs.") "Improve" and "improvement" are also considered dangerous words; they seem to imply there is a problem that needs fixing. That's why corporate lawyers prefer the word "enhancement," as one can always talk about enhancing a program without implying that there is a need to do so.

This blinkered, even upside-down attitude is potentially suicidal in today's world. Surveys show that employees are highly engaged and perceptive readers and analysts of their own company's reports. They know what's going on, and they know about the real problems facing their department or company. But if they see that the party line is "We don't have problems, just opportunities," they will get the message and won't disclose any problems, at least not to management. They may cover them up or talk to those for whom "problem" is not a dirty word, people like regulators, the media, or NGOs, who are not likely to have to have the company's interests foremost in mind.

Conversely, the ability to see yourself clearly—and, even more important, to see yourself the way others see you—is enormously empowering. Only by seeing reality and acknowledging your shortcomings will you stand a chance at real improvement. But honest self-appraisal is a skill that many managers and companies lack. They need to develop it sooner rather than later.

Strong Leadership

When driving a major change, such as the current move toward sustainability, strong business leadership begins with clarity of message. Jack Welch, the longtime CEO of GE, became a uniquely effective business leader because of his understanding of the vital importance of a *clear message, expressed in simple terms, disseminated throughout the organization, and hammered home repeatedly.* Thanks to Welch's insistence on the clear message, concepts like Six Sigma and "Be number one or number two in the market, or get out" became widely known (and practiced) not just throughout GE, with its six major businesses, dozens of business units, and 285,000 employees, but throughout the business world. And Welch's proudest moments were times when front-line GE workers, from secretaries to factory hands, were able to explain in a few sentences the latest corporate strategy—thanks to frequent missives, speeches, exhortations, and occasional explosions from "Neutron Jack."

Today's smartest businesses are applying the same lesson to the concepts behind sustainability. DuPont, for example, uses the admirably short and simple slogan "The Goal Is Zero" to summarize its environmental goals. Nor do DuPont's executives restrict their sustainability message to the top one, two, or three levels of corporate management.[1] Instead, they follow the concept of "felt leadership," which states that "it is not enough for a policy to be written and posted on the walls; everybody in the organization must feel it. This means that it is considered in decisions, it is referred to at management reviews, and tough decisions are made to support the vision." As Travis Engen, recently retired CEO of Alcan, said, "I know a message is taking hold when they are arguing about it at lunch."[2]

Along with a clear message, you need a sense of commitment from the top of the organization if your sustainability efforts are to bear fruit.

It's hard to overstate the psychological and cultural impact that can be achieved when the top leaders of a company get personally invested in sustainability. When PepsiCo decided to launch a sustainability initiative, it could have begun in any number of ways—via a memo, emails, or a company newsletter, or simply by collecting a few names of people "who ought to be involved" and informing them that they'd been chosen to initiate and coordinate the effort. But PepsiCo's CEO, Steve Reinemund, wanted to underscore his personal commitment to sustainability, so he made it a key topic at his annual three-day leadership retreat held in the Colorado Rockies.

Reinemund first introduced William McDonough, a highly charismatic visionary on the subject, to address the leaders. McDonough spoke with clarity and passion, emphasizing the business opportunities in sustainability and the fact that PepsiCo could be both more sustainable and more profitable. At the end of McDonough's presentation, Reinemund returned to the podium. He stressed both his personal commitment to sustainability and the pressing business needs surrounding the issue. Then he called for volunteers to create a sustainability task force to develop a plan for PepsiCo and get it implemented.

Needless to say, Reinemund's approach got the leaders' attention. No fewer than twenty-five of the executives (including all five divisional CFOs, who lead strategy formulation within their businesses) asked to participate. They drove the project forward for a year, after which the task force was whittled down from this unwieldy number. By then, Reinemund's personal commitment, amplified by the way in which he presented it, had catalyzed a lasting change within the company.

Of course, commitment from the top means more than a one-time gesture, however emphatic. As he or she would with any major change at a large company, the CEO must devote regular time to the company's efforts, staying involved and informed, and keeping sustainability near the top of everybody's agenda. If the CEO's commitment is seen to wane, so will the energy behind the company's program. Then sustainability will get hung with the moniker that signals the death of any corporate initiative—the "issue du jour"—and gradually be ignored, then forgotten.

Long-Term Thinking

Many of the stories we've told in this book involve trade-offs between short-term costs and long-term benefits. The word *sustainability* implies long-term thinking, because it focuses on how your company can survive and thrive in the long term, and includes consideration of future generations. It's a time frame that most American businesses—unlike many of their counterparts in Asia and Europe—aren't used to, but one that is increasingly important to businesses today.

Many people blame the financial markets, but the development of the United States may help explain the prevalence of short-term thinking among American business leaders. As historian Frederick Jackson Turner famously wrote in his essay "The Significance of the Frontier in American History" (1893), America has been largely shaped by the idea of the frontier—the notion that there is always new land just over the next hilltop, pristine, limitless, waiting to be discovered and exploited.[3] Even today, more than a century after the closing of the physical frontier and the linking of the continental United States by railroads and a strong national government, the idea of the frontier continues to affect our thinking. Americans still tend to assume that new horizons and new solutions are always just over the next hilltop. For President John F. Kennedy, outer space was "the new frontier." For many Americans of the last two generations, technology is the new frontier leading to new worlds, such as cyberspace, nanospace, and biogenetics.

Thanks to this frontier mentality, many Americans, particularly business leaders, are exceedingly comfortable with short-term thinking and planning. Why worry about the future when America is a land of endless frontiers and limitless beginnings? (By contrast, the Japanese have almost the exact opposite perspective, being relatively short on land and poor in resources.) Combine that mentality with a businessperson's ability to solve difficult problems, often involving scarce resources of some type, and the American tendency to worship those who succeed against great odds, and you have a "Damn the torpedoes, full speed ahead!" view of the future.

This American optimism is very attractive, and because of the enormous influence of the United States on the world stage, it has had a profound impact on business thinking in Europe and Asia. But it's also dangerous. After all, the reality is that the frontier *does* have an end; open space is *not* limitless; natural resources *are* finite; and technology does *not* offer a perpetual escape hatch from any problem or challenge we may create for ourselves.

In recent years, millions of people in the United States and around the world have been gradually coming to recognize these truths—to accept the fact that we live in an age and on a planet of genuine limits, and that as world population nears seven billion there are some problems we simply can't solve fast enough. As the baby boomers age and come to realize that their children and grandchildren are facing financial, environmental, and social crises that the boomers themselves have helped create and for which there are no easy solutions, such as global warming, a sober sense of reality is gradually sinking in. And as this happens, the wisdom of longer-term thinking is becoming more apparent.

Much will have to change for long-term thinking to supplant quarter-by-quarter thinking in American business. U.S. business leaders need to learn from their counterparts in Asia and Europe the wisdom of planning for decades in the future, not just the next three months. Wall Street will need to learn to reward long-term growth, not just beating expectations for a quarter or a year. This will take time—but it *will* happen. We want to be living together here on planet Earth for a long time, and to do so, we will eventually have to change our way of looking at things.

Epilogue

THE FUTURE OF SUSTAINABILITY

> To extend our love and care beyond our narrow
> self-interest is antithetical to neither our human
> nature nor our financial success. Rather, it leads to
> the further fulfillment of both. Why do we not
> encourage this in our theories of business and
> economics? Why do we restrict our theories to such
> a pessimistic and crabby view of human nature?
> What are we afraid of?
> —*John Mackey, founder and CEO, Whole Foods*[1]

An Evolving Concept

Almost two decades after the word was coined, the idea of sustainability continues to evolve. As more and more companies explore its implications in their own industries and businesses and among their own networks of stakeholder connections, new ways of envisioning and creating the sustainable company are being spun off. Eventually, today's idea of sustainability may be viewed as simply one stage in a long journey that all of us—business leaders, consumers, community members, scholars and students, and government representatives—have embarked on together, and whose end is not yet in sight.

To see where we might be going, this closing chapter describes a continuum of four stages of thinking about corporations and sustainability, each stage incorporating prior ones and moving toward deeper corporate transformation. We'll use this framework as a lens through which to glimpse the future and to make some predictions about where sustainability may lead us—as businesspeople and as a society—in the decades to come.

Lean Thinking: Perfecting Business Processes

The broadest mainstream approach to sustainability might be captured in the term *lean thinking*, popularized by authors James Womack and Daniel Jones, who in 1997 founded the Lean Enterprise Institute, based in Washington, D.C.[2]

Lean thinking begins with the concept of minimization, as we defined it in Chapter Nine—the reduction of waste, pollution, resource depletion, and other costs of doing business—and then strives to *broaden* that concept to include every impact that business has on its social, physical, and economic environment. Lean thinking emphasizes *business as process*, examining all the activities that surround the design, production, consumption, servicing, and disposal or recycling of any good in search of ways to improve the efficiency of the flow of value from the beginning of the process through its conclusion.

A lean-thinking company constantly examines the life cycle of every product or service it creates, seeking to manage that cycle in accordance with the following five principles:

1. *Understand the value created by each product:* identify with precision the *real* sources of benefit to consumers and others that are provided by any good your company offers (as opposed to physical materials or human services that do *not* actually contribute to value but merely deplete it).

2. *Identify the value stream for each product:* study your company's processes to determine which activities are contributing to real value, and which are depleting it, and the relative efficiency with which value is created at every stage in the life cycle.

3. *Make value flow without interruptions:* organize *all* your business processes to reduce waste of time, money, energy, and other resources.

4. *Encourage customers to pull value through the entire system:* use modern techniques of communication and information sharing so that the process of creating value can be driven by actual customer needs rather than by arbitrary schedules.

5. *Pursue perfection at every stage:* constantly examine, redesign, and reexamine each step in the life cycle of any product or service in search of incremental improvements in efficiency as well as larger conceptual leaps that can eliminate entire processes along with the associated costs and waste.

The principles behind lean thinking may sound simple, even obvious. But if each principle is applied in the broadest and most detailed way possible, the result is a complex analysis of the total operations of the company that is likely to yield (literally) *thousands* of opportunities to improve efficiency, trim costs, reduce waste, clean the environment, and further enrich all the company's stakeholders, including customers, employees, suppliers, investors, and concerned outsiders.

The auto industry was a progenitor of lean thinking, tracing all the way back to Henry Ford, whose assembly line pioneered the notion of streamlining value creation. From the 1930s through the 1970s, Japanese automaker Toyota experimented with production techniques designed to reduce or eliminate *muda*—a Japanese word that translates as "waste" but which includes, more broadly, "any human activity which absorbs resources but creates no value."[3]

Even after a century of development, however, lean thinking in the car business is still in need of new breakthroughs. The rapidly industrializing nations of China and India are becoming the world's fastest-growing market for automobiles. Bringing the mobility and convenience of driving to hundreds of millions of new consumers in Asia is an exciting prospect (and a fantastic business opportunity for the world's automakers). But it's also a daunting economic and environmental challenge. Goldman Sachs, the Wall Street Investment firm, has forecast that the number of cars in China could rise from 12 million in 2004 to 500 million by 2050, and in India from 5 million to 600 million.[4] With oil prices already at an all-time high, where will the world get the energy to move all those new cars—to say nothing of the metal, glass, plastic, and other materials needed to manufacture them and the landfill space to dispose of them?

The smartest, most strategic way for the auto industry to respond to this planet-altering challenge is to figure out how to design and make cars that are inexpensive to manufacture and operate, produce little or no pollution, maximize the use of renewable resources, and can be completely recycled—in other words, twenty-first-century Chinese cars that *create* value (for manufacturers, resellers, consumers, and the general public) at every stage in their life cycle rather than waste value as today's expensive, polluting, gas-guzzling, dump-filling cars generally do.

This may sound utopian. But companies in the Japanese automotive industry are already deeply involved in the next generation of lean thinking, not only creating hybrid cars, which enhance the efficiency of energy use when driving, but creating cars from recycled materials, a business in which Japanese firms see both profit potential and environmental benefits for years to come. Every year, Nippon PGM Company, a subsidiary of the metal refiner Dowa Mining Company, collects about 14.9 billion yen (equivalent to over $130 million) worth of rare metals, such as platinum and palladium, from used automobile mufflers, which they sell back to the auto industry. Dowa is also the global leader in recycling of indium, a metal used in liquid crystal displays. Thanks to growing demand from the Chinese auto and electronic appliances industries, the price of indium has increased tenfold in recent years, making Dowa's recapturing of this metal extremely profitable—a classic illustration of improved value flow that benefits everyone.

Japanese government officials, who have long been involved in shaping and guiding national industry, see companies like Dowa as harbingers of the future direction of Japanese business. "If we make recycling a global industry, Japan could turn into a resource-rich country," says one such official.[5]

Dematerialization: More Value, Less Product

As companies pursue lean thinking, with its goals of waste reduction, continual value enhancement, and (eventually) perfect efficiency at every stage of the life cycle, some are rethinking certain basic assumptions about how they create value in the first place, which has led some visionary companies to *dematerialization*, a second element in the evolving concept of sustainability.

Dematerialization is based on the surprising—yet ultimately obvious—realization that consumers don't necessarily *want* the physical materials used in manufacturing, shipping, and using many products. When you buy a television, you don't want a box of electrical components—so many pounds of glass, plastic, metal, silicon, and other materials. No—you want the fun, information, and entertainment you derive from watching programs on TV. The physical materials are irrelevant and even *undesirable*, not only to the consumer but to the manufacturer, the shipper, the merchandiser, the retailer, and whoever must dispose of the broken or worn-out TV set a few years down the road. At every stage, the extraction, processing, shaping, shipping, handling, and disposal of those materials creates costs, depletes the environment, and produces streams of waste. If the materials could be reduced or eliminated altogether while keeping the benefits TV provides, everyone would be better off.

Building on this insight (and driven by the availability of computer chips that enable dramatic size reductions for electronic components), many companies are finding ways to reduce the physical presence of the goods they produce. Today's computers, stereo

systems, and telephones are a fraction of the size of their counterparts from twenty or thirty years ago. Today's large, flat-screen tele-
visions contain much less material than the small-screen,
big-cabinet units in most living rooms a generation ago. Cars are
becoming lighter (and therefore less costly to manufacture, service,
and ship, as well as less costly to run) as steel is being replaced by
aluminum, and metals by new ultrastrong plastics. Offices are gradually replacing costly, bulky paper with electronic data flows, and
old-fashioned vinyl record albums have given way, first to smaller
CDs and then to completely dematerialized MP3 files stored by the
thousands in tiny digital players.

From Products to Services

Pushing dematerialization further, many kinds of companies are
exploring ways to transform the goods they sell into services,
thereby providing the same value at less cost, or more value at the
same cost. The concept isn't entirely new. It's analogous to
Theodore Levitt's point in his classic essay, "Marketing Myopia":
rather than selling electric drills, the power tool company should
realize it is selling *holes*.[6] It's a profound change in perspective that
gets the drill company closer to what the customer wants and can
lead to innovative ways of doing business and earning higher profits (because the value-creating, idea-driven aspect of any business
usually produces the highest margins and is less replicable than the
"stuff-assembling" aspect).

Volkswagen (VW) and Toyota are now working on dematerialization, trying to evolve from product manufacturers (that is, car-
selling companies) into service providers (that is, transportation
companies). Imagine if you didn't need to own a car anymore, but
could simply enjoy instant access to a vehicle you need every time
you need it. Think of the convenience and savings you'd enjoy: no
more need for a garage attached to your home, no more costly and
annoying service and maintenance requirements, no more insurance payments, no periodic jousting with the auto salesman about

the deal on your new car and the trade-in on your old one. Welcome to the world of sustainable mobility.

Volkswagen's CEO, Bernd Pischetsrieder, has announced plans to transform the company into a "global mobility group."[7] In pursuit of this goal, VW has bought LeasePlan, a leading auto-leasing firm, from Dutch bank ING. The acquisition has turned VW into the world's second-biggest fleet management company. LeasePlan offers all-in-one plans that include cars, insurance, maintenance, and road tax, thereby serving the large market of customers who don't really want a car but do want a convenient way of getting around.

This goes beyond dematerialization to what one might call the recommissioning of VW. Like the drill company which recognizes that its mission is not selling drills but creating holes, VW is changing its mission from selling cars to providing mobility.

VW will almost certainly enjoy concrete business benefits from recommissioning itself. By some estimates, fully 90 *percent* of profits in the transportation business are not in the sale of cars but in ancillary products and services, from auto insurance and maintenance to the financial fees and interest associated with leasing.[8] Buying LeasePlan allows VW to tap into this vast value pool for the first time in its history.

Meanwhile, other ways of redefining the car business are being developed by smaller, entrepreneurial firms. Take Zipcars, the growing business that leases cars by the hour or the day. First launched in Europe in 1999, Zipcars is now growing rapidly in such U.S. cities as Boston, New York, and Washington, D.C., where car ownership is costly and inconvenient. It's a smart new business model that also creates huge environmental benefits. The company estimates that each Zipcar replaces seven to ten privately owned cars, reducing the amount of material that must be used to manufacture cars, and the number of parking spaces occupied by idle vehicles. Greenhouse gas emissions are also reduced, partly because Zipcar users drive less (they lease vehicles only when they really need them rather than "hopping into the car" just because it's there in the driveway), partly because new Zipcars with stringent pollution controls replace older vehicles that Zipcar customers retire. A not-for-profit version of Zipcars, City CarShare, is now operating in San Francisco, Chicago, and Philadelphia.

Redefining the business in terms of the underlying service provided isn't the sole province of the auto industry. During the 1990s, the oil companies redefined themselves as energy companies. BP has taken this the furthest, turning the meaning of its traditional acronym from British Petroleum into Beyond Petroleum. A gimmick? Yes, in a way. But sometimes a gimmick can be a powerful way of sending a message that is hard for people to ignore—provided, of course, that the gimmick is backed up by substance, as it is in the case of BP.

In 1997, BP set the target of reducing greenhouse gas emissions from its operations by 10 percent as compared to 1990 levels.[9] This target was achieved in 2001, nine years ahead of schedule. As a result, BP gained an estimated $650 million in net value from increased operational efficiencies, technological innovation, and improved energy management.

BP's recommissioning also involves investing in alternative energy technologies, such as hydrogen fuel cells, which have potential as a clean, nonpolluting energy source. BP has partnered with other private and public sector organizations in an initiative known as CUTE (Clean Urban Transport for Europe), which is testing the use of hydrogen-fueled buses in selected European cities. (BP is providing the hydrogen-refueling infrastructure in such cities as London and Barcelona.) BP is also involved in the manufacture and marketing of photovoltaic cells in areas ranging from Germany and the United Kingdom to California and is working on off-grid solar power projects alongside local partners in such developing countries as the Philippines and India.

BP now likes to say that "the environment is our business." It's a broad vision that sounds at first like mere feel-good rhetoric, but grows in meaning the more you study it. Customers don't want energy; they want the virtually infinite number of things it can do, from moving a car or heating a house to amplifying an electric guitar or powering an MRI machine in a hospital. BP is recommissioning itself as the company that helps consumers and society achieve those ends, all of which add up to producing a better environment for human existence. In effect, BP is working to *merge* the circles in the Venn diagram of the sustainability sweet spot, making profit and public benefit almost identical.

Rethinking the Corporation

As the evolution of sustainability continues, the idea that *profit* is the only purpose of the corporation begins to come into question. Are companies simply profit-maximizing machines, as most business thinkers today assume? Or are there other purposes for the corporation that may be equally important?

This question is a natural outgrowth of one basic element of sustainability, and indeed of business generally—namely, the recognition that stakeholders other than shareholders may have a valid claim on the resources of the corporation. Of course, we contend that any company that can find and operate within the sustainability sweet spot—the area of vital overlap between business and social interests—will ultimately make more profit, outcompeting and outlasting its less savvy competitors.

Remember how PPL's management, looking to work with, rather than against, the company's long-time adversaries, aggressively used stakeholder engagement to craft a dam-removal deal in partnership with environmentalists, Native Americans, and the entire community? Whereas some of its competitors have been forced to tear down their dams for nothing, PPL gets to save the salmon and the local economy by removing two dams voluntarily and getting paid $50 million to do it. Everyone will gain, including PPL and its shareholders, who will both reap the financial and reputational benefits and be spared further money- and time-wasting battles over energy production on the Penobscot River—a sweet spot if ever there was one.

By contrast, the Hershey trustees, focused exclusively on maximizing the financial returns to the trust, utterly failed to consider the social and community impacts of their plan to sell the company and, as a result, ultimately forfeited significant financial benefits for Hershey shareholders as well as possible benefits for the town and the employees. And, in that case, missing the sweet spot meant blowing the deal.

Sustainability does not necessarily require companies to deemphasize profit or accept diminished financial results. But it will eventually demand that businesspeople abandon a short-term, single-minded focus on maximizing shareholder value and recognize that corporations exist to serve other stakeholders as well. "Shareholder primacy needs to be tempered with consideration of other stakeholders," says Dr. Allen L. White, cofounder of the GRI, one of its creators, and the organization's first acting director. White's new organization, Corporation 2020, plans to convene a "corporate constitutional convention" in 2007 to discuss how to put other stakeholders on a more even playing field with shareholders. In White's view, a core tenet of defining the corporation is that

> financial capital providers are only one among many investors in the company. Others invest nonfinancial capital and incur risk. Communities invest their natural and social capital. Employees invest their human capital. Suppliers invest their organizational and technical capital. Yet our concept of the corporation—embodied by securities law, charters, fiduciary duty, and principles of governance—appears to focus only on financial investors.[10]

It's not only social activists like White who are urging a rethinking of the classical view of shareholder value or profitability. No company is more closely aligned with the business mainstream than the global consulting firm of McKinsey & Company. In an opinion piece in *The Economist,* Ian Davis, the firm's worldwide managing director, writes about the weaknesses of what he calls the "business of business is business" mind-set, what we referred to as the skeptics' response to sustainability in Chapter Six.[11]

One of these weaknesses, in Davis's view, is that a single-minded focus on shareholder value can lead companies to overlook crucial economic, political, and cultural trends that will have a major impact on the future of their business, involving both risks and opportunities. We quoted his words in Chapter Nine, but they bear repeating:

> Paradoxically, the language of shareholder value may hinder companies from maximizing shareholder value in this respect. Practiced as an unthinking mantra, it can lead managers to focus excessively on improving the short-term performance of their business, neglecting important longer-term opportunities and issues.

Davis is simply making our basic argument that in the long run, the sustainable company is likely to be a highly profitable one as well. But Davis goes further. He suggests another reason to consider scrapping the rhetoric of shareholder supremacy—namely, its inaccuracy. Although starting with the obligatory nod to shareholder value, Davis quickly shifts gears:

> Shareholder value should continue to be seen as the critical measure of business success. However, it may be more accurate, more motivating—and indeed more beneficial to shareholder value over the long term—to describe business's ultimate purpose as the efficient provision of goods and services that society wants.

Notice the powerful implications of Davis's reformulation. If the "ultimate purpose" of business is "the efficient provision of goods and services that society wants" (not just what investors or customers want), then an array of stakeholders, not just shareholders, have a legitimate interest in how a company uses its resources. The "society" Davis invokes as the preeminent judge of the offerings of business is simply a shorthand way of describing those other stakeholders: employees, business partners, neighbors, environmentalists, community leaders, and so on.

So when a company is managed profitably, it provides goods and services in ways that are more efficient and effective—providing greater and greater benefits for shareholders and other stakeholders, with fewer and fewer adverse impacts and more and more positive ones. Davis sees this as a noble purpose, and we fully agree.

Companies might take this one step further and define their missions so as to make them synonymous with the public good, finally arriving at Davis's view that "profits . . . [are] a signal from society that their company is succeeding in its mission of providing something people want." In other words, profits in effect become a reward for enhancing the public good.

The Ennobled Enterprise–Merging Private Profit and Public Good

Let's take Davis's ideas one step further. Imagine an enterprise expressly created both for profit and for social and environmental prosperity—one in which the two circles of business and social interests are completely merged. What would it look like?

We can get a glimpse of what such an ennobled enterprise might look like by considering the current phenomenon of *social entrepreneurship*, a discipline that has found its way into the curricula of some thirty U.S. business schools since the first course in the subject was offered at Harvard in 1995 by Dr. J. Gregory Dees (now at Duke University's Fuqua School of Business).

Social entrepreneurship is so new that students and experts in the field have not yet agreed on a fixed definition, knowledge base, or set of skills for the discipline.[12] Dr. Paul C. Light, a professor at the Robert F. Wagner Graduate School of Public Service at New York University, is currently studying social entrepreneurs in search of the common factors that lead to success. In examining the field, Light has said, "There is very little evidence-based knowledge out there. Right now the field is dominated by a hope and a dream."

Lacking a body of research or a comprehensive theory to fall back on, those exploring social entrepreneurship point to specific organizations that have made a positive difference by deploying for-profit techniques on behalf of social goals—organizations like the Grameen Bank of Bangladesh, whose founder, Muhammed Yunus, launched the microlending movement. By providing loans in tiny amounts (the equivalent of $5 to $100) for start-up capital to poor men and women in rural Bangladesh, the Grameen Bank has helped launch tens of thousands of small businesses and lifted many villages out of poverty. The bank is a profit-making institution, but it has created more social benefits through its innovative programs than have most NGOs.

Today, new ventures in social entrepreneurship are sprouting up all over the world. Some are based in not-for-profit organizations, some in traditional businesses; others involve alliances and partnerships between nonprofits, businesses, and sometimes government.

An ambitious example is the Safe Water Drinking Alliance, which describes itself as "a strategic public-private collaboration" whose goal is to help households in some of the world's poorest countries obtain a regular supply of safe drinking water.[13] Most residents of the developed world take clean drinking water for granted, but an estimated 1.1 billion people around the world have contaminated water supplies, and the related diarrheal diseases result in the needless death through dehydration of some two million children annually.

Launched in late 2003, the Alliance draws on funding from USAID, an independent agency of the U.S. government; expertise from the Johns Hopkins Bloomberg School of Public Health; on-the-ground outreach by two respected NGOs, CARE and Population Services International (PSI); and in-kind and financial contributions from Procter & Gamble (P&G), a for-profit consumer products company.

P&G's involvement is largely centered on the use of its new water-purification product, PuR, specifically designed to be economical and easy to use by extremely poor people in the developing world. A sachet of PuR powder is mixed into ten liters of water, where it combines with pathogens and other impurities and settles to the bottom. After twenty minutes, the water is filtered through cloth, which removes the impurities and yields clean, safe drinking water. Total cost: the equivalent of about ten U.S. cents.

The blend of business and social motives can be seen in the three different approaches to improving water safety that have been developed by the Alliance:

1. A *commercial model*, in which P&G uses its existing commercial distribution infrastructure, along with help from educators and local agencies, to sell sachets of PuR.

2. A *social marketing model*, in which PSI distributes PuR sachets (as well as other antidiarrheal products, such as oral rehydration salts for combating the effects of disease), educates storekeepers and pharmacists about the products, and teaches families about the importance of clean drinking water through street theater, community presentations, and radio and TV ads.

3. A *disaster relief model* in which supplies of safe water along with point-of-use packages of PuR are distributed by relief agencies (such as CARE) to those hit by immediate needs.

In this complexly interwoven network of organizations and efforts, sorting out the precise blend of motivations and purposes isn't easy. Certainly profit-making objectives underlie P&G's involvement. The PuR water-purification technology is a product with a potentially enormous market, and if the commercial distribution program succeeds, P&G will have established a huge beachhead in a burgeoning for-profit business arena. From a social responsibility perspective, this program puts P&G in a whole different category from its competitors, who are shipping bottled water out of water-starved communities to sell it elsewhere at prices that no local can afford.

Other aspects of the Safe Water Drinking Alliance also promise long-term benefits for P&G. For example, the educational programs supported by the Alliance teach poor rural families about the importance of hygienic practices, such as washing hands with soap, in preventing the spread of infectious diseases. It's obvious that a billion developing-world people with a newly formed habit of using soap could represent an enormous source of future growth for companies like P&G.

How, then, do we classify P&G's involvement in the Safe Water Drinking Alliance programs? Is it a charitable contribution? An R&D investment? Or an exploratory marketing program for a new product? It's probably most accurately described as a combination of all three. This means that the long-term success of P&G's involvement must be measured by using several yardsticks, blending profit considerations with other concerns:

- To what extent has the incidence of diarrheal disease been reduced? How many lives have been saved?
- How much useful evidence has been gathered for the effectiveness of PuR as a practical water-purification product?
- How much insight has P&G gathered into the profit-making potential of PuR in the developing nations of Asia, Latin America, and Africa? How much profit is being made today?
- What kinds of inroads into these expanding markets have been made by P&G brands of soap, shampoo, and other hygiene products?
- What has P&G learned about the relative value of the three models for distribution of water-purification technologies in the developing world? What blend of for-profit and not-for-profit enterprise is likely to be most effective?

Perhaps the "redefined corporation" that Allen White and others have been envisioning isn't such a distant prospect after all. We may be seeing the outlines of this new kind of company emerging below the radar in initiatives similar to P&G's safe water program.

Global Problems and Business Opportunities

Throughout this book, we've shown how the role of business is being redefined in an interdependent and interconnected world. In truth, the roles of *all* social institutions today are under scrutiny and facing redefinition. If it was once possible to draw bright lines separating the responsibilities of business, government, and the institutions of civil society, that day is past. In a world of rapid, unpredictable, and dangerous changes in the world, pragmatism is the order of the day, and partnerships that shatter barriers, combine resources from many sectors, and (above all) *get things done* quickly and effectively are increasingly important.

You may have noticed that throughout this book, we have *not* relied on any altruistic or save-the-world justification for sustainability. That's deliberate. We do believe that most people, including most business managers, share at least some degree of what Adam Smith called "universal benevolence" (see Chapter Six)— that is, they care about their fellow human beings and would like to do their part in making the world a better place. But we also know that businesspeople are under intense pressure to produce growth and profits for their companies, and that any suggestion that a business should focus its efforts elsewhere than on profitability isn't likely to be warmly received in most boardrooms today. We've therefore tried to emphasize the sweet spot and the strong, growing evidence that it is possible, through creative management, to overcome any potential conflict between being profitable and being responsible.

Still, we'd be remiss if we failed at least to suggest the tremendous and exciting opportunity for the corporate sustainability movement to make huge inroads in the major problems facing humankind in the twenty-first century. These problems include

- Global warming and climate change
- The worldwide HIV/AIDS epidemic
- Millions of annual deaths from other preventable diseases

- Global hunger and poverty, especially in sub-Saharan Africa
- Shortages of potable water and sanitation in much of the world
- Escalating demand for and dwindling supplies of fossil fuels
- Lack of educational resources for millions of children
- Aging and infirm populations in much of the developed world
- The growing economic gap between rich nations and poor

Today some of these problems affect primarily the peoples of the developing world—Latin America, Asia, and sub-Saharan Africa. But others (such as climate change and the dependence on fossil fuels) have implications for rich and poor alike. And all, unless they are solved, will increasingly trouble the nations of the developed northern hemisphere, as growing desperation in the south leads to increased migration, political and social upheaval, a limitless demand for resources, and war.

Governments and international institutions, from the United Nations to the World Bank, must work to solve these problems. But business must also play a role. Call it altruism if you like, but "enlightened self-interest" would be equally accurate. As Bjorn Stigson, president of the World Business Council for Sustainable Development, likes to say, "Business cannot succeed in a society that fails."[14] And even if it could (for a time), do you really want to live in a world where 30 percent of the population lives in resplendent luxury while 70 percent live in ever increasing squalor and misery and hopelessness . . . even if you happen to be among the fortunate few?

Self-interest in the most straightforward sense may yet play a major role in helping solve the problems of our century. As illustrated by the "bottom of the pyramid" movement, one aspect of the sustainability mind-set involves learning to see the opportunities hidden in problems—even problems as vast and daunting as those we listed earlier.

There's an old business parable that may be relevant. According to the story, rival shoe companies sent consultants to visit a developing tropical nation newly opened for trade, asking that they report back on business prospects. After a week or so, the first consultant wired back to the home office, DON'T WASTE YOUR TIME HERE. EVERYONE IN THIS COUNTRY GOES BAREFOOT. The second consultant, however, had a different reaction. He sent a telegram exulting, FABULOUS BUSINESS OPPORTUNITY. MILLIONS OF PEOPLE AND THEY ALL NEED SHOES!

The seemingly intractable problems of our world are not simply invitations to philanthropy; they are also opportunities for corporate engagement, with the potential of producing benefits for all—provided we open our eyes to see them.

Appendix A

GLOSSARY AND KEY ACTION STEPS

Glossary

This glossary provides definitions for seven key elements that form the basis of a sustainability management system. To show how the elements relate to each other, we give two examples that flow, from a single vision, through the system.

Vision   How you see business, your industry, and your company in terms of the challenges associated with environmental, social, and economic issues. *Example:* "Our vision is to increase shareholder and societal value while decreasing our environmental footprint."

Strategy   A plan of action that puts your vision into effect (in other words, a plan that seeks the sweet spot). *Example 1:* Creating new products that will sell well and biodegrade. *Example 2:* Reducing the amount of energy and water used in manufacturing.

Goals   Specific aspirations or targets related to the strategy. Most useful when designated to be achieved by a certain date. *Example 1:* By the end of the year, develop a new biodegradable plastic with specific characteristics. *Example 2:* Conduct a global assessment of current water and energy use and identify opportunities for efficiencies, within eighteen months.

Procedures and protocols   Procedures that prescribe behavior designed to achieve the goals. Most useful when written down, well understood, and endorsed by affected employees. *Example 1:* Include the development of the new polymer in the annual performance objectives (that is, the incentive plan) of the head of R&D. *Example 2*: Establish procedures that require employees to shut off the lights before leaving work.

Key performance indicators (KPIs)   Measures or mileage markers that indicate whether procedures are actually working to help the company meet its goals. *Example 1*: Has the new polymer been designed and tested for biodegradability? *Example 2*: Have incentives been created to encourage waste reduction and energy savings at the plant level?

Measurement and reporting   Specific ways to account for or measure performance against the goals. *Measurement, Example 1*: Indicia of biodegradability: for example, new polymer biodegrades within eight months when exposed to air, but will not degrade when landfilled. *Measurement, Example 2*: Indicia of resource conservation: company is now using 6 percent less energy and 9 percent less water per employee. *Internal reporting, Example 1*: Provide monthly progress report on polymer creation to vice president for corporate strategy and sales. *Internal reporting, Example 2*: Plants provide monthly reports on water and energy usage and related costs, in standard format, to environmental department and office of the CFO. *External reporting, Examples 1 and 2*: Use GRI reporting indicators, including the following: 1.1, vision and strategy; 2.9, stakeholders; 2.14, significant changes in products; 3.9–3.12, stakeholder engagement; 3.16, initiatives to improve product design to minimize negative impacts associated with manufacturing, use, and final disposal; 3.19, programs related to environmental performance; EN14, significant environmental impacts of principal products; EN3 and EN4, energy use; EN5, total water use.

Stakeholder engagement   Interaction with stakeholders that influences the decisions and behavior of the company, from vision to measurement and reporting. *Example 1*: Meet with environmentalists, regulators, and end users to ensure that that new plastic will actually be discarded in such a way that it will biodegrade. *Example 2:* Work with community to understand the impact of plant water usage on surrounding community.

Key Action Steps

This list expands on the elements discussed in the glossary and serves as a framework for assessment, design, and implementation of a sustainability management system. It follows Part Two of the book.

I.   Self-assessment
    Remember: When doing your due diligence on where your company stands, make sure you look at sources outside the company and at what key stakeholders are saying.
    A. Look at your company's reports.
    •   Are they balanced? (That is, do they contain positive and negative information?)
        •   Are they based on data and objective information?
        •   Are they comprehensive? (Do they "tell the whole story"?)
        •   Do they set forth specific goals, targets, and KPIs?
        •   Do they provide measures and assessment of progress?
        •   Do they include or incorporate feedback from stakeholders?
    B. Look at how your company operates.
        Does your company
        •   Generally comply with laws and regulations and respect the role of regulators?
        •   Have positive relations with the communities in which it operates?
        •   Extend its analysis of impacts to include its value chain (from suppliers to customers)?
        •   Have a good record on labor and human rights issues?
        •   Have a positive relationship with employees?

- Have minimization or optimization programs for environmental, social, or economic impacts?
- Have a good record on environmental protection?
- Consider social and environmental issues before taking major actions and work to minimize adverse impacts and maximize positive ones?

C. Understand the nature of your company's business.

- What are the primary environmental, social, and economic impacts of your company's products?
- What are their secondary impacts? (In other words, what are the company's side effects?)
- Does the company serve any protected or vulnerable customers, operate in environmentally sensitive areas, or deal directly with any critical social issues?
- What specific industry issues is your company facing?

Consider: Organize the findings in a way that is most useful to you in terms of future actions. As you look at where the company stands, it might be useful to identify the organization's strengths, weaknesses, risks, and opportunities as a way of gaining further insight into the design and implementation of your programs.

II. Strategy

Remember: You can develop a sustainability strategy at any level of the organization, from corporate headquarters to departments to plants and offices. Make sure you understand the organization's business objectives and how your part of the organization supports those. Then see if there is a way to contribute to those objectives by incorporating an approach to environmental, social, or economic issues.

A. Analyze strengths—for example, skill sets, material resources, cultural advantages, and stakeholder connections.

B. Analyze weaknesses—for example, missing skills, resource depletions, cultural blind spots, and poor or nonexistent stakeholder relationships.

C. Review and develop possible strategies based on strengths and weaknesses.
- Grab for low fruit:
  Identify customer needs.
  Differentiate from your competitors.
  Leverage your position.
  Anticipate future trends.
  Start with your current skill set and knowledge base.
- Search for the sweet spot:
  Look for overlaps with sustainability considerations.
  Minimize adverse impacts ("be less bad"): identify processes that create waste; look for areas of stakeholder conflict; compare your impacts with those of other companies or of the industry.
  Optimize positive impacts ("be more good"): push or build from minimization efforts; develop new products or service ideas to help; look for new markets "in plain sight."

Consider: Focus on the best three ideas you have and try to create projects by coordinating with other departments that would need to be involved. Make sure you emphasize the "wins" for that department in terms of its existing objectives.

III. Launching your program (goals, procedures, and KPIs)
Remember: Before establishing goals, procedures, and KPIs, look at the GRI guidelines and other reporting frameworks (for example, those of your competitors and in your industry). Also consider education and training on new goals, procedures, and KPIs.
A. Set goals.
- Begin with existing business goals.
- Identify possible environmental, social, and economic goals: Are they reasonable and achievable, clear and understandable, internally consistent and consistent with business goals?

- Determine ways to advance toward business goals by addressing TBL issues.

B. Establish procedures.
  - Ask, What departments, business units, and facilities must participate to achieve the goals?
  - Write simple paragraphs in plain language that describe what needs to happen in order to reach the goals. Use these to identify needed procedures.
  - Identify existing procedures into which new procedures can be embedded, or write new procedures that contain the required language.

C. Develop KPIs.
  - Identify and clearly define all key terms used to describe goals.
  - Identify ways to measure progress toward each goal (consider leading and lagging indicators).
  - Strive to define all KPIs in terms of a number.
  - For nonnumerical KPIs, look for objective descriptors.

Consider: Make sure that your goals, procedures, and KPIs tie together and form a cohesive framework: goals should suggest procedures, which should suggest KPIs, which measure progress toward achieving the goals.

IV. Organization and resources

Remember: Organize your effort in a way that works best for your company or department. Benchmark your competitors or look at how other successful initiatives have been organized within your company.

A. Review your options.
  - Assemble a task force to initiate, coordinate?
  - Find or appoint one or more sustainability champions to drive?
  - Establish a sustainability department?
  - Create a virtual sustainability department?
  - "Piggy-back" on existing department(s) (for example, environmental or community relations)?

Consider: You will need two additional resources—funding and technical. Minimization programs (for example, water and energy conservation) can produce immediate savings, which can be used to support other programs with more long-term payback. Think about leveraging existing technical expertise when you choose what programs to develop.

V. Stakeholder engagement

Remember: Stakeholder engagement is the key to finding and staying on the sustainable path—to identifying and moving into the sweet spot. Even if you could do everything "right" without it, engaging your stakeholders is an indispensable element of "doing business in an interdependent world."

A. Understand your current level of engagement with stakeholders (listed here from best to worst).

Does your company

- Engage in ongoing partnership?
- Engage in project-specific partnership?
- Engage in open, two-way dialogue?
- Listen actively?
- Listen passively?
- Refuse to listen (you talk, they listen)?
- React?
- Ignore?
- Antagonize?

B. Understand your current attitude and approach to stakeholder engagement.

Is it

- Systematic engagement or ad hoc?
- Proactive or reactive?
- Long-term or short-term in its perspective?
- Trusting or suspicious?

C. Map your stakeholders.

- Conduct a target analysis: Who are our stakeholders?
- Create an impact chart: What issues and activities affect our stakeholders?

- Create a priority table: How can our stakeholders affect us? Who is most important, and why?

D. Understand what you want from engagement.
   - Develop and implement simple engagement strategy if you are looking for a mutually beneficial relationship without trying to influence a specific outcome.
   - Develop advanced engagement strategy if you have a specific objective and want to gain support or minimize opposition.

E. Make sure you know whom you are dealing with.
   - Are your stakeholders company focused, policy focused, issue focused, or a combination?
   - How much are they focused on you? (In other words, are they knocking only on your door or on others' too?)

F. Choose the level of engagement.
   - Do your homework and due diligence on stakeholders.
   - Understand the likelihood of success, failure, and middle grounds.
   - Develop a solid exit strategy.
   - Be prepared for the unexpected.
   - Be prepared for the long haul.
   - Set expectations internally and externally—then lower them.

G. Develop radar.
   - Establish networks: identify reliable sources of information on trends and issues that may affect your business in the future, and systematically work those networks.
   - Get online: find and scan the best websites, blogs, and other sources of information on the Web. Consider whether and how to participate in Web-based information forums.

Consider: Think about the three most recent unpleasant surprises that came from outside the company or department. Ask, How did we miss this? What can we do to make sure we are not surprised in that way again?

VI. Measurement and reporting

Remember: Reporting is the tail that wags the dog for many companies; they start with the need to report, then develop programs in order to have something to report, then try to justify what they are doing in terms of the business case. This is backwards.

A. Start with the business case.

- Make sure you have a strong business need or rationale for what you are measuring and how you are reporting or planning to report it.

B. Consider any need that might seem outside the business case for reporting.

- Give thought to your political or relationship reasons for reporting on certain issues, which ought to be considered part of the business case. The important point is to recognize why you are reporting, to whom, and for what purpose.

C. Consider the Global Reporting Initiative.

- Divide the indicators into three categories: strong, moderate, weak business need.
- Look at all the indicators again and figure out whether you have the data, can easily obtain the data, or haven't a clue how to obtain them. Cross-reference data availability with the business case to determine how to proceed.

D. Take an incremental approach.

- Start with the indicators for which there are a strong business (or stakeholder) case and available data. Once those systems are complete, consider other indicators for which there is a strong business case but no available data. Add more information each year until you are reporting on the full range of indicators that pertain to your business.

E. Consider seeking stakeholder input.

- Following steps (A) through (D) will give you the makings of a reporting strategy. Next consider your stakeholders and what they might say about your overall reporting plans.

- Consider how and where you might be flexible in responding to stakeholder requests for additional or different information.
- Anticipate their specific requests and how you will respond.
- Work toward getting stakeholders involved in helping you determine the content and focus of your report.
- Make sure you have a workable reporting plan before you make a public commitment.
- As needed, continue internal reporting (for example, for management purposes) that is not reported publicly, provided this does not contradict your public report.

F. Engage in industry-specific planning.

- Make sure that you look for industry-specific reporting guidance and issues and for helpful technical protocols regarding ways to measure and report specific TBL issues.

G. Assess the costs and risks of reporting.

- Look carefully at the costs of reporting before you make a commitment: many companies underestimate the difficulty of obtaining and reporting information with sufficient precision for public reporting.
- Look at the hidden risks. Are you willing to publish bad news and unflattering information? If not, reconsider whether you want to report at all. Also consider whether you will verify the information in your report and how you will do so.

Consider: Your ultimate goal should be integrated reporting—one unified report that doesn't distinguish financial and non-financial information but rather contains all information that would be relevant to a prudent investor.

VII. Culture

Remember: Sustainability flourishes in companies with certain characteristics. A company's culture is usually set at the top, but sustainability projects are often initiated by middle managers who create a supportive culture within their own departments. You can, too, by moving forward in four areas:

A. Develop a vision. Do you have a vision of what sustainability means to your company or department? Start with the following questions:

- How do your company's goods and services or its processes overlap with the interests of society?
- How is the world enhanced or diminished by your company or department's activities?
- What are your company or department's major positive and negative impacts?
- How does your company interact with today's stakeholders and think about its responsibility to future generations?

Then ask how you would have *liked* to answer those questions. Your aspirations may be the start of formulating your company or department's vision.

B. Gain self-awareness. As they say in politics, "Don't believe your own good press." Answer the following questions:

- Does the company see itself clearly?
- What is the company's capacity for honest self-awareness?
- Is everyone afraid of the regulators or the lawyers?

C. Establish and promote leadership. Behind almost every example and case study we have cited is a strong leader. Not necessarily a CEO, like Mike Morris at NU, but in many cases an inspired and determined mid-level manager, such as Scott Hall at PPL. Companies that support and nurture their leaders and future leaders are far more likely to progress than are those that do not.

- Is there strong leadership for sustainability, as evidenced by a clear message that is expressed in simple terms, disseminated throughout the organization, and hammered home repeatedly?

D. Engage in long-term thinking. Sustainable companies find ways to think and act in their long-term interests, despite enormous pressure to act only in the short-term interest of their investors.

- Does the company think about the long term, or is the emphasis always on the next quarter?

Consider: "You must be the change you want to see in the world" (Mahatma Gandhi).

Appendix B

FOR FURTHER READING

Burke, Edmund M. *Managing a Company in an Activist World: The Leadership Challenge of Corporate Citizenship.* Westport, Conn.: Praeger, 2005.

Elkington, John. *Cannibals with Forks: The Triple Bottom Line of 21st Century Business.* Philadelphia: New Society, 1998.

Fussler, Claude, Aron Cramer, and Sebastian van der Vegt. *Raising the Bar: Creating Value with the United Nations Compact.* Sheffield, England: Greenleaf, 2004.

Grayson, David, and Adrian Hodges. *Corporate Social Opportunity: Seven Steps to Make Corporate Social Responsibility Work for Your Business.* Sheffield, England: Greenleaf, 2004.

Hawken, Paul. *The Ecology of Commerce: A Declaration of Sustainability.* New York: HarperBusiness, 1993.

Hay, Bruce L., Robert N. Stavins, and Richard H. K. Vietor (eds.). *Environmental Protection and the Social Responsibility of Firms: Perspectives from Law, Economics and Business.* Washington, D.C.: Resources for the Future Press, 2005.

Henriques, Adrian, and Julie Richardson (eds.). *The Triple Bottom Line: Does It All Add Up? Assessing the Sustainability of Business and CSR.* London: Earthscan, 2004.

Hollender, Jeffrey, and Stephen Fenichell. *What Matters Most: How a Small Group of Pioneers Is Teaching Social Responsibility to Big Business, and Why Big Business Is Listening.* New York: Basic Books, 2004.

Holliday, Charles O., Jr., Stephan Schmidheiny, and Phillip Watts. *Walking the Talk: The Business Case for Sustainable Development.* Sheffield, England: Greenleaf, 2002.

Jackson, Ira A., and Jane Nelson. *Profits with Principles: Seven Strategies for Delivering Value with Values.* New York: Doubleday, 2004.

Laszlo, Chris. *The Sustainable Company.* Washington, D.C.: Island Press, 2003.

McDonough, William, and Michael Braungart. *Cradle to Cradle: Remaking the Way We Make Things.* New York: North Point Press, 2002.

Paine, Lynn Sharp. *Value Shift: Why Companies Must Merge Social and Financial Imperatives to Achieve Superior Performance.* New York: McGraw-Hill, 2003.

Prahalad, C. K. *The Fortune at the Bottom of the Pyramid: Eradicating Poverty Through Profits*. Upper Saddle River, N.J.: Wharton School Publishing, 2005.

Prahalad, C. K., and Michael E. Porter (eds.). *Harvard Business School Review on Corporate Responsibility*. Boston: Harvard Business School Press, 2003.

Willard, Bob. *The Sustainability Advantage: Seven Business Case Benefits of a Triple Bottom Line*. Philadelphia: New Society, 2002.

Notes

Introduction

1. The story of how the combination of overfishing, declining whale stocks, and the growing availability of alternative fuels (such as kerosene) gradually decimated the Atlantic whaling industry starting in the mid-nineteenth century is told in many sources, including such books as *Men and Whales*, by Richard Ellis (New York: Knopf, 1991).

2. Data are from "North Atlantic US—Overfishing," on the website of the National Undersea Research Center, available online at www.nurc.uconn.edu/about/natlantic.htm, as well as from "Threats to North-East Atlantic Ocean—Overfishing," on the website of the World Wildlife Federation, available online at www.panda.org/about_wwf/where_we_work/europe/what_we_do/ne_atlantic/area/marine_species/overfishing/index.cfm.

3. See *Cannibals with Forks: The Triple Bottom Line of 21st Century Business*, by John Elkington (Philadelphia: New Society, 1998), especially chap. 4.

Chapter One

1. From an interview for J. Mack Robinson College of Business, Georgia State University, Oct. 1, 2004, available online at http://robinson.gsu.edu/video/executive.

2. Our account of the attempted sale of Hershey Foods by the board of the Hershey Trust is based on numerous press accounts as well as interviews with many participants in the events described, including Joe Berning, Millie Landis Coyle,

John Dunn, Michael Fisher, Ric Fouad, Bruce Hummel, John Long, Michael Macchioni, Bruce McKinney, Kathy Taylor, and Dick Zimmerman. A good contemporary account of the controversy can be found in "Hershey: Sweet Surrender," by John Helyar, *Fortune*, Oct. 1, 2002, available online at www.fortune. com/fortune/subs/print/0,15935,366947,00.html. Specific quotations and details are cited in the notes that follow.

3. "Sweet Deal: Hershey Foods Is Considering a Plan to Put Itself Up for Sale," by Shelley Branch, Sarah Ellison, and Gordon Fairclough, *Wall Street Journal*, Eastern Edition, July 25, 2002, page A1.

4. A useful source of background information on Milton S. Hershey and the history of the company he founded is *The Emperors of Chocolate: Inside the Secret World of Hershey and Mars*, by Joel Glenn Brenner (New York: Random House, 1999). A more recent biography, *Hershey: Milton S. Hershey's Extraordinary Life of Wealth, Empire, and Utopian Dreams*, by Michael D'Antonio (New York: Simon & Schuster, 2006), was published as our book was going to press.

5. Interview with Karl Weber, June 2005.

6. Michael Fisher interview with Karl Weber, Oct. 2005.

7. Interview with Karl Weber, June 2005.

8. "How Hershey Made a Big Chocolate Mess," *Business Week*, Sept. 9, 2002, p. 54.

9. "Action Alert (9/12/02)," posted by Essential Action: Global Partnerships for Tobacco Control; online at www.essential action.org/tobacco/letter/us0209.html. (This page has been updated and no longer includes the Action Alert.)

10. Analyst quoted by David Brancaccio on *Marketplace*, National Public Radio, Sept. 18, 2002, available online at http:// marketplace.publicradio.org/shows/2002/09/18_mpp.html.

11. "Hershey Says No, Bankers Cry Foul," by Dan Ackman, Forbes.com, Sept. 18, 2002, available online at www.forbes.com/ 2002/09/18/0918topnews.html.

12. Quoted in "Meltdown in Chocolatetown—Controlling Trust at Hershey Bows to Opposition to Sale; Company Faces Future Alone," by Robert Frank and Sarah Ellison, *Wall Street Journal*, Sept. 19, 2002, p. B1.

13. Quoted in "Hershey Says No, Bankers Cry Foul," by Dan Ackman.

14. Frank and Ellison, "Meltdown in Chocolatetown."

15. "The Best and Worst Managers," *Business Week*, Jan. 13, 2003, p. 84.

16. Interview with Karl Weber, June 2005.

17. *Working Better Together: Our Corporate and Social Responsibility Report 2004*, Cadbury Schweppes, available online at www. cadburyschweppes.com/NR/rdonlyres/8E1AF189-9CC6-4CF8-8FEC-5CAF93CF10B6/0/00_2004CorporateSocial ResponsibilityReport.pdf.

Chapter Two

1. Quoted in "Money and Morals at GE," by Marc Gunther, *Fortune*, Nov. 15, 2004, p. 176.

2. *Boston Globe*, June 3, 2005, p. E1.

3. Quoted in "GE Hotline Gives Workers Some Clout," *Financial Times*, May 19, 2005, p. 19.

4. "Welcome to Ecomagination," GE corporate website, available online at http://ge.ecomagination.com.

5. "Blowing in the Wind," *Fortune*, July 25, 2005, on second page of unnumbered insert titled "Fortune Global 500: The World of Ideas."

6. *Business Week*, August 22–29, 2005, p. 130.

7. "A Consistent Policy on Cleaner Energy," by Jeffrey Immelt, *Financial Times*, June 29, 2005, p. 13.

8. "The Biggest Contract," by Ian Davis, *The Economist*, May 26, 2005, available online at www.economist.com/business/Printer Friendly.cfm?Story_ID=4008642.

9. *Wall Street Journal*, Oct. 15, 2005.

10. "Queen's Awards for Enterprise: Diversity of British Endeavour Wins the Greatest Accolade," by Sarah Murray, *Financial Times*, Apr. 21, 2005, p. 7.

11. "Proud Papa of the Prius," by Chester Dawson, *Business Week*, June 20, 2005, p. 20.

12. "Toyota Develops Hybrids with an Eye on the Future," by Danny Hakim and James Brooke, *New York Times*, Aug. 4, 2005, p. C3.

13. Cited in *Who Cares, Wins: Connecting the Financial Markets to a Changing World*, Investment Financial Corporation/World Bank, 2004, available online at www.unglobalcompact.org/Issues/financial_markets/who_cares_who_wins.pdf.

14. Data from *Sustainability Pays Off: An Analysis About the Stock Exchange Performance of Members of the World Business Council for Sustainable Development (WBCSD)* (Vienna: Kommunalkredit Dexia Asset Management, Oct. 2004).

15. Quoted in *Integral Business: Integrating Sustainability and Business Strategy*, PricewaterhouseCoopers LLP, 2003.

16. *Global Equity Research—Food and Beverages*. UBS Investment Research, Oct. 24, 2005, p. 4.

17. The notion that sustainability can improve your business by helping you protect it, run it, and grow it was originally formulated by the World Business Council for Sustainable Development.

18. Quoted in "The Perils of Doing the Right Thing," by Andrew W. Singer, *Across the Board*, Oct. 2000, p. 18.

19. "GM Food Banned at Monsanto Canteen," Dec. 24, 1999, on *Urban 75 ezine*, available online at www.urban75.org/archive/news099.html.

20. Stock market valuation calculations by James Wilbur, analyst at Salomon Smith Barney, cited in "Is Monsanto's Biotech Worth Less Than a Hill of Beans?" by David Stipp, *Fortune*, Feb. 19, 2001, available online at www.fortune.com/fortune/subs/print/0 15935,368798,00.html.

21. Quoted in *Walking the Talk: The Business Case for Sustainable Development*, by Charles O. Holliday Jr., Stephan Schmidheiny, and Philip Watts (Sheffield, England: Greenleaf, 2002), p. 27.
22. Estimate by U.S. Green Building Council, cited in "Beyond Recycling: Manufacturers Embrace 'C2C' Design," by Rebecca Smith, *Wall Street Journal*, Mar. 3, 2005, p. B1.
23. *The Fortune at the Bottom of the Pyramid: Eradicating Poverty Through Profits*, by C. K. Prahalad (Upper Saddle River, N.J.: Wharton School Publishing, 2005).
24. "The Wegman's Way," by Matthew Boyle, *Fortune*, Jan. 24, 2005, p. 62.

Chapter Three

1. "DuPont: The Enlightened Organization," by Dr. John Kenly Smith, available online at http://heritage.dupont.com.
2. "Henry Ford's Revolution for the Worker," by Christine Gibson, American Heritage.com, available online at www.americanheritage.com/articles/web/20060105-henry-ford-five-dollar-day-model-t-ford-motor-company-assembly-line-james-couzens-highland-park-detroit-automobiles.html.
3. Details on the J&J credo and its history are available at the company website, online at www.jnj.com/our_company/our_credo/index.htm. One of the many accounts of the Tylenol crisis is "The Tylenol Crisis: How Effective Public Relations Saved Johnson & Johnson," by Tamara Kaplan, Pennsylvania State University, available online at www.personal.psu.edu/users/w/x/wxk116/tylenol/crisis.html.
4. *Tasks, Responsibilities, Practices*, by Peter F. Drucker (New York: HarperCollins, 1973), p. 314.
5. "Deal Brings 'Proctoids' to 'Plywood Ranch,'" by Sarah Ellison and Charles Forelle, *Wall Street Journal*, Jan. 31, 2005, p. B1.
6. *2003/4 Corporate Citizenship Report: Our Principles, Progress and Performance*, Ford Motor Company, available online at

www.ford.com/en/company/about/corporateCitizenship/report/
toolsPrint.htm.

7. Interview with Andrew W. Savitz.

8. Useful sources of information about the Kryptonite story include "Why There's No Escaping the Blog," by David Kirkpatrick and Daniel Roth, *Fortune*, Jan. 10, 2005, available online at www. fortune.com/fortune/technology/articles/0,15114,1011763 3,00.html; "The Pen Is Mightier Than the . . . U-Lock," from *BicycleBusiness*, available online at www.bikebiz.co.uk/daily news/article_print.php?id=4637; and "Kryptonite Argues Its Case," weblog diary posted by Shel Israel on July 26, 2005, available online at http://redcouch.typepad.com/weblog/2005/07/ kryptonite_argu.html.

9. *Tomorrow's Markets: Global Trends and Their Implications for Business* (Hertfordshire, England: World Business Council for Sustainable Development, 2002), p. 10.

10. "Students Spread a Worthy Gospel," by Sarah Murray, *Financial Times*, July 11, 2005, p. 10.

11. Study cited in "Campuses with a Cause: Diverse Issues Inspire Students," by Jenna Russell, *Boston Globe*, Oct. 9, 2005, p. B1.

12. Studies cited in "Who's Minding the Store? Global Civil Society and Corporate Responsibility," by Melanie Beth Oliviero and Adele Simmons, in Marlies Glasius, Mary Kaldor, and Helmut Anheier (eds.), *Global Civil Society 2002* (London: Centre for the Study of Global Governance, London School of Economics, 2002).

13. "Critics Press Companies on Internet Rights Issues," by Tom Zeller Jr., *New York Times*, Nov. 8, 2005, p. C7.

14. Data compiled by Investor Responsibility Research Center, cited in "Greening of the Boardroom: Socially Conscious Investors Get Results on Global Warming," by Christopher Rowland, *Boston Globe*, Mar. 3, 2005, p. E1.

15. Information from Investor Responsibility Research Center, Inc., available online at www.irrc.com.

16. "The Growth of Socially Responsible Investing," on the website of the World Resources Institute, available online at http://pubs.wri.org/pubs_content_text.cfm?ContentID=1777.
17. *Strategic Management: A Stakeholder Approach*, by R. Edward Freeman (Boston: Pittman, 1984).
18. Survey by Edelman PR Worldwide/Strategy One 2002, cited in Oliviero and Simmons, "Who's Minding the Store? Global Civil Society and Corporate Responsibility."
19. "The Dark Side of Whistleblowing," by Neil Weinberg, *Forbes*, Mar. 14, 2005, p. 91.

Chapter Four

1. Quoted in "The Debate over Doing Good," *Business Week*, Aug. 15, 2005, p. 76.
2. "Exxon Chief Makes a Cold Calculation on Global Warming," by Jeffrey Ball, *Wall Street Journal*, June 14, 2005, p. A1.
3. Quoted in "The Global Compact: Corporate Citizenship in the World Economy," available online at www.unglobalcompact.org/docs/about_the_gc/2.0.1.pdf.
4. "Substantive Agreements Lead to Surge of Withdrawals," *Corporate Social Issues Reporter*, Apr. 2005, p. 4.
5. Survey information cited in "Recruiters Seek M.B.A.s Trained in Responsibility," *Wall Street Journal*, Dec. 13, 2005, p. B6.

Chapter Five

1. Quoted in "The Perils of Doing the Right Thing," by Andrew W. Singer, *Across the Board*, Oct. 2000, p. 17.
2. Meeting at Northeast Utilities corporate headquarters in Berlin, Connecticut, attended by Andrew W. Savitz, 1997.
3. "Northeast's Guilty Plea Is a Good Business Decision," by Paul Choiriere, *New London Day*, Sept. 29, 1999, p. B1.
4. "Teaching Wal-Mart New Tricks," by Tracie Rozhon, *New York Times*, May 8, 2005, p. C1.

5. "The Race to Save a Rainforest," *Business Week*, Nov. 24, 2003, p. 125.

6. *Collapse: How Societies Choose to Fail or Succeed*, by Jared Diamond (New York: Viking, 2005).

7. *The Economic Impact of Wal-Mart*, report prepared for Wal-Mart by Global Impact Advisory Services, Nov. 2, 2005, available online at http://globalinsight.com/publicDownload/generic Content/11-03-05_walmart.pdf.

8. "J. P. Morgan Adopts 'Green' Guidelines in Lending Policies," by Jim Carlton, *Wall Street Journal*, Apr. 25, 2005, p. B1.

9. Interview with Andrew W. Savitz.

10. A useful concise summary of the Brent Spar episode appears in "Lessons from Brent Spar," by Dirk Maxeiner, on the website of Maxeiner & Miersch, available online at www.maxeiner-miersch.de/lessons_from_brent_spar_e.htm.

11. "Southern Baptists End Disney Boycott," June 23, 2005, on the website of In the Faith, available online at www.inthefaith.com/2005/06/23/southern-baptists-end-disney-boycott.

12. *The Shell Report 2004*, available online at www.shell.com/home/Framework?siteId=shellreport2004-en.

13. Quoted in *Walking the Talk: The Business Case for Sustainable Development*, by Charles O. Holliday Jr., Stephan Schmidheiny, and Philip Watts (Sheffield, England: Greenleaf, 2002), p. 128.

Chapter Six

1. Data available from the website of Responsible Care, online at www.responsiblecare-us.com.

2. Quotation from "A Spear in the Chest," speech delivered in 1998 and available online at www.interfacesustainability.com/video.html.

3. "The Good Company: A Survey of Corporate Social Responsibility," edited by Clive Cook, special section of *The Economist*, Jan. 22, 2005.

4. *Environmental Protection and the Social Responsibility of Firms: Perspectives from Law, Economics and Business,* edited by Bruce L. Hay, Robert N. Stavins, and Richard H. K. Vietor (Washington, D.C.: Resources for the Future Press, 2005).

5. "Of Universal Benevolence," by Adam Smith, in *The Theory of the Moral Sentiments* (1759, pt. 6, sect. 3, chap. 3).

6. Quoted from an interview in "Managerial Correctness," by A. J. Vogl, *Across the Board,* July/Aug. 2004, available online at www.conference-board.org/articles/atb_article.cfm?id=266.

Chapter Seven

1. Quoted in "Dam Builder Becomes a Dam Breaker to Help Save a Species," by Ian Urbina, *New York Times,* Sept. 22, 2004, p. A20.

2. Our account of the Penobscot River restoration project developed by PPL and a consortium of Native American and environmental groups is based on extensive press coverage as well as interviews that Karl Weber conducted with several participants, including John Banks, Laura Rose Day, Scott D. Hall, and Gordon W. Russell, during Aug. 2005. All quotations from these individuals are derived from those interviews. (Also see notes 3 and 4.)

3. This passage and some other details about the history of the Penobscot River are drawn from the website of Penobscot Partners, available online at www.penobscotriver.org/histories.html.

4. "The $345 Bill," full-page advertisement for PPL Corporation, *Wall Street Journal,* Nov. 21, 2005, p. R5.

Chapter Eight

1. From a conversation with Andrew W. Savitz.

2. *Cannibals with Forks: The Triple Bottom Line of 21st Century Business,* by John Elkington (Philadelphia: New Society, 1998), pp. 132–133.

3. Available online at www.geocities.com/Athens/Acropolis/5232/ comicmay97.htm.

4. "Newsmaker: Phil Knight," *The NewsHour with Jim Lehrer*, May 13, 1998, available online at www.pbs.org/newshour/bb/ business/jan-june98/nike_5–15a.html.

5. *Corporate Responsibility Report fy04*, available online at www.nikeresponsibility.com.

6. A summary of the facts in the Kasky case can be found online at http://reclaimdemocracy.org/nike/kasky_nike_justfacts.html.

7. Available online at www.pbs.org/newshour/bb/health/jan-june98/ fat_6–17a.html.

8. Cited in "Obesity-Linked Diabetes Rising in Children," by Sally Squires, available online at www.usda.gov/cnpp/ WP%20Obesity%20Article.htm.

9. Cited on the website of the Centers for Disease Control, www.cdc.gov/od/oc/media/pressrel/r991026/html.

10. The website of the GRI is located at www.globalreporting.org.

11. *Making the Right Choices: Sustainability Report*, 2004, p. 29, available online at www.bp.com/downloadlisting.do?categoryId= 666&contentId=2004066.

12. Interview with Andrew W. Savitz.

13. The website of CSR Wire is located at www.csrwire.com; that of Business for Social Responsibility is located at www.bsr.org; and that of the Interfaith Center on Corporate Responsibility is found at www.iccr.org.

14. See "Chemical Summary: Parabens," on CHEC's HealtheHouse website, available online at www.checnet.org/healthehouse/ chemicals/chemicals-detail.asp?Main_ID=268.

15. *Connecting with Society*, Ford Motor Company, 1999, available online at www.ford.com/en/company/about/corporateCitizenship/ connectingWithSociety/default.htm.

16. "Yale Poll Reveals Overwhelming Public Desire for New Energy Policy Direction," June 9, 2005, on the website of Apollo Alliance, available online at www.apolloalliance.org/apollo_in_ the_news/archived_news_articles/2005/06_09_05_yalepoll.cfm.

17. "China Embarks on Mission to Quench Growing Petrol Thirst," by Geoff Dyer, *Financial Times*, June 29, 2005, p. 5.

Chapter Nine

1. "The Biggest Contract," by Ian Davis, *The Economist*, May 26, 2005, available online at www.economist.com/business/Printer Friendly.cfm?Story_ID=4008642.
2. "Introduction to Unilever," available on the company website at www.unilever.com/Images/Introduction%20to%20Unilever_tcm13-15184.pdf.
3. Information here and in the next four paragraphs is drawn from Unilever's *Social Report 2004: Listening, Learning, Making Progress*, available online at www.unilever.com/Images/Social%20 Report%202004_lowres_tcm13-13239.pdf.
4. *Cradle to Cradle: Remaking the Way We Make Things*, by William McDonough and Michael Braungart (New York: North Point Press, 2002).
5. Information on 3M's 3P program is available online at www.3m.com/about3m/pioneers/ling.html.
6. From interviews with internal human resources consultants at PwC conducted by Andrew W. Savitz.
7. "Breakaway Brands—Subway," by Matthew Boyle, *Fortune*, Oct. 31, 2005, p. 162.
8. "About Brownfields," article on the website of the Environmental Protection Agency, available online at www.epa.gov/swerosps/bf/about.htm; "Developers See Green in 'Brownfield' Sites," by Ray A. Smith, *Wall Street Journal*, June 1, 2005, p. B1.
9. Case study on the website of Business and Sustainable Development, available online at www.bsdglobal.com/viewcasestudy.asp?id=123.
10. "Health Insurers' New Target," by Vanessa Fuhrmans, *Wall Street Journal*, May 31, 2005, p. B1.
11. "Virtual Battle: How a Global Web of Activists Gives Coke Problems in India," by Steve Stecklow, *Wall Street Journal*, June 7, 2005, p. A1.

12. The website of Smoke Free Movies is located at http://Smoke FreeMovies.ucsf.edu.

Chapter Ten

1. Quoted in "At Tokyo Auto Show, a Focus on Fuel, Not Fenders," by James Brooke, *New York Times*, Nov. 4, 2005, p. C1.
2. *Walking the Talk: The Business Case for Sustainable Development*, by Charles O. Holliday Jr., Stephan Schmidheiny, and Philip Watts (Sheffield, England: Greenleaf, 2002), p. 147.
3. "The Matchmaker in the Machine," by Paul Kaihla, *Business 2.0*, Jan./Feb. 2004, p. 52.

Chapter Eleven

1. From speeches attended by Andrew W. Savitz, 2002–2005.
2. Interview with Karl Weber, June 2005.

Chapter Twelve

1. *Corporate Responsibility Report fy04*, available online at www.nikeresponsibility.com.
2. *Cannibals with Forks: The Triple Bottom Line of 21st Century Business*, by John Elkington (Philadelphia: New Society, 1998), p. 196.
3. *Linking Opportunity with Responsibility: Sustainability Report 2004*, available online at www.pg.com/content/pdf/01_about_pg/ corporate_citizenship/sustainability/reports/sustainability_report_ 2004.pdf.
4. Elkington, *Cannibals with Forks*, pp. 134–135.
5. "Corporate Social Opportunity?" Feb. 21, 2005, interview on the website of the World Business Council for Sustainable Development, online at www.wbcsd.org/plugins/DocSearch/ details.asp?type=DocDet&ObjectId=13258. (This web page is no longer available.)

6. Quoted in "Campaigners Use Peace as a Weapon," by Sarah Murray, *Financial Times*, May 5, 2005, p. 4.
7. "French Giant Tries to Convince World Nukes Are Green," by John Carreyrou, *Wall Street Journal*, Nov. 12, 2003, p. A1.
8. Interview with Andrew W. Savitz.
9. *Corporate Responsibility Report fy04*, available online at www.nikeresponsibility.com. A summary of the facts in the Kasky case can be found online at http://reclaimdemocracy.org/nike/kasky_nike_justfacts.html. Also see "Nike Settles Speech Lawsuit," by William McCall, Associated Press, Sept. 13, 2003.
10. *The Shell Report 2004: Meeting the Energy Challenge—Our Progress in Contributing to Sustainable Development*, available online at www.shell.com/home/Framework?siteId=shellreport2004-en.
11. "The Biggest Contract," by Ian Davis, *The Economist*, May 26, 2005, available online at www.economist.com/business/PrinterFriendly.cfm?Story_ID=4008642.
12. Interview with Andrew W. Savitz.

Chapter Thirteen

1. "2003 Toxic Release Inventory Public Data Release eReport" Washington: Environmental Protection Agency, 2005. Available online at www.ep.gov/tri/tridata/tri03/2003eReport.pdf.
2. "Wal-Mart Must Face the Music: Asked for 'Sustainability' Report," by Lynn Moore, *Montreal Gazette*, June 3, 2005, p. B1.
3. *Sustainability Reporting Guidelines 2002*, by the Global Reporting Initiative (Boston: Global Reporting Initiative, 2002), available online at www.globalreporting.org.
4. *Every Day, Around the Globe: The Coca-Cola Company 2004 Environmental Report*, available online at www2.coca-cola.com/citizenship/environmental_report2004.pdf.
5. "Talisman Pulls out of Sudan," BBC News, Mar. 10, 2003, available online at http://news.bbc.co.uk/2/hi/business/2835713.stm. Also see "Oil and the Civil War in Sudan" on the website of

the *Yale Insider*, available online at www.yaleinsider.org/article.jsp?id=14.

6. *Building Public Trust: The Future of Corporate Reporting*, by Samuel A. DiPiazza and Robert G. Eccles (New York: Wiley, 2002).

7. Interview with Andrew W. Savitz.

Chapter Fourteen

1. *Walking the Talk: The Business Case for Sustainable Development*, by Charles O. Holliday Jr., Stephan Schmidheiny, and Philip Watts (Sheffield, England: Greenleaf, 2002), p. 231.

2. Meeting of the Accountability and Reporting working group of the World Business Council for Sustainable Development, attended by Andrew W. Savitz.

3. *The Frontier in American History*, by Frederick Jackson Turner (Ann Arbor: Michigan Historical Reprint Series, 2005).

Epilogue

1. From "Rethinking the Social Responsibility of Business," *Reason*, Oct. 2005, p. 32.

2. *Cannibals with Forks: The Triple Bottom Line of 21st Century Business*, by John Elkington (Philadelphia: New Society, 1998), pp. 202–203.

3. Ibid, p. 203.

4. "At Tokyo Auto Show, a Focus on Fuel, Not Fenders," by James Brooke, *New York Times*, Nov. 4, 2005, p. C1.

5. "Recycling Business Adds Global Value to Trash," *Asahi Shimbun*, June 9, 2005, p. 23.

6. "Marketing Myopia," in *The Marketing Imagination* (expanded ed.), by Theodore Levitt (New York: Free Press, 1986).

7. "Consortium Led by Volkswagen Group to Acquire Dutch LeasePlan Corporation," Apr. 22, 2004, on the website of

Volkswagen Media Services, available online at www.volkswagen-media-services.com/medias_publish/ms/content/en/pressemit teilungen/2004/04/22/consortium_led_by.standard.gid-oeffentlichkeit.html.

8. "VW Chief Tries Tricky Manoeuvre" by James Mackintosh, *Financial Times*, June 11, 2004, available online at http://search.ft.com/searchArticle?id=040611000630&query=volkswagen+leaseplan&vsc_appId=quickSearch&offset=50&resultsToShow=10&vsc_subjectConcept=&vsc_companyConcept=&state=More&vsc_publicationGroups=TOPWFT&searchCat=-1.

9. "BP Tackles Climate Change Threat with £200m Boost for Energy Efficiency," *London Daily Telegraph*, Oct. 25, 2005.

10. Andrew W. Savitz interview with Allen L. White, Nov. 15, 2005.

11. "The Biggest Contract," by Ian Davis, *The Economist,* May 26, 2005, available online at www.economist.com/business/Printer Friendly.cfm?Story_ID=4008642.

12. "A Subject for Those Who Want to Make a Difference," by Alan Finder, *New York Times*, Aug. 17, 2005, p. B9.

13. "Clean Water, No Profit," by Sarah Ellison and Eric Bellman, *Wall Street Journal*, Feb. 23, 2005, p. B1; *Linking Opportunity with Responsibility: Sustainability Report 2004*, available online at www.pg.com/content/pdf/01_about_pg/corporate_citizenship/sustainability/reports/sustainability_report_2004.pdf.

14. From speeches attended by Andrew W. Savitz.

Acknowledgments

Every business book is a collaboration, and many friends and colleagues helped me along the way. I would like to thank them now.

First and foremost, Larry Tye, who, although under a deadline to deliver his own fourth book, gave me the confidence; the road map; and the monthly, weekly, daily, and at times the *hourly* encouragement I needed to start and finish my first. I am grateful for his support, for his friendship, and for the constant energy and inspiration that he provides.

Peter Barash, Mark Green, and the late, great congressman Benjamin S. Rosenthal started me thinking about corporations in terms of their impacts beyond the financial in my very first job. Later, John DeVillars gave me the opportunity to understand the relationship between public and private environmental interests, from the public side of the desk, where he has contributed so much.

Thereafter, PricewaterhouseCoopers let me take my knowledge and experience to the marketplace. I was fortunate to know and work with two of the firm's great chairmen, Gene Freedman and Samuel DiPiazza—who turned out to be a mentor and a friend, as well as a highly involved and committed leader in the service of accountability, business integrity, and meaningful corporate reporting. Chris Hughes, whose constant friendship, soaring intellect, and basic goodness have been a source of strength, read and commented on the final draft of this book, as he has on almost every important word I have written over the past fifteen years. Chris broadens and deepens the meaning of the word "partner" in everything he does, and what splendid good fortune for me that we met and stuck.

Loraine Shuman cheerfully helped me wrestle with the manuscript, as she cheerfully helped me every day at PwC. Thanks also to Greg Bardnell, Dale Jensen, Eric Howe, Karen Ethier, Jessica Shipps, Karen Burnette, and Holly Clack, my loyal teammates and colleagues, and especially to Mike Besly, an early reader, book supporter, and former captain of the Queen's Guard.

The World Business Council for Sustainable Development helped me and thousands of others think clearly and practically about sustainability. Bjorn Stigson, Margaret Flaherty, Travis Engen, Dan Gagnier, and Ron Nielsen (the latter three of whom are setting the standard for sustainability at Alcan), Matt Haddon (of Environmental Resources Management), Ian Goslin (of Caterpillar), Sunny Misser and Tess Mateo (both of PwC), Claude Fussler, Cheryl Hicks, and Laura Sanders, experts all, were generous with their time and thoughts. Bob Massie, Joan Bavaria, Mindy Lubber, and all the good people at CERES, and Allen L. White at Tellus have greatly enriched my thinking.

Speaking of ideas, Bill McDonough from McDonough, Braungart Design Chemistry and Anne Johnson from Green/Blue gave me many, and my collaboration with them continues to be a formative experience that is reflected on many pages herein.

I have had the pleasure to work with some outstanding clients over the years, but none more enjoyable than the fine people running with the sustainability ball, while juggling many others, at PepsiCo. I have learned much about how things actually get done in this world from Elaine Palmer, who is one of those heroic managers who make things happen in large companies through a combination of skill, smarts, and incredibly hard work—in this case moving PepsiCo in a sustainable direction. Tod McKenzie has inspired me (and many others) in every way, and Matt McKenna has impressed me with his personal and professional commitment to this issue. While they were at Northeast Utilities, Mike Morris was the first CEO I ever heard talk about managing based not so much on rules as on values; Dennis Welch was the first person I ever saw do it; and Greg Butler, Cheryl Grisé, and Barry Ilberman were each in their own way contributors to my understanding of that management philosophy. For two years, Stan Twardy, of Day, Berry, & Howard, gave me weekly tutorials on the science and art of environmental law enforcement. Keith Miller and Sara Ethier at 3M have been stalwarts. Roy Deitchman, Stan Bagley, and Bob Noonan at Amtrak helped me understand how responsibility works in the field. Thanks also to the environmental professionals at Sony and Shell, who are also among those in the book with whom we have worked.

I owe an enormous debt of gratitude to Morgan McVicar, a fine writer, who helped me with not one but twenty book proposals. Mark Katz introduced me to Evan Schwartz, who introduced me to Rafe Sagalyn, who has been far more than just a superb agent. Rafe gave me a world of good advice, and to the extent that this book rings true, he had a lot to do with it.

Many individuals were helpful to me and to my collaborator, Karl Weber, as we researched and reported the contents of this book. In particular, we want to thank those with past or present connections to the town of Hershey, Pennsylvania, and to the company after which the town is named, whose insights helped inform our chapter on Hershey. They include Joe Berning, Millie Landis Coyle, John Dunn, Michael Fisher, Ric Fouad, Bruce Hummel, John Long, Michael Macchioni, Bruce McKinney, Kathy Taylor, and Dick Zimmerman.

Thanks, too, to the people involved in the saga of PPL Corporation and the revitalization of the Penobscot River, who were generous with their time and advice. In particular, we want to thank John Banks, Laura Rose Day, Scott D. Hall, and Gordon W. Russell.

Naturally, our narratives concerning both Hershey and PPL reflect our own perspective, which shouldn't be identified with that of any individual we may have interviewed.

When we finished what I thought was a first readable draft, I looked around for actual readers and thought, "I'd better start with an immediate relative." Fortunately, my cousin Jeffrey Trachtenberg was more than willing. A lifelong pal and an accomplished author, journalist, and fisherman, he told me to "write it like a letter to your aunt." He gladly read the draft, gave me more helpful comments, and, most important, told my aunt that it *was* readable, knowing that his mother would pass that compliment along to *my* mother, who already knew the book was great, *without having to read it.*

My other reader-coaches, Mindy Lubber, Dawn Rittenhouse, Allen L. White, and Elizabeth Ames, provided shockingly targeted and diverse insights, all of which changed the book for the better, and did so over their holidays, for which I will be forever grateful. Penny McGee Savitz, my wife, provided me with uncountable mornings, evenings, and weekends of quietude (no mean feat with six-year-old Noah and four-year-old Zuzzie), and offered some excellent editorial suggestions. Brother Peter gave me the Wall Street perspective, which led to some late-night discussions and positive changes.

Max Bazerman spent many of his precious hours reading and commenting, chapter by chapter, concept by concept, case by case, with the thoughtfulness, balance, and rigor of a world-class thinker, scholar, and business consultant, and with the fierce integrity that he brings to every aspect of his life and, by a happy osmosis, to many around him.

Our editor at Jossey-Bass, Susan Williams, has been a staunch supporter from beginning to end and an astute guide through the writing, editing, and publication process. She has supported this first-time author with all the help he needed, providing it in a firm, low-key, and generous way, with incredible dexterity and insight. Thanks for her insights and advice on the book itself, which have added significantly to the quality of the work.

Thanks also to Mark Linton, who helped with the research; Scott Cohen, the publisher of *Compliance Week,* who provided some last-minute assistance and encouragement; Rabbi William Hamilton; Kert Davies; Dutch Leonard; Jane Nelson; Ralph Earle; and Rob Stavins, who got me thinking about fishing.

Finally, my collaborator and now friend, Karl Weber, was magnificent in every way. A clear thinker and writer, a gentle editor, and a fellow follower of baseball and politics, he took my ideas and my words, added some of both (and cut some too, thank goodness), and helped arranged them into what we both hope is a compelling, informative, and entertaining book.

To all of you—my friends, my family, my collaborators—go my heartfelt thanks.

A.W.S.

The Authors

ANDREW W. SAVITZ, president of Sustainable Business Strategies, helps organizations think creatively about opportunities and risks related to sustainability. As a partner in Environmental and Sustainable Business Services at PricewaterhouseCoopers LLP, he assessed, designed, and helped companies implement environmental and sustainability programs. He represented PwC on the World Business Council for Sustainable Development and the Townley Environmental Center of the Conference Board.

Savitz was the general counsel of environmental affairs for the Commonwealth of Massachusetts and a staff member of the U.S. House Committee on Commerce, Consumer and Monetary Affairs, where he worked on corporate governance, labor, and consumer protection issues.

Savitz served on the U.S. National Environmental Education Advisory Council and currently serves on the Steering Committee of the Environmental and Natural Resources Program in the John F. Kennedy School of Government at Harvard University. He is a member of the board of the Environmental League of Massachusetts and the Advisory Council of Zoo New England. He currently serves as board chair of the Massachusetts League of Environmental Voters.

Savitz was graduated from The Johns Hopkins University; New College, Oxford (Rhodes Scholar); and Georgetown University Law Center, where he was an editor of the Law Review. He lives in Brookline, Massachusetts, with his wife, Penny, and children, Noah and Zuzzie. He is an avid, lifelong Boston Red Sox fan.

KARL WEBER is a freelance writer specializing in nonfiction, with a focus on business and current affairs. He has coauthored several acclaimed books on management and strategy by noted consultant Adrian Slywotzky (most recently, *How to Grow When Markets Don't*) and also coauthored the best-selling book *The Power of We* with Jonathan Tisch, CEO of Loews Hotels.

As an editor, Weber has helped develop books by such figures as former U.S. president Jimmy Carter; former representative Richard Gephardt; U.N. ambassador Richard Butler; and the national director of the Anti-Defamation League, Abraham Foxman. He lives in Chappaqua, New York, with his wife, Mary-Jo, and he writes on social and political topics on his blog, www.worldwidewebers.net.

Index